You need this book! It's chock-full of highly relatable examples and tips, and a must-read for anyone who has emotions. Dr. Veilleux uses cutting-edge science and her trademark humor and clinical wisdom to explain what emotions are, and how we can decipher the messages they have for us about how to become our best selves.

—**JAMES GROSS, PhD,** PROFESSOR OF PSYCHOLOGY,
STANFORD UNIVERSITY, STANFORD, CA

open to

EMOTION

JENNIFER C. VEILLEUX, PhD

open to
EMOTION

How Acknowledging, Understanding,
and Regulating Your Feelings
Can Improve Your Mental Health

AMERICAN PSYCHOLOGICAL ASSOCIATION

Published by
American Psychological Association
750 First Street, NE
Washington, DC 20002
https://www.apa.org

Order Department
https://www.apa.org/pubs/books
order@apa.org

Typeset in Sabon by Circle Graphics, Inc., Reisterstown, MD

Printer: Sheridan Books, Chelsea, MI
Cover Designer: Mark Karis

Library of Congress Cataloging-in-Publication Data

Names: Veilleux, Jennifer C., author. | American Psychological Association.
Title: Open to emotion : how acknowledging, understanding, and regulating your feelings can improve your mental health / by Jennifer C. Veilleux.
Description: Washington, DC : American Psychological Association, [2025] | Includes bibliographical references and index.
Identifiers: LCCN 2024047040 (print) | LCCN 2024047041 (ebook) | ISBN 9781433844157 (paperback) | ISBN 9781433844164 (ebook)
Subjects: LCSH: Emotions. | Mental health.
Classification: LCC BF511 .V45 2025 (print) | LCC BF511 (ebook) | DDC 152.4--dc23/eng/20250111
LC record available at https://lccn.loc.gov/2024047040
LC ebook record available at https://lccn.loc.gov/2024047041

https://doi.org/10.1037/0000461-000

Printed in the United States of America

10 9 8 7 6 5 4 3 2 1

I dedicate this book to my husband, Doug, and our goobers, Rowe and Celene. They are the inspiration for and the witnesses to my emotional messages because they are the core of my value of Belonging.

CONTENTS

Acknowledgments ix

Introduction: Mail, or Junk Mail? 3

Chapter 1. Emotional Sensitivity 7

Chapter 2. Emotional Awareness 27

Chapter 3. Clarify Your Values 53

Chapter 4. Emotional Labeling 81

Chapter 5. Coping Ahead 105

Chapter 6. Opening the Envelope 131

Chapter 7. Actively Regulating Emotions 163

Chapter 8. Expressing and Sharing Emotions 191

Chapter 9. Putting All the Pieces Together Flexibly 225

Afterword 253

Contents

Glossary of Key Terms   255

References   263

Index   293

About the Author   309

ACKNOWLEDGMENTS

I thank all of the clients I've worked with over the past 2 decades, whether directly or indirectly (e.g., via the graduate student therapists who I supervised). They have helped me hone my therapist skills and helped challenge me in figuring out how to explain emotion science concepts in an accessible way.

I also thank all of the students I've mentored, supervised, and/or taught, many of whom have their names in this book. They asked questions about how emotions work, pushed me for resources, and contributed to some of the science reported on here. Some have also successfully used the techniques and metaphors described in this book with their own clients!

Mount Sequoyah Center (https://mountsequoyah.org) is a tranquil oasis where this book was written. I'm indebted to the center for providing artist studio spaces and a beautiful quiet place to walk (and see baby deer!) when I needed a break from writing.

I thank my dad, who sends me stunning Grand Canyon pictures and always tells me when an Amazon package is scheduled to be delivered, and my mom, who is the reason I love musicals and supplies me with the sweaters that keep me warm.

open to
EMOTION

MAIL, OR JUNK MAIL?

When I was a kid, I loved getting mail. I still do. Going to check the mailbox at the end of the day is a tantalizing experience. Could I have a package, or a magazine, or a holiday card from friends? Getting mail feels like someone knows I'm out there and cares enough to communicate with me. What's not to like about that?

But most of the time, the mailbox is either empty or full of junk mail: coupons I have no interest in using, catalogs with products I'm not interested in, postcards for political candidates I have no intention of supporting, and bills. Ugh. Bills.

Over the past several years, I've realized how emotions are pretty similar to mail. You might suspect that an emotion is coming, just like you can anticipate the mail truck, but you rarely know exactly what the mailbox will contain. Just like mail, emotions can be pleasant or unpleasant. They can feel helpful, or they can feel useless. The unpleasant emotions in particular can feel burdensome and stressful—like a bill you don't have enough money to pay. Some unpleasant feelings just seem like junk mail—who wants to feel angry, disgusted, anxious, sad, ashamed, or embarrassed? These feelings certainly seem worthless and pointless, just like that catalog for tools I threw out last week.

Yet, just like mail, emotions have a purpose. In fact, I'd argue that emotions have a far greater purpose than much of the mail in my mailbox. Emotions are trying to tell us something, even the unpleasant emotions. In fact, people can't have emotions about things that don't matter.

Emotions are messages about what matters. This book is about trying to understand these emotional messages, so you can understand what matters and what to do about it. If you are someone who struggles with your emotions, or someone who suffers from depression or anxiety, or someone who just wants to understand how emotion science can apply to human mental health, this book is for you.

THE SCIENCE OF EMOTION

As a licensed clinical psychologist and professor of psychology, one of my tasks is to train aspiring psychologists in conducting therapy and performing psychological assessments. A few years ago, I was working with a graduate student who wanted desperately to be a good therapist, but she questioned whether she was doing the "right" thing. As a result, she had a lot of questions about best practices in therapy. Off-handedly one day, I mentioned something about emotion science and she said, "Wait. There's a *science* about *emotion?*"

There is, in fact, a thriving science of emotion and emotion regulation, and it has experienced exponential growth in the past 20 years. It's great that more people are interested in studying emotion and emotion regulation! However, there is so much research that it's virtually impossible to keep up with it all. Not to mention that academic articles tend to be full of jargon, are not particularly easy to read, and often lack practical implications for how to apply the knowledge to actual life.

I've made it my mission to try to get a handle on the central messages of this ever-growing science, and I occasionally contribute to the science myself with my own research. I've also worked to find ways to apply the knowledge of emotion and emotion regulation science, both as a therapist working with my own clients or training students to work with their clients.

THE EMOTIONAL SELF

And, if I'm being honest, I've tried to apply the scientific research to my own emotional life, too. My emotions often confuse me. As a teenager, my friends called me emotionally dramatic, because I made myself cry on the sidelines at school dances so that someone would come talk to me. Yet, sometimes I could be emotionless. I didn't cry at my grandfather's funeral when I was 8. My junior year of college, my boyfriend called me an unfeeling "ice queen"; to me, he seemed like a fire-breathing dragon.

I wondered, "How can one person be both overemotional and underemotional? What is normal for emotions?" I looked around at others in my life, and at people in TV shows and movies, and I started noticing the variety in people's emotions. Some people seemed to be perky and peppy all of the time, and others seemed to be easily hurt or emotionally wounded. Some people showed sadness but not anger, and others showed anger but nothing else. Why?

EMOTIONAL HEALTH

The science of emotion and emotion regulation doesn't have answers to every emotional question. Some of the science doesn't neatly apply to individual people. And science can't answer "why" questions about why you are the way you are, or why I am the way I am. But the science of emotion and emotion regulation has much to offer for cultivating emotional health.

One of the most common phrases I hear from my therapy clients is "I'm bad at coping; I need better coping skills." What people typically mean by this is "I need to find better ways to push my too-strong feelings away before they destroy me from the inside out, because what I'm doing now isn't working." But what if learning new skills is only part of the solution?

The assumption of this book is that you want emotional health. You want to feel comfortable in your skin, and you want to know how to connect to other people. You want to know how to stop wallowing in self-critical thoughts. You want to feel less depressed or anxious—or both. You want to know how to cope with your feelings—you want to know how to circumvent or wash away those pesky negative emotions.

Yet, if emotions are messages, then maybe part of the pathway to emotional health is understanding emotions a little bit better. If people can't have emotions about things that don't matter, then emotions are a guide to what matters. The real question is, where do these messages come from, and what can they tell us about what matters?

Each chapter in this book is geared to help you understand your emotional world a bit more. The goal is to help you develop some compassion for your emotions, and the emotions of people around you, by digging deep into understanding these emotional messages.

Throughout the chapters, I use examples from my own life and from clients I've worked with. All of the client names and details have been changed so that they aren't identifiable. In fact, the names in this book are the names of students I've worked with over the years, many of whom have helped shape these ideas. Their names are used with their gracious permission.

Let's get started.

CHAPTER 1

EMOTIONAL SENSITIVITY

Consider two wildly different people, the Princess and the Detective. The Princess is extraordinarily sensitive, in both emotion and physical sensation. She is so sensitive, in fact, that she is able to feel a tiny pea hidden beneath 20 downy mattresses.

The Detective, however, is extraordinarily logical. He solves crimes by ignoring emotion and examining the facts and then pointing out how the answer was elementary all along.

The Princess and the Detective represent two ends of the sensitivity spectrum. In the classic children's story *The Princess and the Pea* (Andersen, 1835/1985), sensitivity is desirable: It is the Princess's sensitivity that marks her as fit to marry a prince. But to Detectives, like Sherlock Holmes, emotional sensitivity is undesirable. Emotions reduce logic, and rationality reigns supreme.

Which is it? Is sensitivity good or bad?

The answer, of course, is neither. There is nothing inherently wrong with either the Princess or the Detective. Yet people on both poles of the sensitivity spectrum tend to get feedback that their sensitivity is wrong. Perhaps the Princess left her own kingdom because she was told that she was "too touchy" and that she should "just calm down and stop complaining." No doubt someone told Sherlock Holmes that he was "uncaring" or "a cold fish."

Emotional sensitivity matters because it reflects a personality-like tendency that provides the backdrop for how emotions are experienced in daily life. How people experience emotions is core to who they are, and some people are simply more emotional than others. Two people who land on a different part of the emotional sensitivity spectrum experience the emotional world differently, and there are different pros (and cons) to being high versus low in sensitivity.

There are two overarching lessons to take from this chapter. Remember going to birthday parties as a kid and you got a gift bag to take home? The first lesson of this chapter is that even though the purpose of this book is to help you understand, cope with, and manage your own emotions, the "gift bag" to take with you is a greater compassion for other people's emotions. Your spouse, neighbor, best friend, and parents experience the emotional world differently than you do, and that's just as OK as the way you experience your own emotions.

The second lesson is that even though it sounds like emotional sensitivity is a long-standing, stable, inborn trait, sensitivity can indeed change. Yes, emotional sensitivity is a biologically based part of personality that is evident in infancy (Rothbart et al., 2000). If you were a baby who was easily frustrated or scared, you're probably still easily frustrated and easy to scare! However emotional sensitivity is not set in stone. Traumatic experiences (e.g., sexual violence, war, a natural disaster, watching a family member die) can alter emotional sensitivity. So can small events, like getting cuddled and snuggled, having opportunities to explore new surroundings (Fu & Depue, 2019), experiencing racism, or living in poverty (Myin-Germeys et al., 2003).

If emotional sensitivity can change because of life events, it can also be changed intentionally, whether with therapy (Sauer-Zavala et al., 2017) or with the kind of reflection and learning that are included in this book. As a therapist as well as a professor who teaches new therapists, I've had the privilege of watching many people change the way they deal with emotions.

Let's get started by learning about your own emotional sensitivity. But before we do that, you first need to understand what exactly emotions are.

WHAT IS AN EMOTION?

I truly wish I could provide you with a clear, precise definition of an emotion that you can remember easily and share with your family at the dinner table. However, no such simple definition exists. In fact, there is no one universally agreed-upon definition of "emotion," even by scientists who study emotion (Izard, 2010; Russell, 2012). Instead, experts think of emotions as personally relevant states that have multiple components. Let's break down exactly what that means.

First, emotions are **states**, a temporary change in the mind and body in response to a situation (Scherer, 2005). States, which shift and change over time and across situations, stand in contrast to **traits**, which are more stable characteristics. Emotions come and go; in fact, they tend to be fairly brief. They last a few seconds or a few minutes, rarely longer than a few hours (Verduyn et al., 2009).

Emotions are also personally relevant. A situation has to be interpreted as relevant, salient, and important to a person for them to have any kind of emotional response (Lazarus, 1984). This element is crucial because, again, people can't have emotions about things that don't matter to them.

Emotions have multiple components. Emotions activate parts of the brain that call out to the body to prepare for what might be needed next. Subjectively, this feels like a change in heart rate, sweaty palms, or a clenched stomach.

Emotions also include expressions—people imbue their body language, facial expressions, and vocal tone with their feelings.

Emotions have action tendencies (Frijda, 1988), which means that emotions prompt people to do things that are consistent with a particular feeling. Happiness and joy prompt people to play, fear prompts a retreat to safety, anger prompts an attack to correct a perceived injustice, sadness prompts reflection and comfort-seeking. It is certainly possible to ignore these action tendencies and act differently than what the emotion prompts, but the action tendency is, in essence, baked in to the emotion.

Finally, emotions have thoughts attached to them, with different patterns of thoughts associated with different types of feelings. We'll dig into the thoughts associated with each emotion in later chapters, but it should make sense to you that you have different kinds of thoughts when angry ("How dare that *@#%$% cut me off in traffic!") versus when guilty ("I really shouldn't have done that. . .") versus when anxious ("What's going to happen? Is he going to be OK?").

These components together—the combination of physiological changes, expression, action tendencies, and thoughts—coalesce into what we think of as a subjective feeling (Izard, 2010; Scherer, 2005), such as "upset" or "happy" or "disappointed-but-also-grateful."

TERMS OF EMOTION

Many people use the term "feeling" as a synonym for emotion, but there are actually several different terms that scientists use to refer to emotion: **emotion, mood, feeling,** and **affect.** Feeling tends to refer to the subjective experience of an emotion, whereas emotion covers all of the components of an emotional state. Affect is an umbrella term that covers basic feelings of pleasantness (e.g., positive affect) or unpleasantness (e.g., negative affect). For the purposes of this book, we will ignore the small distinctions among feelings, emotions, and affect.

The distinction between emotion and mood, however, is important. Emotions happen in response to some kind of situation or stimuli (Gross, 1998b; Scherer, 2005), whereas moods are free-floating.

Emotions are triggered. The trigger could be something that happens in your environment, for example, a deer running in front of your car at dusk. Triggers do not have to be big events. People feel emotions when listening to music, seeing a social media post, or having a conversation. The trigger could also be internal, like when you spontaneously remember a funny skit you saw on YouTube last week. Emotions are anchored to triggers, which start the emotion off, but each emotion also has a middle and an end. Like waves, they rise up, crest at the peak, and then come back down.

Look at the chart in Figure 1.1. This is an emotional wave chart of a former client of mine, Regina (Reggie). She was an artist, and she had a diagnosis of bipolar disorder. She was also a recovering

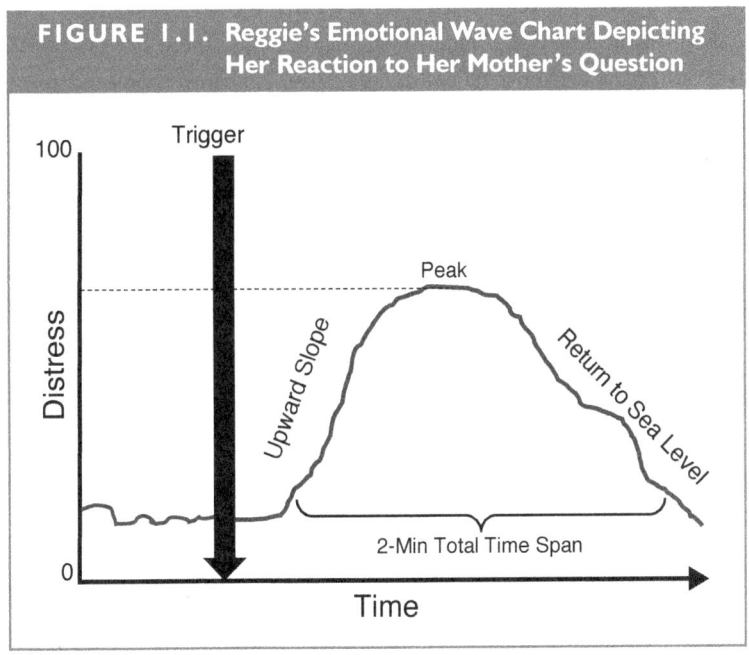

FIGURE 1.1. Reggie's Emotional Wave Chart Depicting Her Reaction to Her Mother's Question

alcoholic. On this particular day, which was about a year into our working together, she'd had a strong emotional response to a discussion with her mother. Before she talked to her mother, she had been feeling pretty good. This is the baseline level, and Reggie's chart is pretty typical. Most people walk around feeling mildly positive most of the time (Yik et al., 1999).

The y-axis in Figure 1.1 represents a simple emotional rating scale like ones I often use in therapy, on which 0 represents no distress at all and 100 indicates extreme distress, the worst it could possibly be (Tanner, 2012). Reggie's baseline was about a 15 here, which is pretty typical. In my research and my clinical practice, when I ask people to chart emotions, they usually report a low level of baseline distress (10–15 is common).

Reggie had a strong emotional response when her mother asked her when she was planning to settle down and have kids. This was a hot-button issue for Reggie, who very much wanted her boyfriend to commit to her, but she also wasn't sure if she even wanted to be married, or to have kids. Reggie experienced all the components of emotion here—she felt her face flush, her heart started racing, she felt the urge to hang up on her mother, and she started thinking what she called "unhinged" thoughts.

The components of emotion all coalesced quickly into a strong subjective feeling. Her mother got the sense that her question had upset Reggie, and she changed the subject, where the emotion quickly returned back to what I call "sea level."

Unlike emotions, moods are free-floating feeling states that are often not triggered by anything. A person can just be in a good mood or in a crappy mood. Mood states tend to be less intense than acute triggered emotions. Think of it this way: If emotions are waves, then moods are the tides.

Moods can make emotional waves feel stronger. Figure 1.2 is another of Reggie's charts from earlier in our therapy. She understood

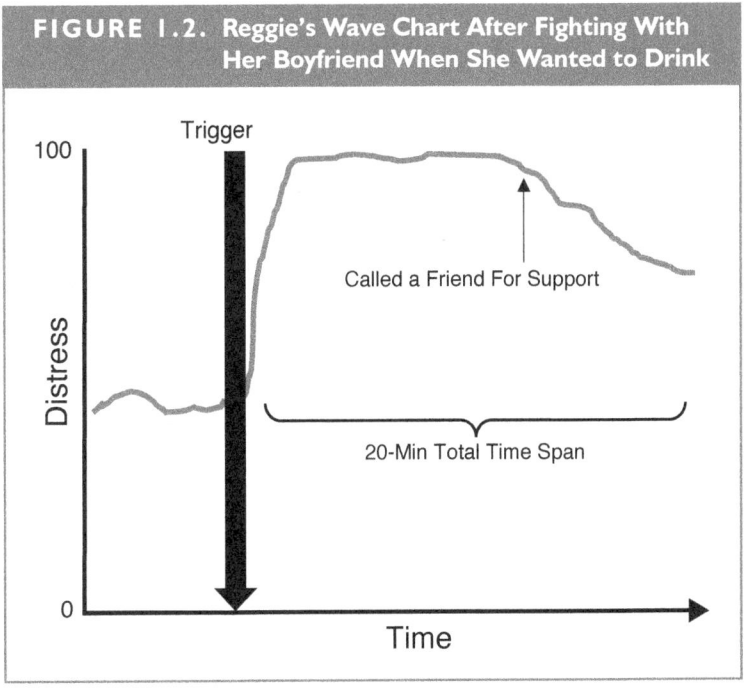

FIGURE 1.2. Reggie's Wave Chart After Fighting With Her Boyfriend When She Wanted to Drink

her feelings a lot less at the beginning of therapy, and she tended to be in bad moods more often. On this day, her mood, or her tide of distress, had started higher, at a baseline of approximately 40–45. She was feeling generally anxious about the direction of her life— not about anything specific; she just felt uneasy quite often. Then she had a fight with her boyfriend, and she really wanted to drink alcohol. Her distress level shot up to a 98. It stayed there because she kept thinking about the fight and her urge to drink until she thought to call a friend to help distract her, which is when her distress started to decrease.

Emotions can also resolve into moods. In the first situation, with Reggie's mom, if her mom hadn't recognized what was going on and changed the subject, Reggie might have stayed in a funk after the conversation for the next several hours, just feeling blah and off.

Sometimes when I ask therapy clients (or participants in my research studies) how long a particular emotion of theirs lasted, I get the answer "days." I understand what people mean when they say this. Maybe they felt cranky (i.e., were in a bad mood) for days on end. Or—and this second one is more likely—the person had multiple emotional waves related to the same trigger.

For example, if Reggie had replayed the conversation with her mother over and over in her mind, she would actually have experienced repeated emotions, not one long-lasting emotion. The first emotional wave was triggered by the conversation itself, and the subsequent waves were triggered by Reggie's memory of the conversation. But the emotion itself doesn't last for days. The physiological responses, action tendencies, thought patterns, and expression components that are baked in to the emotion are fleeting, not long lasting. Reggie might find herself caught in an emotional storm with multiple waves.

Why, exactly, does the distinction between moods and emotions matter? It matters because emotional sensitivity is much more about the experience of emotion than of mood.

WHAT IS EMOTIONAL SENSITIVITY?

Now that we have an understanding of emotion, it's time to dig into the main topic of the chapter: **emotional sensitivity**.

Emotional sensitivity refers to (a) how quickly a person experiences an emotion in response to a trigger, (b) how intense their emotion becomes, and (c) how their long emotion lasts (Nock et al., 2008). These are the same parameters that are shown in the emotional charts from my former client Reggie (Figures 1.1 and 1.2). In these charts, the speed is indicated by the upward slope, the intensity is the peak, and longevity is the return to sea level. People who are highly emotionally sensitive tend to experience emotions easily and quickly (e.g., a strong upward slope), and they have strong and intense feelings (e.g., a high peak) and the emotions stick around for a while (e.g., return slowly to sea level).

To use a different metaphor, picture a hollow body filling with orange juice. How quickly does the juice level rise, how much of the body is filled, and how long would it take for the juice to drain out? People who are highly emotionally sensitive have juice faucets that turn on quickly and fill the body fast. The body is filled all the way to ear level (or higher!) with juice, the drain spout doesn't work well, and it takes quite a while for the juice to fully drain out.

In contrast, someone who is not very emotionally sensitive might have a delayed-onset emotion faucet that doesn't turn on quickly. Or the emotion juice level might rise only to their knees, and/or the drain spout empties out the juice quickly.

Emotional sensitivity specifically refers to the internal feeling of having an emotion, not whether the emotion is observable to an outside eye. However, people who are highly emotionally sensitive do tend to show their emotions more readily (Veilleux et al., 2024). If the body is too full of emotion juice, it's going to leak out somewhere, right? Like out of the eye sockets, perhaps, in the form of tears?

However, it is also possible to hide or mask feelings (Shapero et al., 2016), which some people get quite good at (Cheli & Cavalletti, 2021). Picture someone who is walking around doing things, but their insides are filled to the neck with emotion juice. Unless the person is shaking, crying, talking about their feelings, or otherwise acting on their emotions, an observer would never know just how much emotion is sloshing around inside that body.

Emotional sensitivity is about the feelings going on inside yourself, not what you do with the emotion you're feeling.

THE SPECTRUM OF EMOTIONAL SENSITIVITY

You probably know if you are emotionally sensitive. But just in case you don't, a brief measure of emotional sensitivity is included in Exhibit 1.1. Rate yourself honestly on all of these items with the scale provided and add up your responses.

Scores on this measure can range between 0 and 24. Emotional sensitivity is a spectrum or dimension. There are people with scores of 0, people with scores of 24, and people with every score in between.

EXHIBIT 1.1. The Brief Emotional Reactivity Scale

Look at each of the items below and rate them on this scale. Add up your total score.

0	1	2	3	4
Not at all like me	A little like me	Somewhat like me	A lot like me	Completely like me

_____ 1. I tend to get very emotional very easily.

_____ 2. When I feel emotional, it's hard for me to imagine feeling any other way.

_____ 3. Even the littlest things make me emotional.

_____ 4. When I am angry/upset, it takes me much longer than most people to calm down.

_____ 5. My moods are very strong and powerful.

_____ 6. I often get so upset it's hard for me to think straight.

Note. From "Development and Validation of a Brief Version of the Emotion Reactivity Scale: The B-ERS," by J. C. Veilleux, R. E. Schreiber, E. A. Warner, and K. H. Brott, 2024, *Current Psychology, 43*, p. 12597 (https://doi.org/10.1007/s12144-023-05323-4). Copyright 2024 by Springer Nature BV. Reprinted with permission.

My graduate students and I have given this test to thousands of people, and the average score is an 8. Scores of 15 and above would be considered very emotionally sensitive (only 15% of people score in that range), and scores of 2 and below would be considered very emotionally nonsensitive.

Before you take your score on this little test as gospel, there are a few caveats to keep in mind.

First, there are emotionally sensitive people who wouldn't score highly on this test because they are aversive to the word "emotional." For example, I once worked with a client named Garrett who was quite emotionally sensitive. I could tell because whenever he got emotional in a therapy session—which was essentially every week—he would start to squint as if he were trying to stop himself from crying, and he would try to change the subject. I eventually called him out, and he vehemently denied experiencing any kind of emotion. Instead, he would say that he was "stressed." Now, "stress" is a term that conveys a kind of overwhelmed and anxious feeling. For Garrett, stress was a word that was acceptable to him as a businessman and a father, whereas "emotion" was a word he associated with weakness and hysteria. It took a considerable amount of discussion before Garrett acknowledged that stress was a kind of emotion and that, because he was sensitive to stress, maybe he was emotionally sensitive, too.

Second, perhaps you struggled to answer the statements in Exhibit 1.1 because your responses "depend on the day." This measure, and others like it, assesses trait-like tendencies. They try to determine how you usually are. But people do vary. I am definitely more emotionally sensitive when I've had less sleep, when I'm sick, or when I'm already overwhelmed. In comparison, it takes more to rile me up when I'm rested, healthy, and keeping up with all of my tasks. If you are also someone who varies in your emotional sensitivity, that's OK.

Third, there are different flavors of emotional sensitivity. The measure in Exhibit 1.1 refers to emotions but really asks about unpleasant feelings, not pleasant feelings. This is a test of **threat sensitivity,** sometimes called "punishment sensitivity" (Pickering & Corr, 2008; Smillie et al., 2006; Waller & Wagner, 2019), covering sensitivity to all negative (i.e., unpleasant) emotions, including anxiety (Taylor, 2003), disgust (van Overveld et al., 2006), and social rejection (Chapman et al., 2012).

It is also possible to be sensitive to pleasurable stimuli, which is called **reward sensitivity** (Fu & Depue, 2019; Torrubia et al., 2001; Waller & Wagner, 2019). People who have a higher level of reward sensitivity tend to have stronger experiences of wanting or anticipating future rewards and get more enjoyment (i.e., liking) out of pleasant activities (Berridge et al., 2009; Fu & Depue, 2019). Those who are extremely high in reward sensitivity can be vulnerable to engaging in thrill-seeking and impulsive behaviors (e.g., substance use, risky sexual behaviors; Bresin & Mekawi, 2022). Those who are very low in reward sensitivity are vulnerable to depression (Carver et al., 2008).

Think about your own sensitivity to threats and rewards. Do you get excited about upcoming events, and can you experience strong joy when things go well? If so, you likely have high reward sensitivity. Are you often fearful of what might go wrong and quick to sense when your environment might be unsafe? Then you likely have high threat sensitivity. A person could be high in both, low in both, or high in only one type of sensitivity. For example, the Princess (of *The Princess and the Pea*) seems highly threat sensitive, but we know little about her reward sensitivity. The Detective seems low in both threat and reward sensitivity.

IS THERE A CORRECT AMOUNT OF EMOTIONAL SENSITIVITY?

Earlier in this chapter, I suggested that the Princess (who is highly emotionally sensitive) may have left her own kingdom because she was told she was too sensitive, too dramatic. Maybe the Detective has been told he is "dead inside" and "an insensitive, callous jerk."

Perhaps you have been judged for your emotional sensitivity, too, whether high or low. Or both! These types of statements suggest that there is a correct amount of emotional sensitivity. Is that true? No, it is not! It is more common to have a moderate level of emotional sensitivity; about two-thirds of people score between 5 and 11 on the measure in Exhibit 1.1. There is also some evidence that people in the middle tend to feel more satisfied with their lives and generally feel less distress (Rush et al., 2024). However, this doesn't mean there is anything wrong with either very high or very low sensitivity. There are both pros and cons on each side of the spectrum.

High Emotional Sensitivity

There are many positives associated with high emotional sensitivity. Experts think that high emotional sensitivity can be a kind of superpower (Fiori et al., 2023), because people who are highly emotionally sensitive and learn how to manage their feelings well tend to be more emotionally intelligent. People who are highly emotionally sensitive tend to be empathic (Eman et al., 2019), because they can easily tune in to (and feel) the feelings of others. For example, my friend Katie is quite emotionally sensitive. She is someone people often turn to when they are feeling emotional because she asks questions, gets righteously mad on her friends' behalf, and can sit with her friends in their pain. People who are highly emotionally sensitive are also often passionate and deep, and their strong emotions can enhance others' experiences. I personally love going to haunted houses with Katie, because she jumps and screams whenever someone pops out at her. I tend to be more skeptical and amused by haunted houses, but going with Katie makes haunted houses scarier, which enhances the fun.

There are also clear cons to high emotional sensitivity. High threat sensitivity in particular is associated with increased vulnerability to a variety of mental health problems, including depression (Bylsma, Morris, & Rottenberg, 2008), anxiety (Keough et al., 2010; Macatee & Cougle, 2013; Michel et al., 2016; O'Bryan et al., 2017), panic attacks (McNally, 2002), posttraumatic stress (Taylor, 2003) and borderline personality disorder (van Zutphen et al., 2015; Wall et al., 2018). Highly emotionally sensitive people also can become overly reliant on alcohol and/or other drugs for coping (Shaver et al., 2013). Strong unpleasant feelings are hard to manage. It is harder to think clearly when experiencing a strong feeling, and strong feelings are just not fun to experience. People who are highly sensitive have to actively learn how to effectively navigate their strong feelings (Southward et al., 2021), which is tricky because there are no mandatory "How to Deal With Feelings" classes in school!

Many people who are highly sensitive consider their sensitivity more of a curse than a blessing. For example, my client Reggie often bemoaned her emotional sensitivity. She said things like, "I shouldn't take this so personally," and "I'm too touchy, too flighty." She internalized things that people told her throughout her life. Other people—her parents, her friends—had told her, both implicitly and explicitly, that her feelings were "too much." What she heard was "Your feelings are more than a normal human being is supposed to have."

Being called "sensitive" has a negative connotation. It means "You're too dramatic," or "You have a thin skin," or "You're over-reacting." If you have ever been called "too sensitive," you know full well that these phrases don't feel good to hear. They convey the subtle (or perhaps not-so-subtle) message that you are not experiencing the world correctly.

Being told that your feelings are incorrect or inappropriate is called **emotional invalidation** (Zielinski et al., 2018). Unfortunately, people who are high in emotional sensitivity tend to experience quite a bit of emotional invalidation (Wall et al., 2018). Emotional invalidation can also turn inward: Over time, people who are frequently invalidated by others begin to self-invalidate themselves and feel less worthwhile as a person because of their emotionality (Schreiber & Veilleux, 2022).

Reggie engaged in self-invalidation. She had thoughts like "My emotions make me a weak person" and "I don't have a good enough reason to be as emotional as I am." One of the reasons why people who are highly emotionally sensitive tend to see their sensitivity as negative is because they have internalized the "too sensitive" messages given to them by others.

Low Emotional Sensitivity

What about people low in emotional sensitivity? There are pros and cons here as well. People who are not especially emotionally sensitive tend to be good in a crisis because they can continue to think logically in emergency situations. People who are not especially emotionally sensitive are also less afraid of risks, and they often are good leaders because they can make decisions easily without being swayed by others or by heightened feelings.

However, there is a sizable drawback to low emotional sensitivity. People with low emotional sensitivity can have difficulty connecting to other people. If emotional sensitivity is a kind of superpower (Fiori et al., 2023) then people with low sensitivity lack that power to know themselves and to attend to the emotional nuances of other people.

People with low emotional sensitivity are sometimes called cold-hearted, mean, or uncaring (Waller & Wagner, 2019). These kinds of phrases are also emotionally invalidating, but the message here is that this person doesn't have enough emotion. The feedback that a person with low emotional sensitivity is broken or emotionally deficient can also be internalized: People can begin to view themselves as unworthy of love or believe that they're somehow less of a person because of how little emotion they experience (Schreiber & Veilleux, 2022).

EMOTIONAL SENSITIVITY AND SUPERTASTERS

How can you respond to people who imply that there is a correct level of emotional sensitivity? To answer this question, we will first take a bit of a tangential journey into discussing *supertasters*.

About 10 years ago, psychology conferences were all about testing people for super-tasting. My friend Katie and I went to a teaching-focused conference together in 2013. Walking down the conference hallway one day, someone asked us if we wanted to know if we were supertasters. The researcher handed us thin slips of paper about the length of my index finger, but slimmer, kind of like a litmus test strip. The researcher said we should place one side of the tip of our tongue. When I followed the instructions, it tasted to me like slightly bitter paper: not delicious, but not awful. I shrugged.

But then I watched Katie put the little super-taster paper on her tongue. She almost gagged. The researcher said, "Yep, you are a supertaster!"[1]

Supertasters have more taste buds on their tongues than the average person (Bartoshuk et al., 1994), and these taste buds are particularly attuned to bitter flavors. Supertasters tend to find most flavors more intense than nonsupertasters (J. E. Hayes & Keast, 2011). Supertasting is also a spectrum on which people vary. Some people (nontasters) can eat pretty much anything and barely taste any flavors. Most people are in the middle, and the supertasters are at the extreme high end.

---

[1] If you are interested in finding out if you are a supertaster, there are instructions available online. Just go to your browser of choice, type in "are you a supertaster" and follow one of the many sets of directions!

Despite the parallels to emotional sensitivity, supertasting simply doesn't have the same negative connotations as emotional sensitivity. Both reflect a spectrum on which people vary, and both are a type of sensitivity. But no one is telling a supertaster that they have an incorrect number of taste buds—they just have more taste buds. In essence, a taste bud is a group of receptor cells that provides messages to your nose and mouth about the flavors of the food and drink you consume. Taste buds are like the mailboxes of flavor: People with more taste buds get more flavor messages than people with fewer taste buds. Supertasters are people who are good chefs and food critics because they can taste more of the flavors in a dish. For example, I am personally not someone who can taste a new dish and say, "Hm; what is that I taste in there? Is that . . . thyme?" But supertasters can often do just that.

What if we considered emotional sensitivity as a spectrum where people vary with regard to "feeling buds"? Or, to use the mail metaphor of emotional messages, people with emotional sensitivity just get more mail. Just like some people get more emails than others, and some people are on more mailing lists and get more catalogs than others, some people have more emotional messages. My friend Katie is both a supertaster and a high-sensitivity "super-emoter." I can't know what that's like, but I can certainly understand that she's getting more emotional catalogs than I am.

To be clear, I am not making any claims about what is actually happening in the brain here, because there is mixed evidence for whether people high in emotional sensitivity have more brain activation in response to emotional stimuli (van Zutphen et al., 2015). Instead, I'm saying that if we talked about emotional sensitivity the way we talk about taste, perhaps people very high or very low in emotional sensitivity would not feel as invalidated. Perhaps if we talked about how people high in emotional sensitivity are super-emoters, then having high sensitivity would actually feel more like a blessing and less like a curse.

All of this is important because emotions are personal. We can try to put ourselves in other people's shoes and imagine what their emotions are like, but we cannot really step into someone else's body and feel things the same way they feel them. You can only be you.

I suspect that people with low emotional sensitivity sometimes look at those who are high in emotional sensitivity and think, "But you are asking for these messages. You could just ignore them. Or don't sign up for as many catalogs!" This is a form of blaming, isn't it? Yet, haven't you ever found yourself getting emails or catalogs you never signed up for? I once woke up to find that more than 400 emails had landed in my inbox overnight, from companies that got hold of my email address. My inbox was flooded with ads I hadn't asked for and didn't want. It took a long time to unsubscribe from those messages. We just can't assume that people are feeling emotional on purpose. Perhaps that's why thinking about emotion *receptors* or *buds* is less invalidating, because it feels like less of a choice.

Exhibit 1.2 provides some suggestions on what you can say the next time someone tries to invalidate your emotional sensitivity.

REFLECTING ON EMOTIONAL SENSITIVITY

Truly, it is OK to be anywhere on the emotional sensitivity spectrum, whether high, or low, or anywhere in between. Whether you are someone who experiences frequent, intense, fast feelings that tend to linger, or someone who experiences infrequent, small blips of feelings that barely register, you are worthwhile. Or, if you are more like me, perhaps you have weeks during which you have only small, blip-like emotions and then phases with big, intense, long-lasting waves. That's OK, too. Your emotional sensitivity is part of who you are, but how you experience feelings is not all of who you are, and the point of this book is to help you integrate emotions into your overall sense of self in a healthy way.

EXHIBIT 1.2. How to Respond to Emotional Invalidation

What can you say when someone implies that you are *too* sensitive, or not sensitive enough? Try these responses!

For Those High in Emotional Sensitivity:
- "Just because I'm really sensitive to emotions doesn't mean that my experiences are wrong. Would you say that someone who has a lot of taste buds tastes 'too much' flavor?"
- "We clearly differ here. I'm feeling something because I'm highly sensitive to emotional situations; maybe you're just different than me. It doesn't mean my experience is wrong."
- "When you imply that I'm dramatic or 'too' sensitive, you are discounting my reactions. Yes, they are stronger than yours. Would you tell a weightlifter they are 'too strong'?"

For Those Low in Emotional Sensitivity:
- "I'm clearly not recognizing the emotional elements in this situation, maybe because I'm lower in emotional sensitivity than you. Help me understand what is emotional for you."
- "I'm not cold or unfeeling; I just have a different sensitivity than you. It takes me longer to recognize when situations are emotional."

SUMMARY POINTS

- Emotions are brief experiences with a trigger that crest and fall like a wave, and they have multiple components (physiological responses, thoughts, action urges, expression, and subjective feelings). Emotions are different from moods, which are longer lasting and more free-floating states.
- Emotional sensitivity refers to the degree to which you experience emotions easily and intensely and how long they last.
- People vary on emotional sensitivity from very low to very high and everywhere in between.

- There is no correct amount of emotional sensitivity, and there are pros and cons to both high and low sensitivity.
- Perhaps if we thought about emotional sensitivity the way we think about taste sensitivity (supertasters), there would be less stigma against high emotional sensitivity (super-emoters).
- Sensitivity changes with life experiences, which means you can change your level of sensitivity if you want to, or at least come to better accept the amount of sensitivity you already have.

CHAPTER 2

EMOTIONAL AWARENESS

One afternoon in early 2004, I was sitting alone in my car, in a parking lot in St. Paul, Minnesota. It had been a pretty typical day, and nothing notable had happened up to that point.

Suddenly, I noticed that my heart was beating quickly, far faster than it should have been for just sitting around. My breathing was heavy, and I felt a little lightheaded. I started thinking, "What's wrong with me? Am I dying? Am I having a heart attack?" I started tuning in to my body even more. Was that tingling in my left hand? What if I passed out in the parking lot?

I freaked out. I called my then-husband (now ex-husband), who took me straight to the emergency room. The doctors hooked me up to an electrocardiogram machine and listened to my heart. They asked me if I'd felt anxious lately.

I knew what they were asking about. I was currently in the middle of applying to graduate school for psychology, and I'd taken courses about mental health problems. I scoffed at the doctors and said, "I know you're asking me if this was a panic attack. It's not. I'm studying psychology. I would know if I had panic attacks."

I was wrong. Many months later, after multiple doctor visits and heart workups, I admitted to myself that I'd been incredibly anxious. I acknowledged that those health freakouts were panic attacks.

Panic attacks are quite common; over 10% of adults in the United States experience at least one panic attack in a given year (Kessler et al., 2006). Panic attacks come out of the blue, and they involve sudden feelings of fear with a strong physical component. It is not unusual for a person having a panic attack to experience chest pain, racing heart, and trouble breathing and think they are having a heart attack. Just like what happened to me.

One of the most prominent things about panic attacks is that it is basically impossible to be unaware of them. As far as emotional messages go, a panic attack is a punch in the face.

At the same time, though, sitting in a parking lot wasn't emotionally triggering for me. What set off those physiological changes that I interpreted as a health emergency? Why did I have such trouble acknowledging the emotional part of my response?

What was I unaware of?

WHAT IS EMOTIONAL AWARENESS?

Emotional awareness is the state of being attentive to and aware of an emotional response (Boden & Thompson, 2017; Hoemann et al., 2021; Mankus et al., 2016; Palmieri et al., 2009; Thompson et al., 2009). It is the recognition that "Yes, I am feeling a feeling right now." From an emotional-messages standpoint, emotional awareness is knowing there's mail in the mailbox.

In general, higher levels of emotional awareness are associated with qualities most people want. High emotional awareness is associated with being emotionally intelligent (Salovey & Grewal, 2005). People who are more emotionally aware are more empathic, less impulsive, and tend to make more progress in therapy (Lane, 2020; Smith et al., 2018). People with lower emotional awareness tend to have more symptoms of depression, anxiety, posttraumatic stress disorder, eating disorders, and borderline personality disorder (Weissman et al., 2020).

Emotions can influence a person's thoughts and actions regardless of whether that person is aware of the emotion (Smith & Lane, 2016; Winkielman & Berridge, 2004). In fairness to our brains, it wouldn't be helpful to be consciously aware of every single thing experienced throughout the day. Our brains are magnificent largely because they do a lot of work under the hood, outside of conscious awareness (Tversky & Kahneman, 1981; Västfjäll et al., 2016). However, because emotions can prompt irrational thinking (Veilleux et al., 2022) or impulsive behaviors (Carver & Johnson, 2018), awareness is useful for helping people shift their thinking and refrain from acting impulsively (Lambie, 2009).

Awareness is important enough that it's a prerequisite for doing much of the other work in this book. To figure out what to do with the mail, you have to know you've received a message. And to cope effectively with your feelings, you have to know you're having a feeling.

ASSESSING YOUR EMOTIONAL AWARENESS

How aware are you of your feelings?

Exhibit 2.1 provides some questions to help you ponder your level of emotional awareness. The first few questions ask about general awareness of feelings, and awareness of fluctuations in feelings, and can give you a general overview of your awareness.

The second set of questions are aimed at different levels of awareness (Lane, 2020; Smith et al., 2018). Some people are quite unaware they are having a feeling at all (the lowest level of awareness). Some people are aware of bodily sensations only (a low level). Some people are aware of bodily sensations plus action urges (e.g., "I felt a tug in my gut to get the hell out of there"), and others are aware of bodily sensations, plus action urges, plus at least some indication of a subjective feeling that is pleasant or unpleasant.

EXHIBIT 2.1. Emotional Awareness Questions

Questions to ask yourself about emotional awareness in general:

- If someone asked me how I am feeling right now, could I respond quickly and easily?
- Am I aware of small shifts in my feelings throughout the day?
- Am I attentive to potential threats or danger?
- Do I instinctively expect other people to feel the same as I do in a given situation?

Questions to ask yourself to figure out your general level of emotional awareness:

- Do people sometimes surprise me by asking if I'm OK, when I feel fine? Have people told me that my body or face conveys feelings that I don't feel inside?
- Am I drawn to feeling tension or sensations in my body? Am I aware of my heart rate, the sweatiness of my palms, and tension in my muscles? (If so, you may be attuned to the physiological components of emotion.)
- Do I sometimes feel strong urges to act (even if I don't actually perform the action) in response to situational or mental triggers? Do I sometimes feel the urge to attack, or to hide, or to jump up in the air? (If so, you may be attuned to the action urge component of emotion.)
- Do I change my thinking patterns when emotional triggers happen? Do my thoughts get more extreme, or do I get particularly self-critical? Do I find it hard to stop thinking about myself, my future, and my past? (If so, you may be attuned to the thinking component of emotion.)
- Am I able to tell when I feel different from my normal self? Can I say that I'm feeling good or bad (or possibly one or more specific emotions, e.g., angry, sad?)

Getting a sense of your starting place in the realm of emotional awareness can let you know about areas of growth. Higher levels of awareness involve being cognizant of more components of emotion and more nuance in emotional experience.

EMOTIONAL AWARENESS IS—GOOD?

When I have told therapy clients that increasing emotional awareness is a crucial part of emotional health, I've gotten some pushback. For example, I once worked with a woman named Casey who was highly emotionally sensitive. In our first therapy session, I worried that she was in the midst of a manic episode. She talked so loudly I thought everyone in the entire building would be able to hear her. She barked laughs that sounded forced. She also spoke quickly and in half-sentences, where she commented on her own words and switched topics in the middle of a thought. She barely made sense.

A few sessions later, we discussed the idea of improving emotional awareness. Casey balked at this. She said, "I'm TOO aware of my feelings! I feel every little thing, I know those body sensations, and I recognize my action tendencies and I ABSOLUTELY know when I'm feeling bad, which is most of the time. You want me to do MORE of that?"

Casey made a reasonable point. It is certainly the case that some people—typically, people with a high level of emotional sensitivity—have emotions that flare up quickly and experience feelings that have too much power over the person's life. It is certainly the case that some people are overly attentive to their emotions.

However, when it comes to emotion, *awareness* and *attention* are not entirely the same thing. We'll talk a bit more about how emotions often direct attention toward important information in Chapter 3.

Right now, the task is to understand that overattentiveness to emotions is a problem, but awareness is what you actually want to cultivate.

To understand this point, we first need to understand how emotions come to be. We need to understand how emotions are generated.

STAGES OF EMOTION GENERATION

As much as emotions seem to pop up from out of nowhere, they really don't. There is a clear process for how emotions are generated (Gross, 1998b, 2015; Gross et al., 2019). This process has implications for awareness, because people also vary in how aware they are of the stages of **emotion generation**.

In Chapter 1, we talked about emotional wave charting and how emotions are triggered, rise to a peak, and then fall again. Most people think that emotions are caused directly by a trigger, when a situation (or another person) creates an emotion. Listen to how people talk about emotions, and you'll hear people say things like "He made me mad!" or "This assignment makes me so anxious."

However, if a situation or another person actually caused an emotion, then everyone would have the exact same reaction to the same situation. But two people often respond to the same situation very differently. For example, some people feel scared watching horror movies, and other people are amused by them. The situation itself doesn't cause the feeling. There are a few crucial steps between the trigger and the experienced feeling, namely, attention and appraisal. These are the core processes that result in your specific, personal, emotional experience (see Figure 2.1).

Before you have an emotional response, you have to attend to some aspect of the situation. What you attend to is what gets into your mind. Our brains are amazing and can soak up a lot more information than we consciously recognize. The pieces of a situation

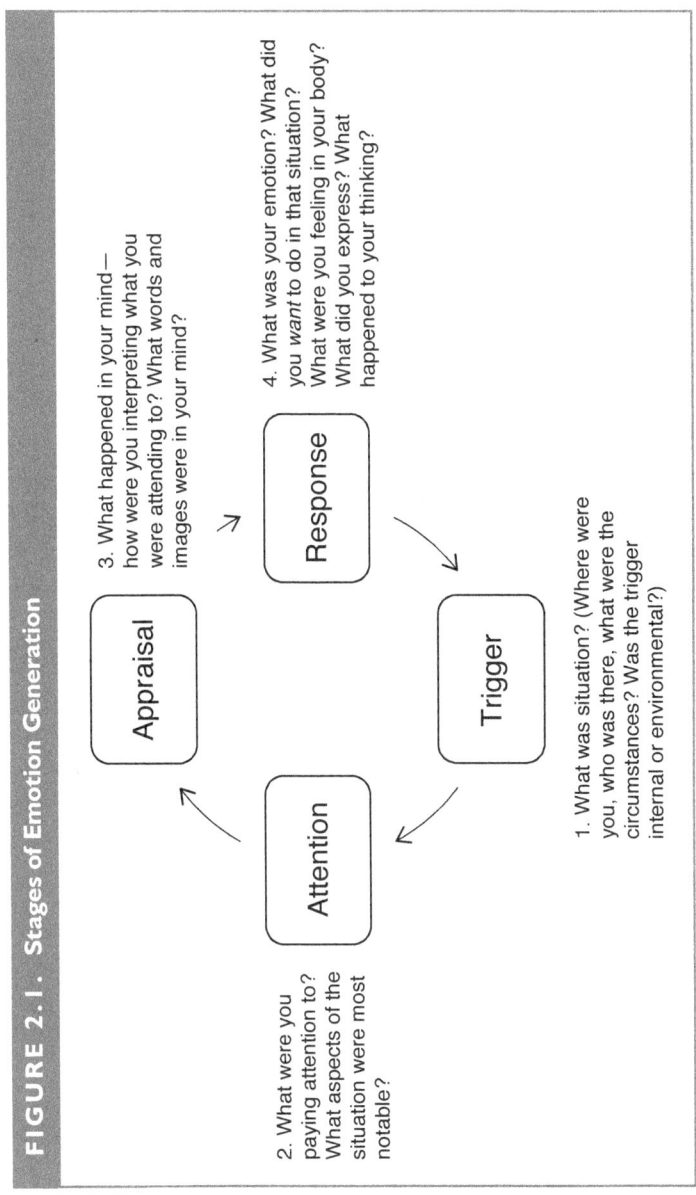

FIGURE 2.1. Stages of Emotion Generation

Appraisal

Response

Attention

Trigger

3. What happened in your mind— how were you interpreting what you were attending to? What words and images were in your mind?

4. What was your emotion? What did you *want* to do in that situation? What were you feeling in your body? What did you express? What happened to your thinking?

2. What were you paying attention to? What aspects of the situation were most notable?

1. What was situation? (Where were you, who was there, what were the circumstances? Was the trigger internal or environmental?)

your brain latches onto—conscious or otherwise—are the ones that will contribute the most to your emotional experience.

After attention comes **appraisal.** Appraisal is a fancy word for "interpretation": We appraise or interpret the information about the situation that our mind attended to. We will talk more about the appraisal process in Chapter 3. For now, what's important to know is that different patterns of interpretation tend to lead to different types of emotions. For example, think about getting stuck in traffic or in a long line and feeling frustrated or angry. Anger is associated with interpreting the situation as unpleasant or unfair and realizing that a goal you want (e.g., to get to where you want to go) is blocked.

For example, when I was sitting in my car having that panic attack, I was attending to my physical sensations, tuning in to my heart rate and breathing. I interpreted, or appraised, those physical sensations as dangerous and an indicator of a serious health problem.

Attending to other aspects of the situation, or making different interpretations (or both), can change the emotional response. If I had not attended to my physical symptoms, I never would have gone to the emergency room. If I had attended to my physical symptoms but interpreted them differently—for example, if I'd said, "Wow, I drank too much caffeine at lunch; I'd better have more water"—I probably wouldn't have freaked out (and I wouldn't have gone to the emergency room).

You might have noticed that, in relating the story of my panic attack, I skipped over discussing my trigger. That's because at the time, I didn't notice any trigger. I was just sitting in a parking lot! There was a trigger, though—I just wasn't aware of it at the time. I had to work to increase my awareness, both of the emotional response and of the processes that generated it.

ATTENTION VERSUS AWARENESS

Attention functions as a spotlight. We can't take in all of the information in our environments at once, so our attention helps us select what we want to zoom in on (Matthews & Wells, 1999). In contrast, awareness is conscious: People can report on what they are aware of. Much of the time, attention and awareness go together, because we're aware of what we pay attention to. However, they can be separated. The brain processes information faster than our conscious brains can articulate, which suggests that attention can occur without awareness (Hsieh et al., 2011).

The entire idea of subliminal messaging is based on the notion of people attending to information of which they aren't consciously aware. Here is an example. My 10-year-old child still sucks his thumb. Some part of his brain is attending to his thumb-sucking desire, because his hand makes its way to his mouth, but he's often unaware that he's doing it. Just this morning, I watched him suck his thumb four times in a 2-minute period and I asked him, "How many times did you suck your thumb just now?" He had no idea. His mouth was sure attending to his thumb, but he was unaware that he was doing it!

When considering emotional awareness, there are three different profiles to discuss. The first two are associated with problems with attention. I'll talk about each profile briefly and then dig into each in more detail.

The first profile reflects *involuntary attention with narrowed awareness*—this is what my client, Casey, was talking about when she said she was "too" aware of her emotions. Involuntary attention can be a hazard of high emotional sensitivity. We'll call this the *Watching the Mailbox* problem. The Watching the Mailbox problem occurs when attention is zoomed onto the emotion. The attention seems to have a mind of its own, and even if you wanted to look somewhere else the light just keeps shining back on the emotion. From an emotional-message standpoint, this is like checking the UPS delivery app every 5 minutes, trying to track exactly when to open the door to greet the delivery driver. And even when someone tells you that checking the app and waiting at the window will not make your package arrive any faster, you feel like you're not even doing it on purpose—it's just something you have to do.

The second profile reflects *low awareness*; this is what I experienced with my panic attack. We'll call this the *Delivery Unsuccessful* problem. From an emotional-message standpoint, this means the messages are never getting delivered. It's like you can't hear the delivery driver knocking at your door because your music is on too loud, or you never actually trudge to the mailbox. This involves difficulties attending to the emotional trigger, or unclear appraisal processes that cause you to not actually recognize that an emotion has occurred.

Finally, we have the profile we're aiming for, a *broad and balanced awareness* with the ability to at least somewhat control attention. We'll call this the *Mindful Awareness* profile.

The Watching the Mailbox Problem

Watching the Mailbox is associated with overattentiveness to the process of emotion generation, and it coincides with a related issue, the "Mail With Sticky Glue" problem, which involves overattentiveness to an emotion that has already been generated. In the Mail With Sticky Glue problem, it is as if a prankster has put a thin line of superglue onto the mail pile so that when it's picked up, you can't put it down, and all of your attention goes to this mail that's now stuck to your hand.

Both Watching the Mailbox and the Mail With Sticky Glue are problems of involuntary attention to emotion. Casey did not want to be thinking about her emotions, and she did not want emotions to be a prominent part of her identity, but they were. This is why she said she was too aware of her emotions, because her emotions captured her attention without her willingness. She would have readily endorsed involuntary-attention-to-emotion items such as "Paying attention to my emotions is not something I can control" or "I find myself paying attention to my emotions even when I don't want to" (Huang et al., 2013).

Greater involuntary attention to emotion is associated with more mental health symptoms (Ingram, 1990), including, but not limited to, depression and anxiety (Huang et al., 2013). Although sometimes called *self-focused attention*, this does not mean that people who are depressed or anxious (or have any other mental health diagnosis) are selfish or self-centered—far from it. In fact, many people who are depressed and anxious give so much to others that they lose sight of what they need for themselves (O'Connor et al., 2007). The terms *self-focused attention* and *involuntary attention to emotion* simply refer to an active mind that often latches onto thoughts and feelings that are self-relevant.

I made the case in the previous section that attention is different from awareness, and here's where that distinction is most notable. With involuntary attention to emotion, attention snaps onto potentially threatening and dangerous information. There are all kinds of cognitive biases at work here, which simply means that as emotions are being generated, the brain automatically and unconsciously processes some kind of information (THREATS! BAD MEMORIES!) more readily than other kinds of information (neutral, positive, balanced, holistic information).

Involuntary attention to emotion is also associated with imbalanced appraisals; that is, interpretations are likely to be more extreme. They are more negative (e.g., "This situation is horrible"), global (e.g., "It will always be this way"), and self-critical (e.g., "It's my fault, I'm to blame, this never would have happened if not for what I did").

I hope you can see that the Watching the Mailbox problem and the Mail With Sticky Glue problems are strongly associated with involuntary attention to emotion. Involuntary attention to emotion feels like too much awareness, but really attention is spotlighted onto the emotion and the perceived threats those emotions convey, rather than a broad view of the whole stage.

If you are someone who watches the mailbox or gets stuck in your feelings, is there any way out? Yep. Paradoxically, the primary solution is pretty much the same as the solution for increasing awareness in people with the Delivery Unsuccessful problem.

The Delivery Unsuccessful Problem

The Delivery Unsuccessful problem is an issue of low emotional awareness. Note that there are people with low emotional sensitivity who just don't get a lot of mail. The Delivery Unsuccessful problem isn't that. Instead, this problem is about people who are emotional but are simply unaware of their emotions. People prone to the Delivery Unsuccessful problem might say that they are low in emotional sensitivity and don't experience many subjective feelings; however, if you watch them closely enough it becomes evident that they do experience substantive emotional shifts, or they act in emotional ways. Garrett, my client from Chapter 1 who would admit he felt "stressed" but wouldn't acknowledge that "stress" was a feeling, definitely fits in this group.

The scientific term for people who are prone to the Delivery Unsuccessful problem is **alexithymia**. Alexithymia is not a disorder but a personality-like characteristic that describes up to 10% of the population (Koven & Thomas, 2010; Samur et al., 2013). The word *alexithymia* comes from the Greek and means "without words for emotions." It is associated with problems recognizing and understanding feelings, which are problems of emotional awareness. Alexithymia is also associated with difficulties labeling and expressing emotions. We revisit alexithymic tendencies in Chapters 4 and 8. For now, what's important to know is that alexithymia is a risk factor for a wide variety of mental health concerns, including schizophrenia (O'Driscoll et al., 2014), autism (Kinnaird et al., 2019), depression (Hemming et al., 2019), substance use (Honkalampi et al., 2022), and eating disorders (Nowakowski et al., 2013).

When considering the stages of emotion generation, alexithymic people tend not to appraise or interpret information in their environment as emotional. Then, alexithymic people operate at low levels of emotional awareness once an emotional response has been generated (Luminet et al., 2021), and they struggle to distinguish between physical and emotional sensations (Bagby et al., 1994).

Men are more likely to have alexithymia than women (Levant et al., 2009), because men and boys are socialized to push away and restrict emotions, in particular vulnerable emotions such as sadness and anxiety (Levant, 1995). "Strong" and passionate feelings associated with anger, aggression, and lust are perfectly acceptable according to masculine ideology. This isn't to say that men are always less emotionally aware. I know plenty of men who are emotionally sensitive and quite aware of their feelings. What's important here is that in some cultural subgroups, including men in the United States, not attending to emotions is pretty normal. When people are taught to push their emotions away, are never taught to develop and use a rich emotional vocabulary, and are discouraged from openly sharing their emotions (Edwards et al., 2017), alexithymia can occur.

Women (and nonbinary folks) can be alexithymic, too. In fact, one of the big revelations I had while writing this book is that I myself am high on alexithymia! I have a very hard time knowing what I'm feeling.

When viewed through a Delivery Unsuccessful lens, my panic attack and reactions to my panic attack make a lot of sense. I was aware of only the physical aspects of my feeling, which corresponds to a low level of awareness.

Alexithymia is usually, but not always, associated with low emotional sensitivity. There is evidence, in fact, that psychological disorders that are yoked with strong emotional sensitivity (anxiety, depression, borderline personality disorder) have higher proportions of individuals who show evidence of alexithymia (Preece et al., 2020). Some people think that highly sensitive people develop an alexithymic style to blunt their sensitivity. (Garrett, the client who only felt "stressed," was probably one of these people.)

If you are someone with high levels of alexithymia who doesn't get deliveries of emotional messages, can you learn to better listen for the mail truck? Can you turn up the volume on the notifications for your email inbox? Absolutely. Many strategies have been suggested to help people with alexithymia, including those covered in this book: emotional labeling (Chapter 4) and emotional expression (Chapter 8) in particular. Therapy helps, too (Cameron et al., 2014).

People with low levels of awareness can also start with the components they are aware of and use that low-level awareness to tune in to other aspects of an emotion. I've had to train myself to figure out what I might be feeling. For example, I involuntarily clench my stomach muscles when I'm feeling anxious, tense, angry, or sad. But I also feel sensations in my stomach when I'm hungry, or sick. And don't get me started about how confusing my belly barometer was during pregnancy! I typically know when something is happening in my body, but I don't always know it is a feeling. I have to explicitly ask myself, "Am I hungry? Could I be sick? Is the baby kicking? Or, wait—am I nervous?"

I also look for other clues to help me figure out if I'm experiencing an emotion, usually after tuning in to my physical sensations.

I ask myself "Am I thinking differently than usual, or do I have an urge to act?" If my urge is to eat, I'm probably just hungry. (Though that might not be an ideal clue; some people have the urge to eat when they are sad; see Heatherton & Baumeister, 1991). If my urge is to problem-solve, or look information up online, or if I notice that I'm especially self-critical, I'm probably feeling an emotion.

There is one strategy that works particularly well to combat the Delivery Unsuccessful problem, and it works for the Watching the Mailbox problem too. Mindfulness is the key to balanced emotional awareness, and it is a crucial component of the third profile, Mindful Awareness (Edwards et al., 2018; Norman et al., 2019).

MINDFUL AWARENESS

The third awareness profile, and the one to aim for, is Mindful Awareness. This profile represents a balanced approach to emotional awareness. A mindfully aware person has at least a moderate level of emotional awareness and can distinguish between physical and emotional symptoms. This person also knows—at the very least—that a feeling is occurring and can say whether it is pleasant or unpleasant. A mindfully aware person can pay voluntary attention to their feelings, rather than only involuntary attention.

MINDFULNESS AS A USEFUL PRACTICE

The good news is that if you have a Watching the Mailbox or Delivery Unsuccessful profile, practicing mindfulness can help you achieve a Mindful Awareness profile.

Mindfulness is the practice of paying attention to the present moment without judgment (Bishop et al., 2004). I've provided two classic mindfulness activities for you to practice: mindfulness to breath (Exhibit 2.2) and mindfulness to sound (Exhibit 2.3). These activities

---

EXHIBIT 2.2. Mindfulness to Breath

This mindfulness activity involves practice observing your breath, without trying to change how you breathe. Start by doing this for 2 minutes, and slowly increase the time to 5 minutes once you get the hang of it.

- Sit with your feet firmly planted.
- Close your eyes, or focus them on a point on the floor in front of you.
- Pay attention to your breath going in and out; do not count your breaths or try to change your breath in any way.
- Curiously observe how your breath moves in and out of your nose and mouth.
- What are the texture and temperature of your inhales? Are your inhales short and shallow, or are they slow and deep?
- Is your breath residing in your chest or your belly?
- Notice your exhales. Do you naturally exhale out of your mouth or your nose? Do you exhale completely, or do you hold a little breath in?
- Observe all of these without making judgments. If you find yourself making a judgment, label it as a judgment and let it go, returning to observing your breath.
- When your mind wanders away from your breath, gently turn your mind back to your breath without judging yourself.
- Do not do this activity while driving!

---

differ in terms of where attention is focused: either inward, on breath (Exhibit 2.2), or outside the self, on a part of the environment (Exhibit 2.3). Each of these exercises takes only 2 minutes, and ideally you should try to practice one of them every day.

Both exercises are intended to help people practice tuning into a specific aspect of the current moment. The specific part matters because it is difficult, maybe impossible, to be truly aware of all aspects of the current moment (e.g., sight, sound physical sensations, feelings, urges, thoughts, and everything going on in the immediate environment). The brain is capable of paying attention to only a few

---

EXHIBIT 2.3. Mindfulness to Sound

This mindfulness activity involves observing sounds in your immediate environment. Start by doing this for 2 minutes, and slowly increase the time to 5 minutes once you get the hang of it.

- Sit or stand with your feet firmly planted on the ground.
- Close your eyes, or focus them on a point on the floor in front of you.
- Pay attention to all the sounds around you, both near and far away.
- Describe the sounds. Are they short and shrill? High pitched or low pitched? Loud or soft? Rumbling or sporadic? Natural or technological?
- Observe the sounds without making judgments. If you find yourself making a judgment, label it as a judgment and let it go, returning to observing the sounds.
- If you find yourself caught up in other people's conversations or the content of speech, forgive yourself and try to focus on what the speech sounds like rather than what is being said. Is the voice low or high? Slow or pressured?
- When your mind wanders away from sounds, gently turn your mind back to observing sounds without judging yourself.

---

things at a time. When practicing mindfulness, pick one thing (e.g., breath or sound) to intentionally train your mind to follow.

The nonjudgment part of the definition is also important. You want to be able to describe what you're attending to (e.g., "The bird is chirping") without making any kind of attribution of goodness (e.g., "That birdsong is so pretty!") or badness (e.g., "That wood-pecker is so annoying").

I can't tell you how many times, after I have explained mindfulness to someone, that they say either "I don't need mindfulness skills because I'm already really good at it; I'm mindful all the time" or "I hate mindfulness." I'm skeptical of both of those responses, because each suggests a lack of understanding of what mindfulness truly entails. Let us unpack each of these mindfulness myths.

So, You're Good at Mindfulness: Are You Sure About That?

I struggle with what it actually means to be good at mindfulness. Yes, there are people who are better at focusing their mind on the present moment without getting distracted, but it's perfectly acceptable to get distracted during a mindfulness activity. In fact, it's expected. Why? Because minds think. That's what minds are supposed to do. Thoughts and images float (or speed) through the mind, and the mind wanders. When I try to pay attention to my breath, I sometimes end up thinking about what TV show I'm going to watch later, or whether I have popcorn stuck between my teeth.

Having distracting thoughts doesn't mean you are bad at mindfulness; neither does the absence of those thoughts necessarily mean you are good at mindfulness. The whole point of mindfulness is to tune in to what the mind is doing, to try to focus on something specific, and when your mind moves away, as it inevitably will, to notice what your mind is doing and gently bring it back. So, when I find myself thinking about a TV show, I make an effort to recognize and redirect. I say to myself "Oops, thanks for your curiosity about pop culture, but let's go back to focusing on breath again. Come over here, mind."

When people tell me that they are good at mindfulness, and I ask them to explain what they mean, a good chunk of the time they say something like, "I can just get into whatever I'm doing. This mindfulness-to-sound thing? I do this all the time when walking. I just listen to the birds chirping, and I lose track of where I even am."

That's not mindfulness. "Losing yourself" in a task or activity is called **flow** (Nakamura & Csikszentmihalyi, 2002). When in a flow state, you are so absorbed in the activity that you lose all sense of time and self. In this state, action and awareness are merged. A person in a flow state is one with their actions.

Don't get me wrong—flow is great. Think about an athlete in the zone during an Olympic trial, or an artist losing hours of time while painting. People get into flow states during video games, too. Flow states are associated with deep enjoyment of the activity, because attention is absorbed into the activity (Nakamura & Csikszentmihalyi, 2002).

In reality, flow and mindfulness are actually very different. A major distinction is that when being mindful, a person has the capacity to know what they are paying attention to. I sometimes explain mindfulness as having "one foot in and one foot out." To be mindful, you have to be aware of what your mind is doing. The one-foot-in side of your mind is trying to pay attention to breath or sound. The one-foot-out side of your mind is watching and observing the "in" side. With a flow state, your mind becomes fully absorbed into an activity. A flow state is "all in." In fact, one of the defining characteristics of flow is that you don't even know you were in a flow state until after it's over. That idea of "Oh, I lost track of time because I was so into playing Mario Kart" is flow, but it can't be mindfulness. With mindfulness, you try to be aware of what you're doing while you're doing it.

Having one foot in and one foot out is hard! Mindfulness to breath involves part of your mind attending to your breath (one foot in) and another part tracking where your mind is going (one foot out). The inward foot wants to pull along the outward foot, and it often does. That's what happens when I think about a TV show or popcorn kernels in my teeth during a mindfulness activity: My one-foot-in mind wandered away, and my one-foot-out mind tagged along automatically. Mindfulness practice helps train that one-foot-out mind to be more aware and less of a follower.

So, You Hate Mindfulness: Are You Sure About That?

When a person says they hate mindfulness, what does that mean? Maybe they mean that practicing mindfulness is either unpleasant, or difficult, or both. I get it. I personally despise mindfulness to breath (Exhibit 2.2). I find it unpleasant and difficult. I start thinking,

"Am I breathing normally? Am I supposed to be breathing deeper or more slowly than usual? Is it normal for my heart to be beating this fast? Am I doing this right?" Mindfulness to breath makes me feel incompetent at doing something that I do literally all of the time without thinking about it: breathing. I hate feeling incompetent!

Yet, mindfulness to breath is one of the most helpful activities for me. Is it fun? No. But remember that mindfulness is about paying attention to the present moment in a nonjudgmental way. I epically fail at nonjudgment when I say, "I hate mindfulness to breath." *Hate* is a strong judgment word, and I have a very hard time not judging myself when doing mindfulness to breath. It is exactly for this reason that mindfulness to breath is useful for me—not fun, but useful. When I do mindfulness to breath, I find myself thinking, "This sucks. This is boring. I'm so bad at this." Then the "one foot out" part of my mind can label those thoughts as "judgment, judgment, judgment." The important part, in particular when first learning to practice mindfulness, is to acknowledge and recognize the judgments. Just noting when you make judgments is a good first step.

In contrast, I really love mindfulness to sound. Tuning in to small nuances of sound makes me realize how much is happening in the world around me. Even in a quiet office, you can hear the hum of the lights, which is about a B-flat in pitch in the United States (Andrei, 2021). When I'm outside, I hear the sound of the wind, the chirping of birds and scampering of squirrels, and occasional traffic noises. I can get distracted by my own thoughts when trying to mindfully attend to sounds (because minds wander!), but I don't get tugged into judgments. Mindfulness to sound is fun and relaxing for me.

There was a trick in that last paragraph. Did you catch it?

Judgments can be opinions of either badness or goodness. My liking mindfulness to sound is actually a positive judgment. I'm judging mindfulness to sound as good and mindfulness to breath as bad. Positive judgments are judgments, too, and so when practicing mindfulness to sound I have to watch myself to ensure that I remain descriptive (e.g., "I feel the wind on my face") and avoid even positive judgments (e.g., "This wind on my face feels so great!").

My dislike of mindfulness to breath and my enjoyment of mindfulness to sound also relates to one other reason many people say they hate mindfulness: because they think mindfulness doesn't work. What does it mean for mindfulness to work? I personally like mindfulness to sound because it is relaxing. It gets me out of my head, and I find that relieving. If I define "working" as "helping me feel better," then yes, mindfulness to sound definitely works, and it works far better for me than mindfulness to breath.

But if "working" means "helps me become more of the person I want to be," then mindfulness to breath is really the activity that works, because it pushes me to be aware of and to shift my own judgmental tendencies and actively confront my distaste for feeling incompetent. Mindfulness to breath is more difficult, and so it is a skill that builds my emotional strength the more I practice it.

Most people who I've encountered don't think mindfulness works because they don't see an immediate effect of mindfulness on their mood. But that's not actually the purpose of mindfulness. Mindfulness helps train that one-foot-out side of the mind to observe without judgment and to help people feel as though they have a bit more control over what their mind is doing. The purpose of mindfulness is not to influence momentary mood; it is to train voluntary attention. Mindfulness is a type of emotional strength training. Can you see the effect of physical strength training in a gym right away? Nope!

So, if you're someone who dislikes mindfulness, I hear you. But engaging in regular mindfulness practice can help you even though you dislike it. If you can commit to doing it every day for 2 minutes (or maybe even three times a week, if every day is too much), check back in with yourself after a month. What have you learned? Is it possible that maybe the idea of the practice working can be more than just what feels good in the moment? Is it possible that perhaps greater awareness of your thoughts and emotions is a worthy outcome even if you don't "feel better"?

Different Mindfulness Activities for Different Awareness Problems

Mindfulness is a valuable practice for just about everyone, because mindfulness helps train emotional awareness. However, the function of mindfulness is slightly different for people who tend toward the Watching the Mailbox problem versus those with the Delivery Unsuccessful problem.

I intentionally included two mindfulness activities that differ in focus between attending to sensations inside the body (mindfulness to breath) versus attending to sensations outside of the body, external to the self (mindfulness to sound). People who involuntarily pay too much attention to their feelings should practice mindfulness to external sensations because intense emotions often involve excess attention to internal sensations, like feelings, thoughts, and physiological changes. That means the brain needs to be trained to shift attention to momentary sensations outside of the body.

On the other hand, people low in emotional awareness (e.g., those who have alexithymia) benefit most from increasing attention to internal sensations. Practicing tuning in to internal physical sensations (e.g., mindfulness to breath, body scan mindfulness, as described in Exhibit 2.4) can help a person with low emotional sensitivity start to recognize small fluctuations in their internal experience. Greater attention to internal nuances can help people identify when an emotional response might be occurring. Mindfulness is a crucial tool for helping people with alexithymia gain more awareness and understanding of their feelings (Norman et al., 2019).

What if you have a moderate level of emotional awareness? Mindfulness is still a useful skill to practice. Try both mindfulness to

---

EXHIBIT 2.4. Other Mindfulness Activities

Mindfulness to Internal Experiences (for Delivery Unsuccessful Problems)

- *Mindfulness to thoughts.* Observe where your thoughts go. For this activity, there is nothing specific to train your focus on; instead, you are the observer watching what your mind does. Are your thoughts linear, or are they jumbled? Do you think in words or images? Do your thoughts jump around from topic to topic, or are they connected?
- *Mindful body scan.* Lie on the floor and start with mindfulness to breath (see Exhibit 2.2). Then, starting from your toes, try to feel all parts of your body. Begin with your toes and slowly work your way up your body (feet, ankles, calves, knees, thighs, pelvis, belly, chest, shoulders, arms, wrists, neck, head), attending to the feel of each body part and what it is connected to. Is it touching the floor? What does it feel like from the inside?
- *Mindfulness to feelings.* This is useful to do when some kind of conflict occurs, thoughts feel different, or physical sensations are occurring. Turn inward and curiously look for places of tension. Do you feel tension in your neck, hands, stomach, chest? Is your breathing shallow or deep? Is your heart racing, or has it slowed? Do you feel the urge to approach or avoid others?

Mindfulness to External Experiences (for Watching the Mailbox Problems)

- *Mindful eating.* Focus on the colors, textures, and smell of your food (or drink). Take small bites or sips, and attend to the sensations in your mouth. What does it feel like to chew and swallow your food? (Note: This may be triggering for high-sensitivity people with eating pathology.)
- *Mindful walking.* Take a walk outside (or inside, in a place that has more than one room, if possible), without your phone or any other devices. Notice how your feet feel against the ground. Notice how your arms swing or stay still at your side. What does the air feel like as your body passes through it? What do your feet sound like as you take steps?

breath and mindfulness to sound, and check your judgments. Which was more difficult for you? Practice the harder skill to help train your mind to have more flexibility. Practice the easier skill to gain confidence and maybe even derive moderate enjoyment from mindfulness. I practice mindfulness to sound to keep my attitude toward mindfulness positive, but I practice mindfulness to breath for growth.

FINDING THE "SWEET SPOT"

In the 1980s, a famous psychological study assessed the relationship between emotions and life satisfaction (Schwarz & Clore, 1983). Researchers called participants on the phone and found that people reported being happier and more satisfied with their life when they were asked questions on a sunny, nice day versus a cloudy, rainy day. Because people are happier on sunny days and gloomier on cloudy days, people tended to report higher life satisfaction when it was sunny outside.

However, the life satisfaction differences between rainy and sunny days disappeared when the researchers innocently asked, "How's the weather there?" In essence, once people were consciously aware of the weather, the weather had less influence on their feelings and thoughts (Schwarz & Clore, 1983). To extend this idea, once people are consciously aware of their feelings, those feelings can be harnessed and used with intention, or intentionally set aside, instead of affecting thoughts and behaviors unconsciously. The "sweet spot" of emotional awareness is when you know a feeling is occurring and you have some agency or control over your attention.

Awareness of Triggers

When I had that panic attack in a parking lot in 2004, I was unaware of the **trigger**, which is the situation that prompts the emotion-generation process (Figure 2.1). In retrospect, it was my lack of awareness of the trigger that was the core of the problem. I assumed that any physiological reaction had to be associated with my health because I wasn't aware of any other possible trigger. Further reflection, though, helped me become aware of everything else that was going on.

In the winter and spring of 2004, I was in the process of applying to graduate school. Clinical psychology graduate programs are incredibly competitive, and because I had majored in theater as an undergraduate, and I didn't have clinical psychologist mentors, I wasn't aware of the hidden expectations of the application process. Also, I was married to my ex-husband at the time, and I'd made a deal with him that if I didn't get into graduate school, we'd try to start having a family. But if I did get into graduate school, we'd have to move across the country. Oh, and I was also trying to train a puppy to stop peeing on the carpet in our apartment.

It was a high-pressure time. I wasn't ready to have kids, and I desperately wanted to become a clinical psychologist. The puppy peeing on the floor was stressful, too. Although I don't recall exactly what I was thinking about in that parking lot in 2004, I'm guessing I was thinking about my chances of acceptance and the implications for my future, and these thoughts increased my heart rate, which I then attended to and interpreted as dangerous. A panic attack ensued.

In this discussion of emotional awareness, we have focused primarily on awareness of the emotional response. However, true awareness involves recognizing all of the stages of emotion generation: knowing what the trigger was and having an idea of what was attended to, what your interpretation was, and the emotional response.

I hope I've convinced you that emotional awareness matters for overall emotional health and that it's important to recognize that you are feeling something, and maybe where the feeling is coming from, but to not pay too much attention to your emotions. You want to get the delivery but not watch the mailbox!

SUMMARY POINTS

- Emotional awareness is the state of being attentive to, and aware of, an emotional response. From an emotional-messages standpoint, emotional awareness is knowing there's mail in the mailbox.

- Being aware of the stages of emotion generation can be helpful. An emotion stems from a trigger (either an internal trigger or a trigger from the external environment), which is then attended to and interpreted, and an emotional response blossoms.

- Awareness is broader than attention. Attention is a specific focus (like a spotlight) and is used to get information into the brain. Attention can be unconscious and involuntary.

- Low levels of awareness are associated with noticing the physiological aspect of emotion, and high levels are associated with noticing more of the components of emotion.

- One profile of emotional awareness involves an involuntary, out-of-control attention to emotion, typically to the unpleasant or threatening aspects of emotion. This profile is associated with the Watching the Mailbox and Mail With Sticky Glue problems. People high in emotional sensitivity are vulnerable to this.

- Another type of emotional awareness issue is the Delivery Unsuccessful problem, which is associated with alexithymia. People high in alexithymia tend to have difficulty attending to emotional stimuli, and they struggle to interpret information from an emotional lens.

- Practicing mindfulness is helpful for all of the problems related to emotional awareness. In particular, mindfulness to breath (i.e., internal sensations) is useful for alexithymia, and mindfulness to sound (i.e., external sensations) is useful for involuntary attention to emotion.

CHAPTER 3

CLARIFY YOUR VALUES

I once worked with a woman I'll call Casey, who I talked about a little bit in Chapter 2. Casey, who was in her mid-20s, was highly emotionally sensitive. She felt her feelings very strongly and intensely. She was also overly attentive to her emotions. She was aware that when she felt emotional it was obvious to her, and she thought that other people could tell how she was feeling, too.

Casey also didn't know what she wanted to do in life. She'd been a star athlete in high school and had received a scholarship to play in college. But she wasn't interested in playing sports professionally, and after she graduated from college she didn't know what career to pick. This was a regular theme of discussion in our sessions. She worked as an Amazon delivery driver to pay the bills, but she didn't want to do that long term. She thought about becoming a firefighter, or a social worker. Every time she thought about a new career direction, she'd take a few steps toward that goal and then pivot to something else.

She lacked persistence in her personal life, too. She talked about wanting to be in a relationship, and she occasionally went on dates with people she met on dating apps, but nothing stuck. She'd go on a few dates and find someone who really liked her, and then she'd break it off.

Casey was stressed out not knowing her life purpose. What was she meant to do? Why was she here, on this earth? How would she leave her mark for future generations?

These are questions about meaning and fulfillment. When people feel as though their lives are full, meaningful, and psychologically rich (Oishi & Westgate, 2022), they report greater well-being and life satisfaction.

Finding meaning, fulfillment, and psychological richness seems like a daunting task. These aren't attributes that you can just wait to stumble into, and you can't expect that they'll come looking for you. You have to cultivate meaning. You have to search for fulfillment. Meaning, fulfillment, and psychological richness are embedded in the actions, situations, and interactions with people whom you choose (Oishi & Westgate, 2022).

So, how did Casey figure out her purpose? And what on earth do meaning, fulfillment, and psychological richness have to do with emotions and dealing with emotional messages? The answer to the second question is "everything." The answer to the first question is "values." Before we talk about values, though, we need to talk about why people even have emotions in the first place.

FUNCTIONS OF EMOTIONS

Most people would agree that happy feelings are good. Feeling joy, excitement, love, contentment, interest, relaxation, pride, and awe is generally enjoyable. But what about the unpleasant feelings? What is the point of those?

If your instinctive response is, "NOTHING, they are USELESS and downright HORRIBLE," you would be in good company. It is certainly true that unpleasant emotions (e.g., anxiety, sadness, fear, anger, disgust, shame, guilt, embarrassment) are, by definition, unpleasant. They are not usually fun to experience, outside of the occasional horror movie. Yet, there are lots of things in the world that are not fun but are ultimately helpful to getting you where you want to go. Like exercise. And airports.

So, How Are Emotions Helpful?

There are at least three major functions of emotions (Izard, 2010). First, *emotions prepare the body for action.* The classic example is encountering a bear in the woods: Do you run away (flight), attack (fight), or play dead (freeze)?[1] In Chapter 2, we talked about how attention is a spotlight, and emotions can help serve as the spotlight operator. High-energy emotions, like anger and feeling threatened, help narrow our attention onto potential threats (Friedman & Förster, 2010), and low-energy emotions, like sadness and contentment, broaden attention so we see what and who else is nearby (Gable & Harmon-Jones, 2010). Emotions direct our attention and speed up or slow down our nervous system to prepare for what's next.

The second function of emotion is to *facilitate communication.* Facial expressions, body language, and tone of voice can provide a host of information much faster and more efficiently than words (Kennedy-Moore & Watson, 2001). Also, because sharing emotions with others is one of the best ways to forge strong bonds with another person (Tackman & Srivastava, 2016), emotions are a powerful tool for social connection. We'll talk more about this function in Chapter 8.

The third function, which is the main focus of this chapter, is that *emotions signal when something is important.* Emotions allow us to learn about our reactions to the world and to ourselves. This is

---

[1]Apparently the answer depends on the kind of bear, and whether the bear is attacking or just investigating. Playing dead (freezing) around a brown or grizzly bear who attacked you is smart, but if a black bear attacks you it's better to fight back. Be prepared and learn bear identification when going into the wilderness!

because people cannot have emotions about things they don't care about. Let me repeat that, using slightly different words: *People only have emotions about what matters.*

Emotions Signal What Matters

Consider 16-year-old identical triplets Megan, Lisa, and Jessie.[2] They all go to a party one weekend and watch two of their classmates get into a physical fight. Megan doesn't particularly care about either classmate, and she isn't concerned about being in close proximity to a fight, so she has no emotional reaction at all. Lisa has a crush on one of the people in the fight, and she feels righteously angry that her crush was attacked. Jessie, who cares about peace and togetherness, is anxious about the fight escalating.

In Chapter 2, we talked about the stages of emotion generation, and how two—or three—people can have extremely different responses to the same situation because of what they *attend* to and how they *appraise* the situation. Consider Lisa (who feels angry) and Jessie (who feels anxious and sad). They attended to and interpreted different elements of the situation on the basis of what matters to them, which is why they have distinct emotional responses.

The interpretation of a particular situation is critical for determining whether an emotion is experienced and which emotion is felt. This perspective reflects the *appraisal theory* of emotion (Moors, 2014; Roseman et al., 1996; Smith & Ellsworth, 1985). Appraisal theories of emotion highlight the cognitive interpretation (or appraisal) of a situation as important to the emotional experience. There are many ways you can interpret a situation. Who caused the situation: you,

---

[2]These are the names of the triplets in the made-for-television movies *The Parent Trap III* (Miller, 1989a) and *The Parent Trap IV: Hawaiian Honeymoon* (Miller, 1989b).

someone else, or the circumstance? Is the situation positive or negative? Is the outcome certain or uncertain? Is the outcome controllable or uncontrollable? Is the outcome deserved?

The answers to these questions shape which emotion a person experiences. For example, for a person like Lisa, who believes that someone else is the cause of an upsetting situation and the outcome is unjust, the emotion felt is usually anger. A person like Jessie, who interprets the situation as uncertain, feels anxious. Also, remember that the most important interpretation determines whether an emotion is experienced: Does this situation even matter to you? If a situation isn't salient or relevant to you, you won't experience an emotional response (Moors, 2014; Smith & Kirby, 2001). For example, Megan didn't interpret the fight at the party as relevant to her, so she didn't feel anything at all. The flip side, then, is also true: When you have an emotional response, something matters to you. Emotions signal that something is important. The difficult part is figuring out what, specifically, is important.

Part of the difficulty in figuring out what is important is that sometimes the situation itself is not actually important or relevant to you at all, but an emotion occurs anyway. When that happens, the situation likely reminded you (maybe even unconsciously) about something important that happened in the past. Or, sometimes emotions signal that something important might happen in the future and are thus worth paying attention to. In subsequent chapters, we'll dig into figuring out what specific emotions might be telling you. For now, what is important is that emotions tell you that something is important.

The other crucial thing is that emotions signal that something matters *to you*. People differ in what they find important. Are there some things that tend to elicit an emotional response in just about everyone? Sure. Life-threatening situations, for example, are important because not attending to them can, quite literally, end in death.

Being in the midst of a natural disaster, such as an earthquake, a wild-fire, or a hurricane, prompts an emotional response in most people, because most people find their own lives to be important. Even those who intentionally pursue activities that are life threatening, like people who chase tornadoes or go BASE jumping (the sport of jumping off tall cliffs, buildings, or bridges) do so because they get a thrill (a type of emotional response) from those actions.

Different people care about different things, and so what is emotional to one person is not necessarily emotional to someone else. For example, I have a quick, visceral, angry response when I receive an email from a student addressed to "Mrs. Veilleux." I also know that in the South, where I live, kids are taught to say "Mrs." as a sign of respect. The people sending me emails addressed to "Mrs. Veilleux" are not trying to piss me off; they are trying to be polite. However, to me it feels disrespectful to assume that I'm married and to prioritize my theoretical marital status over my education. On the basis of my education and my professional title, I should be called "Dr. Veilleux," or "Professor Veilleux." But do all of my colleagues have a similar reaction when they receive emails that don't include a professional title? Nope, because not everyone cares that this happens to women far more often than it does to men.

The point is that when any emotion occurs, your feelings are basically nudging you to say "Ahem. Something important is afoot. Pay attention. Something matters to you right now."

INTRODUCTION TO VALUES

Another way to think about things that matter is to think about **values**. Values indicate what a person cares about and what is important to them. Values are also related to what a person chooses to organize their life around (DeYoung & Tiberius, 2023). We're going to deviate from talking about emotions for a little bit and really dig into values, but don't worry, we'll circle back!

Values are distinct from goals (Dahl, 2015). Goals can be checked off. Daily task lists are full of small goals ("Buy stamps," "Call to schedule mammogram," "Finish work project"). Bucket lists ("See Machu Picchu," "Try zip-lining") are full of larger goals. All of these goals or tasks can be completed. Even big-picture life goals, like "Watch children grow up and become successful adults," though not completely controllable, still fit the general definition of a goal.

Values, on the other hand, are "chosen life directions" (Thompson et al., 2013). Think about directions on a compass. You can head East, but you never actually get East. You can get to a place that is east of you right now, but you can't just arrive at East. East cannot be checked off. Similarly, values guide you to select and pursue check-off-able goals, but they themselves are never complete, never done. Values can be fed or nourished through engaging in values-consistent activities (e.g., going to that easterly place), but because values represent the core of what matters you have to keep feeding them to really feel the benefit.

For a less abstract example, one of my most cherished values is independence. I do not particularly like being told what to do. Just ask my parents, or my current husband (or my ex-husband)! I like figuring things out on my own, and I like making my own decisions. Independence has shown up throughout my life. When my advisor in graduate school suggested it would be a bad idea for me to take on a part-time job, I ignored him and took a job selling shoes at a big department store because I thought I could handle it, and I wanted the extra money. Even now, I do things that feed my value of independence. I figure out how to conduct a new statistical analysis, and I buy the new coat I want. Independence has been important to me since I was a child, and likely will continue to be, because it's core to who I am.

IDENTIFYING YOUR VALUES

Clarifying your values can help you navigate your emotions more effectively in many ways. But values identification is not as simple as saying "Well, I value having a good job, I value my family, and I value my free time." Although some people do talk about values in terms of life domains (Wilson et al., 2010), specific identities (e.g., some people see themselves as neurodiverse, athletic, a sports fan, a gamer), or skills (e.g., "good at woodworking"), I think it is generally more useful to think about values as the personal principles you live by (Schwartz, 2012). Exhibit 3.1 is a values clarification activity that you can do right now. There are five rules to completing this activity.

EXHIBIT 3.1. Values Clarification Activity

Look at the list of values below and choose your top 10, and then your top five. Remember to consider the values that matter but are unmet in your life. Be honest about what matters to you always and what matters to you now. Don't ignore a value that you think sounds bad if it is something you truly care about.

1. ACCEPTANCE	To accept people and things as they are
2. ACHIEVEMENT	To have important accomplishments
3. ADVENTURE	To have novel, unusual, and exciting experiences
4. AMBITION	To be hard working, aspiring toward goals
5. AUTHORITY	To have the power to make changes and have people listen

---

EXHIBIT 3.1. Values Clarification Activity (*Continued*)

6. BEAUTY	To appreciate beauty in nature, the arts, and people
7. BELONGING	To have a sense of belonging, the sense that others care
8. CARING	To take care of and help the people close to me
9. CREATIVITY	To create new things or ideas, use my imagination
10. CURIOSITY	To seek out, experience, and learn new things
11. DEFENSE	To make sure that my community and country are well defended
12. DEPENDABILITY	To know that friends and family can rely on me, trust me to keep my word
13. DOWN-TO-EARTH	To be practical, realistic, and satisfied with what I have
14. DUTY	To follow the rules and do what's right even when no one is watching
15. EQUALITY	To promote fair and equal treatment for all
16. ESTEEM	To be seen highly by others, to avoid humiliation
17. FAITH	To be devout, follow spiritual or religious beliefs

(continues)

EXHIBIT 3.1. Values Clarification Activity (*Continued*)

18. HEALTH	To be well and healthy
19. HELPFULNESS	To work for the welfare of others
20. HONESTY	To be genuine and sincere
21. HUMILITY	To be humble and never think I deserve more than others
22. HUMOR	To see the humorous side of myself and the world
23. INDEPENDENCE	To be self-reliant and self-sufficient, to choose my own goals
24. INTIMACY	To share my innermost experiences with others
25. LEADERSHIP	To inspire and guide others, to take command
26. LEISURE	To take time to relax and enjoy the good life
27. LOYALTY	To be loyal and true in relationships
28. OBEDIENCE	To obey all the laws and rules
29. PLEASURE	To feel pleasure from having desires gratified, including sexual pleasure
30. PROSPERITY	To have the resources to get whatever I want and need

EXHIBIT 3.1. Values Clarification Activity (*Continued*)

31. PROTECTION	To make sure that those in my community and country are safe from harm
32. PURPOSE	To choose my own goals and work toward them in ways I want
33. RECOGNITION	To be well liked and approved of by others
34. RESPECT	To honor parents and older people, to show respect to others
35. RESPONSIBILITY	To be accountable for my actions, reliable and able to be trusted by others
36. SAFETY	To make sure I and my loved ones are safe and secure
37. SOCIAL JUSTICE	To protect and seek justice for the most vulnerable in a society
38. TOLERANCE	To listen to and understand people who are different from me
39. TRADITION	To preserve time-honored customs
40. UNITY WITH NATURE	To feel connected to the Earth and to nature
41. VARIETY	To have a life with different experiences and situations (avoid monotony)
42. WEALTH	To have plenty of money

First, your job is to select 10 of the most important values to you, and then within those top 10, your special, most personal top five. This is a hard task for most people because none of the values are bad. In fact, this list represents values that people all over the world have indicated are important (Schwartz, 2017). I've given this activity to therapy clients, workshop participants, and students in my classes. They tend to find only a few of the values fairly irrelevant or unimportant, which means the majority of these values are important to most people. The task is to figure out which are the most important to you. What are the values that you feel are crucial to you, that are core to who you are? Those are the values you want to select to be in your top 10.

The second rule is that you are not allowed to ignore values that are meaningful to you but aren't evident in your life right now. For example, I did my clinical internship at a Veterans Affairs medical center, and I co-led a group for female veterans with chronic pain. Meredith was in that group. Meredith was paralyzed from the waist down and in a wheelchair. She had significant back pain virtually all the time. When Meredith did her values activity, she talked about how, before her accident, she had cared deeply about Adventure— about traveling, hiking, and exploring (see Exhibit 3.1). She said it was her love of Adventure that had prompted her to join the military in the first place, because she thought that she'd be able travel and see the world. Yet because of her injury she felt completely cut off from this value, and so she hesitated to select it. Don't hesitate! The point is to consider what values are core to who you are, even if a particular value isn't evident in your life right now.

The third rule is that you should be honest with yourself. No one is watching! It is tempting to pick values that represent who you wish you were. Maybe you really want to be Down-to-Earth, and you try to come across as practical, calm, and chill, but inside you are actually a ball of nerves. Or perhaps your parents told you to respect your elders and your community, and so you feel like a jerk not picking Respect as one of your core values. Ultimately this is your set of values and no one else's. Remember that none of the values on the list in Exhibit 3.1 are bad! If you look through the list and feel like you are supposed to value X, or wish you had Y, maybe mark it with a dot and come back to it after you've gone through the rest of the list. You can also think about what you are really willing to work toward. If there is a value you wish you had, think about what it would be like to put effort toward that value. Does it scare or excite you in a way that gets your blood moving faster, or do you just think "Meh, that sounds like a lot." If the latter is more of what you think, that's probably not one of your core values.

The fourth rule is that you want to think about what values matter to you now, with the recognition that values may change over time. For example, I spent my teenage and young adult years perpetually crushing on male friends who weren't interested in me romantically. I spent a lot of time yearning for these guys to love me. At the time, I would have told you that I valued Intimacy. In some ways, I nourished that value through friendships—I spent a lot of time talking, laughing, and joking with those guys. But I desperately wanted a romantic spark. Nowadays, however, I am in a very stable and happy marriage with my second—and, I hope, last—husband. I don't crave intimacy the way I used to, probably because I have it now. Instead, now I value Belonging—an interpersonal value similar to Intimacy but one that seems to better fit my life right now. Some values are consistent over the life span, and others may shift on the basis of life experiences. That's OK. What's important is to tune in to your current defining values.

The fifth and final rule also requires being honest with yourself about your judgments about some of the terms. Perhaps you roll your eyes at the term "Social Justice," and so you don't want to pick it, even though when you read the description you realize that you do in fact care about protecting those whom you think are marginalized by society. Or perhaps you do feel that Recognition is crucial to you—you want to be liked, respected, and recognized for your actions, but you wish you didn't because you've been told that you're "too arrogant." I'll say it again: None of these values are inherently bad. Be honest with yourself! Which values make you feel more alive (Barney et al., 2019)?

Your top five values are your *Top Tier values*: You can write them down in order in a table like I did in Table 3.1. The other remaining values in your top 10 are your *Near Tier values*. These are also very important to you, but not quite as crucial as the Top Tier.

You might notice I have six values, not five, on my Near Tier list. I had a hard time picking between Humor and Responsibility. I initially just kept Humor, but I ultimately went back and added Responsibility back in. Remember, this task is to help you, not to

TABLE 3.1. Example Top and Near Tier Values

Jenn's Top Tier	Jenn's Near Tier
Independence	Creativity
Achievement	Humor
Curiosity	Authority
Honesty	Belonging
Acceptance	Variety
	Responsibility

limit you. Do you have eight values on your Near Tier list? Fine. Do you need 12 to really feel like your values are well represented? Go for it. It is good to try to hone in on the values that truly matter the most, which is why I suggest intentionally narrowing your list to 10, but a little flexibility never hurt anyone.

VALUES AND EMOTIONS

Do you think I'd forgotten about feelings and emotions? Not at all. We took that crucial journey through Values Land for a few reasons. Values and emotions are inextricably linked (Schwartz, 2012). That is because your emotions are a guide to your values, and your values are a guide to your emotions. You cannot feel emotions about stuff you don't care about. If you want a different phrase, consider this statement from Steven Hayes, who developed acceptance and commitment therapy: "You hurt where you care, and you care where you hurt" (Hayes, 2019, p. 24). My amendment is, "You *feel* where you care, and you care where you *feel*." You feel things when your values are triggered, and your values are evident in the feelings you have, if you look for them.

From an emotional-messages standpoint, values are where the messages are coming from; they are the senders of the messages. If feelings occur only when you care, and values are what you are about, then values are the forces sending you your feelings. Values can send emotional messages in lots of ways, but we're going to talk about four of them here. First, *well-nourished* values send pleasant emotional messages. Second, when values are *malnourished*, people tend to feel emotions like sadness, guilt, and shame. When values are *challenged*, or *triggered*, messages of anxiety and anger tend to erupt. Finally, emotions are also evident when values collide or *conflict*. Let us talk about each of these in turn.

Well-Nourished Values

People who engage in actions that are consistent with their values tend to be happier and more satisfied, and they experience fewer distressing feelings compared with those whose values are less nourished (Oppenheim-Weller et al., 2018). When I walk 250 steps every hour, for 10 hours in a row, and I see my little arc of lights on my Fitbit, I feel a sense of Achievement. When I finish cataloging my family's year in a photo book, I feel both Achievement and Creativity. When my kid asks me why some people choose to end their own lives, I answer with Honesty and Acceptance. In these small moments, I feel good about myself. Sometimes I feel happy, but feeding my values also results in other positive emotions, such as pride, relief, and awe.

One way to think about how and whether your values are well nourished is to consider the activities that you already do. It is important to note here that "activity" can mean a small behavior, like smiling at passersby as you walk down the street, or an outing, like going to a baseball game, or everything in between. Think about the activities you do on a daily basis, and ones you do regularly (e.g., at least twice per week, even if not every day). Which of these activities might be feeding your values?

There might be some idiosyncratic relationships here. I once worked with a client who had the value of Achievement but had been fired from her job. She initially felt like she was a loser—that her Achievement value was malnourished. Yet when she looked at her life, she noted that she had little achievements all over the place. She asked, "Does showering and getting dressed count as an achievement?" It sure can! She also lifted weights at the gym, cooked new meals, and applied for new jobs; all of these things were related to her Achievement value. She'd felt so badly about herself that she ignored where her values were still being fed. She wasn't listening to the smaller messages her Achievement value was trying to send.

Malnourished Values

Values that are stagnant and malnourished send messages of depression, sadness, guilt, and shame. Depression has been described as a disorder of *disconnection* (Hari, 2018) because people tend to feel sad or numb when their lives lack meaning, lack value. Malnourished values are sending the message, "Something is missing here; please attend to this."

When you look at your list of values, are some of them not as evident in your life as others? What kinds of things could you do to beef up that value? You might have to get creative. For example, remember Meredith, the woman with chronic pain who I worked with at the Veterans Affairs hospital? Meredith, who valued Adventure, used to feed her value by booking last-minute trips to new destinations—she'd go wherever the cheapest ticket could take her. After her paralyzing accident, she couldn't really do that anymore, and she felt sad, disconnected, and depressed. When we talked about what Adventure meant to her, ultimately it came down to novelty: She liked seeing new places, talking to new people, doing things she'd never done before. Someone in the therapy group suggested that she watch travel shows so she could see new places. She tried it, but watching travel shows made her feel sad that she herself would never get to see those places.

Instead, Meredith had to figure out different ways to pursue her value of Adventure. She could still travel, but it would take more planning to make sure that hotels and excursions were wheelchair accessible. For her, the planning part of travel diminished the fun of Adventure. Thankfully, Meredith's wife, Yun, was able to take on the planning elements so that Meredith could experience the surprise and novelty of new experiences on their trips. And Yun knew Meredith well enough to build in some choices so that, on a given day, she could say, "Meredith, do you want to go to a castle or on a boat ride today?"

Beyond trips, Meredith also cultivated her Adventure value much closer to home. She used to love hiking and trail running, and although she couldn't hike on the kinds of trails she used to, she made it her mission to visit every park and walking trail in her city. She also decided to go to every single greasy spoon diner in search of the best patty melt in town. Finally, she started taking Chinese language classes as another way to feed her desire to experience new things. Over time, and the more Meredith engaged in these activities in her day-to-day life, not only did she feel more fulfilled, but also her almost-constant chronic pain seemed to turn its volume down. She still felt the pain, but it wasn't as strong. The point here is that directly addressing values that are malnourished can bring not only pleasure, but also meaning and fulfillment, to your life.

There is another way to look at malnourished values, and that is by identifying *ignored* values—values that are so malnourished they are hidden from view. Something I've neglected to tell you until now is that the values listed in Exhibit 3.1 aren't just isolated attributes; some of the values share more similarities than others. The most prominent theory of values (Schwartz, 2012, 2017) suggests that values can be organized in a circular pie chart, as seen in Figure 3.1.

The values that fall within each wedge of the pie chart in Figure 3.1 are more similar to each other than to values in other wedges. Some of the values represent motivations that are consistent with a desire to grow, change, and explore (Openness to Change; top right). These are quite different than values in the opposite wedge (Conservation; bottom left), which represent values associated with protecting and maintaining the status quo. The other two wedges represent values associated with moving the self forward, enhancing and prioritizing one's own goals (Self-Enhancement; bottom right), and values that involve prioritizing and putting effort toward the growth of others (Self-Transcendence; top left).

FIGURE 3.1. Specific Values Organized by Overarching Value Dimensions

Note. Data from Schwartz et al. (2012).

Also, when you look at the values in each wedge, you'll see that those that are closer together are more similar than those that are farther away. The values Respect and Loyalty (in the Conservation wedge) both represent deference to others, avoiding upsetting or harming other people, whereas Defense and Protection, while in the same overall wedge, are more about taking actions or prioritizing the safety and stability of a community or society. Respect and Loyalty are more similar to each other than they are to Defense and Protection.

If you map your values onto this pie chart, where do they fall? For example, my top 10 values are circled in Figure 3.2. My Top Tier values are enclosed in solid circles, and my Near Tier values are enclosed with dashed lines. You can see that half of my Top 10 values (Curiosity, Creativity, Independence, Variety, and Humor) are in the Openness to Change section. These are values that typically go with each other, because they all relate to self-direction and interest in novelty and newness. These also feel related to me—I like to ask questions (Curiosity) of different types (Variety) and find inventive solutions (Creativity) on my own (Independence). Doing all of those things with Humor makes them better for me.

Do most of your values fall into one quadrant, or are they spread out? I've done this activity with countless people, and most of them have values in at least three of the quadrants, but not everyone does. Some have all their values clustered very tightly together, and some have values spread out all across the pie.

One purpose of mapping your values onto this pie chart is to think about where you might have clusters of values (which are often fed together, like a mama bird feeds multiple baby birds from the same worm), and where you might actually have values that you've failed to articulate or recognize.

A therapist friend of mine told me about a guy she used to work with. We'll call him Jake. Early on in their work together, Jake and his therapist did a values activity like the one in Exhibit 3.1,

FIGURE 3.2. Jenn's Top Tier (solid line) and Near Tier (dotted line) Values

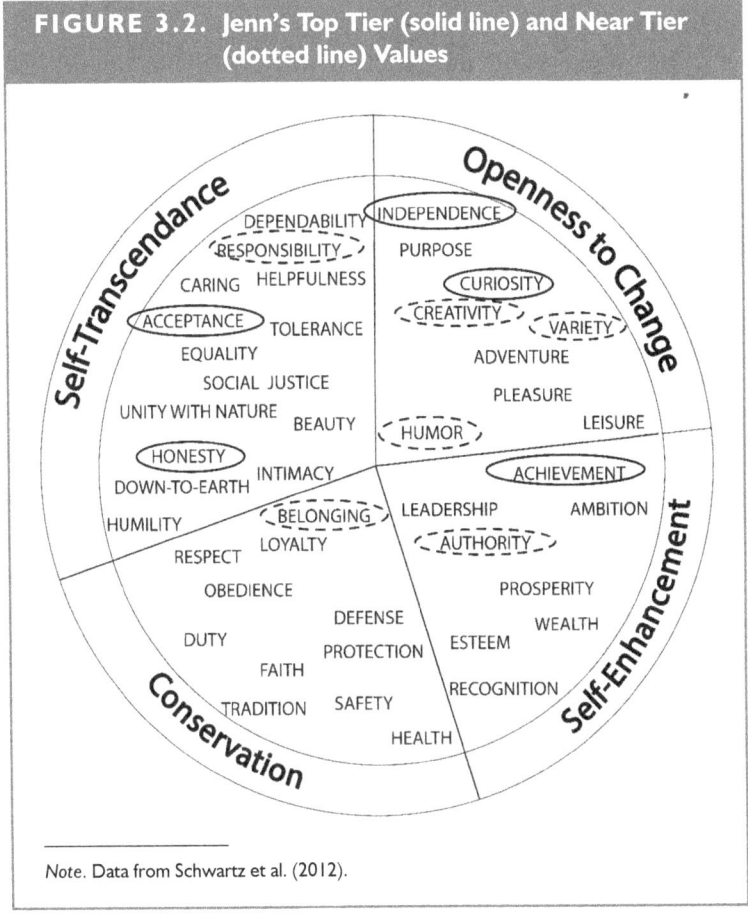

Note. Data from Schwartz et al. (2012).

and Jake selected Purpose, Achievement, Authority, Prosperity, and Recognition as his top five values. His next five were Independence, Health, Ambition, Responsibility, and Leadership. If you look at the pie chart in Figure 3.3, you'll note that most of the values are grouped together.

Jake was a college student who cared a lot about doing well in school. He was majoring in business and wanted to be a successful CEO someday. When he looked at his values and his activities, they all coincided. Yet Jake was deeply lonely. He had a few friends, but none he considered especially close. He said that his mother was his best friend. His therapist nudged him to think about his pain in the context of interpersonal relationships. He couldn't understand why, when he went on dates, the women he went out with typically didn't agree to go on a second date.

It wasn't until Jake's therapist pointed out to him the discrepancy between his nourished values and his state of loneliness that he began to think about what values he might have inadvertently ignored. He cared so deeply about Ambition, Achievement, and Recognition that it felt awful to him to hold a value that he just couldn't conquer. When he thought about it and saw the almost-empty Self-Transcendence section, he realized that he craved Intimacy and Acceptance. Seeing the pie chart helped Jake and his therapist identify the values that were buried deep. Only after he acknowledged his true values was he able to work on how to nourish them.

Challenged Values

Almost the opposite of when a value is malnourished is when a value gets triggered or challenged. A challenged value is one that has ingested some hot sauce. When a situation is value laden and extremely important (i.e., a value is triggered) but another person, or

FIGURE 3.3. Jake's Top Tier (solid line) and Near Tier (dotted line) Values

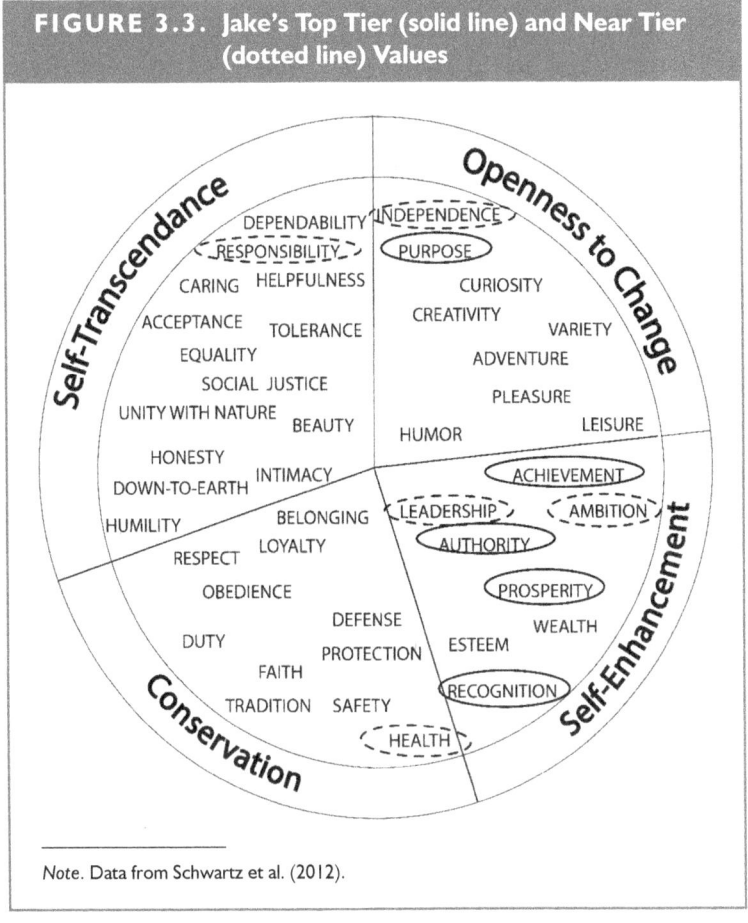

Note. Data from Schwartz et al. (2012).

the circumstances, blocks you from nourishing your value, emotions can erupt. This is your values saying, "Hey! Someone or something is thwarting me! My value is challenged!"

For example, consider someone with a value of Safety. People who value Safety want to—by definition—feel safe, calm, and cozy. Situations that are deemed unsafe, like giving a presentation in front of a class, or walking alone at night in a deserted area with a lot of shadows and alleyways, or being in a situation that reminds them of a prior trauma (i.e., a trauma trigger), challenges this value. Anxiety or fear are the likely responses. In fact, people who tend to hold more values in the Conservation domain (which is where Safety lies) report wanting to feel more calm and less afraid yet also report more feelings of anxiety (Tamir et al., 2016).

Consider another example. People who value power tend to desire to feel more pride as well as more anger (Tamir et al., 2016). When power is thwarted—when a person who values power feels powerless—they are likely to feel a sense of injustice that fuels anger.

Sometimes, negative emotions emerge because values are challenged. If values tell you what matters to you, then when someone (or a situation) tries to keep you or block you from what matters to you, you will certainly not feel happy! Can you think about a situation in which your values were triggered, or activated, but you were not able to nourish them because of that situation? What kinds of situations does that happen in, for you?

Notice that I'm using the word "challenged" and not "threatened." It can feel like values are being threatened in these situations, but interpreting these triggered values as challenges to deal with rather than threats trying to attack you is a small but important tweak you can make for yourself. Why? Because threats must be vanquished, but challenges are opportunities for growth (Jamieson et al., 2012).

Conflicting Values

The final way values relate to emotion is when values conflict. Values on opposite sides of the pie chart in Figure 3.1 tend to be difficult to nourish at the same time. Self-Transcendence values are all about attending to the needs of others, whereas Self-Enhancement values are all about attending to the needs of the self. Openness to Change involves seeking out novelty and newness, whereas Conservation is about keeping things the same.

The most common values conflicts occur in relationships. That's because we each get to have our own values. But our individual values may differ from the values of our parents, grandparents, or even our friends. Think about arguments in your families—might some of them relate to values conflicts?

For example, consider Roselee, a 17-year-old of Bolivian heritage who struggles a lot with her family. Roselee values Creativity, Independence, and Beauty, which all play into her goal to become a fiction writer. Roselee wants to pursue creative writing in college. Her mom, who immigrated to the United States while pregnant with Roselee, values Tradition, Respect, and Safety. Roselee's mother wants her to pursue a practical college major or to forego college and just get a job after high school. Roselee feels invalidated and misunderstood by her mother. Roselee's mother feels that Roselee is abandoning her family and their cultural traditions, and she worries about the stability of Roselee's future. They fight all the time, and both Roselee and her mother feel sad and angry after these fights. Yet when viewed through a values lens, both of their perspectives make sense. Roselee wants to nourish her Openness to Change values, and Roselee's mother emphasizes her own Conservation values. Neither is wrong, but they struggle to let each other hold different values, which is where the relational conflict comes in. Accepting that they each care about different things, and care about each other, could help them repair their fractured relationship.

Values conflicts can also occur within a given person, when two opposing values are hard to nourish simultaneously. For example, my values of Belonging and Independence often conflict. I want to be independent and do my own thing. I also want to belong in my family, which sometimes means keeping my mouth shut or choosing to be home for dinner instead of working late. When these conflicts occur, I can feel torn and like I lose out no matter what I do.

To be clear, values on opposites sides of the pie chart don't have to conflict. Consider a person who uses their values of Authority and Achievement to advance social justice causes. Authority is on the opposite side of the circle from Social Justice, but these two values can in fact work well together. Sometimes values closer together can conflict, too, such as for someone who values Purpose but is rigid rather than Curious about pursuing their life goals.

What can you do when values conflict? That could be an entire book on its own! The short answer is this: Balance them. If you have opposing values, make sure that when they conflict, one doesn't always get attended to over the other. For example, if someone holds values of Variety and Safety, and when Safety is threatened or challenged that person always attends to Safety, Variety will suffer. The idea is to make sure that both values get attention, maybe at different times and in different ways. The same goes with values conflicts across people.

VALUES SEND EMOTIONAL MESSAGES

Emotions serve functions in our lives. They help prepare our bodies for action, they help us connect to other people, and they help us tune in to what matters. This chapter was primarily about the last function: Emotions are intimately connected to values. Understanding your values helps you to understand your emotions, and when your emotions make more sense you can understand where emotional messages are coming from.

Remember Casey, back at the start of this chapter, who didn't know what she was meant to do? A values exercise helped her a lot. She recognized that Purpose was a core value for her that was malnourished, which is why she was so upset about not knowing her path. Yet she also had the value of Variety, and through discussions of her values she realized that she didn't want one sole purpose if that meant cutting off other potential pathways to meaning and fulfillment. She also held values of Esteem, Obedience, Safety, and Belonging. She recognized that her value of Esteem drew her to dating partners who liked her and held her in high regard, but she felt fake in these interactions, like she didn't really belong. She didn't feel safe, or like herself. In talking through her values, she added Authenticity; she wanted to be liked for who she was, but she didn't feel safe being her authentic self much of the time. Values work was a real turning point in Casey's therapy, as she began to feel less angry with herself for not being further along in her career. She recognized that her values were trying to tell her something, and she hadn't really been listening.

Now that you have started to think about your values and how your values are enacted in your life (or where your values could use some attention in your life), it is time to turn back to explicitly discussing emotions. Keep your values list handy, though, because we will continue to talk about how recognizing and identifying emotions can help you nourish your core values!

SUMMARY POINTS

- Values are not only core to finding happiness, meaning, and fulfillment in life; they are also the senders of your emotions. Values send you emotional messages because values are what matters to you, and you can only have emotions about what matters.

- Emotions serve several functions. They help prepare people for action (e.g., fight vs. flight vs. freeze), they facilitate communication, and they highlight what matters.
- Values are chosen life directions, not goals. Goals can be checked off, but values continue to guide the selection of goals and direct where a person wants to go in life.
- Values are the senders of emotional messages and relate to emotions in multiple ways.
  - Well-nourished values tend to send positive emotional messages of excitement, joy, gratitude, awe, love, and relaxation.
  - Malnourished or languished values send emotional messages associated with loss, including sadness, guilt, shame, and regret.
  - Challenged or triggered values send emotional messages associated with threat—typically anger, fear, frustration, and anxiety.
  - Conflicted values can be associated with all kinds of emotions, because one person's values can conflict with another person's values. Values can also conflict within the self.

CHAPTER 4

EMOTIONAL LABELING

Picture two college students, Jenny and Harrison. They are friends who live in the same dorm. They've been talking a lot about their mutual friend, Doug, who they think has been drinking too much and smoking too much weed. One night, they confront him about his escalating substance use. Doug blows up, screaming at them for not understanding that his mother is sick and that he's just trying to blow off steam. He then insults both of his friends and storms off. A resident assistant sees the whole thing and tries to talk to Jenny and Harrison about what happened, asking them how they feel. Harrison says, "I'm hurt by what he said, and concerned about what he's going to do. I'm sad and worried." Jenny shrugs and says, "I dunno. I guess I feel . . . bad?"

Most human beings don't spend much time thinking about the words we choose, the implications those words have for our psyches, or the effects our words have on others. Yet there are real implications for how people speak, write, and think about their emotions.

This chapter is all about **emotional labeling**, that is, naming the message. Is this a postcard, a letter, a catalog, a bill (ugh), or a package? Different kinds of messages require different kinds of responses, so learning how to categorize and distinguish among the messages can help you figure out what to do next.

LABELING, CLARITY, DIFFERENTIATION, AND GRANULARITY (OH MY!)

Up to this point, we have mostly focused on feelings in general, with a bit of discussion about how some feelings are pleasant and feel good, whereas other feelings are unpleasant and generally feel bad. Of course, there are different varieties of feelings even within those larger categories, and they feel qualitatively distinct. Can you tell the difference between the pleasant feelings of love, excitement, pride, relaxation, and awe? Are you aware of when your unpleasant feelings have a flavor of fear, disgust, sadness, anger, embarrassment, or guilt? The process of assigning a specific term or terms to your emotional experience is called *emotional labeling*).[1] It is the difference between "I'm upset" and "I'm embarrassed." Or the difference between "I feel good" and "I feel excited and grateful."

Before you can identify what you are feeling, you first need to know that you are feeling something. Emotional awareness is a necessary precursor to labeling. If you skipped Chapter 2, now might be a good time to go read it!

To be clear, it's OK if you aren't always aware of your feelings, or if you think you might be alexithymic; difficulties with awareness and emotional labeling are both a part of alexithymia (see Chapter 2). In general, though, some level of awareness is required before you can label what exactly you might be feeling.

---

[1] Emotion scientists also use the terms "emotional clarity," "emotion differentiation," and "emotional granularity" to refer to the process of identifying the specific type of emotion experienced. The distinctions matter only if you want to search the academic literature for research on this topic.

THREE REASONS FOR LABELING

I'm going to let you in on a little secret: Emotional labeling might be the most important skill covered in this entire book, but it is also the most underrated. Being clear about what you are feeling is crucial for emotional health, but the benefits are not obvious.

There are three main reasons why emotional labeling is so vital. First, emotional labeling is itself an emotion regulation strategy. Also, emotional labeling helps people choose more effective and adaptive methods of dealing with their emotions. Finally, emotional labeling can help you highlight your values. Let us review each of these in detail.

Emotional Labeling IS Regulation

Emotional labeling is a behind-the-scenes emotion regulation strategy (Torre & Lieberman, 2018). Unlike some other coping and emotion regulation strategies (like those we'll discuss in Chapter 7), emotional labeling isn't something people do intentionally to try to regulate their emotions, like they might with distraction, or venting to a friend, or even trying to think about the situation from a different angle. Instead, emotional labeling operates in a stealthy way. It's like the navigation function on your phone—provided you have your location turned on, it's running all the time and knows where you are. But you really only notice it when you are trying to find a nearby restaurant on Yelp.

When people label their feelings, their emotions shift subtly, even when they aren't intentionally trying to change them! Some of these changes are automatic and physical; for example, physiological reactivity tends to go down after labeling (Kassam & Mendes, 2013). The idea is that labeling helps people resolve their feelings faster and has effects on the brain that are similar to those of more intentional regulation strategies. For example, labeling is associated with activation in parts of the brain associated with self-regulation and with decreased activity in the amygdala, a part of the brain known for emotional processing (Burklund et al., 2014). Labeling is particularly helpful when emotions are intense (Levy-Gigi & Shamay-Tsoory, 2022).

One of the most fascinating things about emotional labeling is that it helps even when people think it will not. In a particularly clever set of studies, researchers had some people rate their responses to emotionally evocative and disturbing pictures (dirty toilets, images of violence, mutilated bodies, etc.). Another group of people looked at the same pictures while intentionally labeling their feelings (Lieberman et al., 2011). The people who labeled their feelings reported less intense negative emotions than those who didn't label them.

But that isn't even the most interesting part. A completely separate group of people predicted how they would feel if they were to do the same activity. Rather than looking at pictures, they were given brief verbal descriptions of the content of the picture and were asked to rate how distressing the pictures would be. A final group predicted their level of distress but were also asked to provide emotional labels. The researchers found that in the group of people who did not see the pictures but predicted their distress, those who provided labels thought that labeling would make them feel worse. That's right—people thought that it would make them feel more distressed, but labeling actually produced less distress.

The fear of labeling makes sense, even if it's unfounded. In my experience as a therapist, I've noticed that some people think that if they put a name to their feelings, then their feelings are more real. They think that naming the feeling will make a fuzzy, amorphous cloud into a sentient monster. And monsters are far scarier than clouds, right? The problem with thinking this way is that monsters could be reasoned with, fought with, hugged, or otherwise dealt with, whereas it's pretty hard to figure out what to do with a cloud. This is one of the times in human psychology when the assumption and fears about what might happen is not an accurate depiction of what will happen.

Emotional Labeling Facilitates Regulation and Goal Pursuit

The second reason why labeling is helpful is that putting words to emotions can help you figure out what to do next. As I keep pointing out (feel free to revisit Chapter 3 if you've forgotten), emotions have functions. Knowing what you are feeling can help you figure out if your feeling is helpful or harmful to you.

Consider Hannah, who wants to get a raise at work. She does a good job, and she gets good evaluations from her supervisors, but she has never asked for a raise because her parents taught her that "hard work will be rewarded." She feels gross even thinking about asking for more money. But then several of her coworkers are promoted ahead of her. When her coworker John announces his raise and promotion, she feels incredibly upset because she's worked at the company longer, and she knows John hasn't had the same kind of spotless record she's had.

When Hannah complains to her therapist about being passed over for a promotion again, her therapist pushes her to think about what kind or variety of upset she feels. In their conversation, Hannah realizes that she feels angry. She is mad at her bosses for not recognizing her hard work and talent. Feeling angry is much more helpful than feeling upset. "Upset" is just a general term for feeling some vague kind of unpleasantness, but "angry" is a specific emotion that is associated with a sense of unfairness. Research shows that anger can help people approach their goals, such as by confronting and approaching the source of the injustice (Ford & Tamir, 2012; Kim et al., 2015).

This is not a situation where Hannah needs to down-regulate her anger, she needs to use her anger. She talks with her therapist about how to fuel her anger to give her the courage to ask directly for what she knows she deserves. At the next week's session, she reports that she had talked to her boss, and they have started negotiations for her to move into a position with more responsibility—and a bigger paycheck.

Hannah's example highlights the idea that if you know which emotion you are experiencing, you might have a better idea of whether the emotion is useful or not. Importantly, even when the emotion is not helpful, labeling the feeling can provide guidance for what to do next. We'll address how to use emotional labels to figure out what to do next in Chapter 6, but cultivating emotional labeling skills is an important first step.

Emotion Labeling Highlights Values

One of the things therapy clients often want to know is "Why am I feeling this way?" What they often really mean is "What's wrong with me that I feel like this?" The implication is that feelings are irrational and that they shouldn't be feeling what they are feeling.

Feelings aren't logical, but they also aren't really irrational. There are good reasons why you feel what you feel. These reasons were the central focus of Chapter 3. Remember that I said that values are a guide to emotions? Well, the inverse is true, too: Emotions are a guide to values. Because you can't have a feeling about something that doesn't matter, that means when you have a feeling, something matters. The question is: What is it that matters? Emotional labeling can help you start figuring that out.

I'll let you in on a little secret: Although there are approximately 500 words in the English language that refer to emotions (Storm & Storm, 1987) there are not actually 500 unique emotions.

Emotions come in *families*. Emotion researchers like to argue about how many basic emotions there are (Izard, 2007) and how emotions are distinct from one another. For example, there are small differences between hate and anger (van Doorn, 2018) and between shame and guilt (Tangney et al., 1996). Yet hate is in the anger family, just as shame is in the guilt family.

Each family of emotions has a thematic message built into it. A list of these common messages is provided in Table 4.1. These messages are written vaguely, with "something" in almost every message. That's because the "something" activating the emotion is typically value related. When you realize you feel an emotion in a particular emotion family, you can use the message to self-reflect on what value is sparking the emotion.

For example, Dylan has a history of what he calls "failed" romantic relationships. At age 27, he is interested in getting married and starting a family, but he hasn't been in a relationship for longer than 6 months. When he finally enters a relationship with someone he really likes, he feels very insecure. He freaks out about his girlfriend leaving him for someone younger, prettier, and more successful. He also thinks, "I'm just being irrational; I shouldn't feel this way." Yet after recognizing that "freaking out" isn't a specific emotion, Dylan realizes that he feels jealous of the other men in his girlfriend's life (friends, coworkers, etc.), who all seem more together than he is, and as a result he feels anxious about whether his relationship will last.

He looks at the list in Table 4.1 and sees that both jealousy and anxiety are related to threats: a relationship threat for jealousy and a looming anticipating threat for anxiety. He asks himself, "What is threatening? How are my values getting activated?" He had chosen Intimacy, Belonging, Safety, Esteem, and Caring as his values (see Chapter 3). He realizes that his values are heavily wrapped up with wanting a romantic relationship and with having a family (Intimacy, Belonging, Caring) but that moving in that direction threatened his

TABLE 4.1. Messages of Emotions

Basic emotion	Message of the emotion
Surprise	Something new and unexpected is happening!
Anger	There has been an injustice; someone I care about has been wronged.
Fear[a]	Something threatening is nearby; I am in danger.
Anxiety[a]	Something potentially threatening is looming in the future.
Sadness	I have lost or lack something I care about.
Guilt	I have done something morally wrong.
Disgust	Something or someone harmful (physically or morally) is nearby.
Jealousy	A valued relationship is being threatened, or someone has something I want.
Joy	I have more resources right now, and more positive energy.
Contentment	I feel satisfied and secure right now.
Pride	I've accomplished something that matters to me.
Awe	I feel small in relation to the wide world around me, and/or this situation is challenging my worldview.
Gratitude	Someone has done something nice for me, and I want to give back.
Amusement	I'm noticing something unexpected that makes me playful with others.

[a]Fear and anxiety are in reality in the same family of emotions because both are related to threats. But fear (which is often more visceral and physical) is about a current threat, and anxiety (which is often more mental and cognitive) is about an anticipated threat.

sense of Esteem and of Safety. He was in a real values conflict zone. Threats to Safety sparked his anxiety, and threats to Esteem sparked his jealousy. Identifying his specific emotions helped him recognize that because all of his core values were activated, his emotions actually weren't irrational at all. Thinking about his values helped Dylan have compassion for himself and helped him admit his threats to his girlfriend. She agreed to provide him reassurance about her commitment to him, and he agreed to learn skills to help him manage his jealousy and anxiety.

HOW ADEPT ARE YOU AT LABELING?

To know if you are someone who could benefit from labeling improvement, ask yourself the questions in Exhibit 4.1. If you look at these questions and say "Huh, I really don't use many of these words to

---

EXHIBIT 4.1. Self-Assessment of Emotional Clarity

Ask yourself these questions:
- Do you almost always know how you are feeling? (Or do you recognize that you are feeling something but either struggle to name or don't bother to name it?)
- Do you use a wide range of words to refer to your emotions, or do you tend to use words like "bad" or "upset" or "stressed," or rely on one word (e.g., "anxious") to refer to all of your emotions? Look at the emotion word lists in Tables 4.2 and 4.3. Do you use these words to refer to your own feelings?
- Do you understand where your emotions are coming from, what prompted them, or do your feelings seem to come out of the blue?
- Are you able to match your emotional vocabulary (e.g., knowledge of the different emotion words) to your emotional experiences? Do the emotion messages presented in Table 4.1 seem distinct to you?

---

refer to myself. I basically just feel 'stressed' all the time," then maybe you could put in some effort to increase your labeling skills.

If you are someone who almost always knows what you are feeling and uses specific emotion words (e.g., "sad," "angry," "frustrated," "disappointed," "guilty") and you understand how your emotional, physical, and cognitive experiences map onto those emotion terms, then you're probably pretty good at labeling. However, it is worth noting that a lot of people tend to say they are adept at knowing what they are feeling and have a strong emotional vocabulary but then do not actually discriminate among the different emotion terms (Boden et al., 2012; Erbas et al., 2019). In fact, I'd put myself in this category!

For that reason, even if you think you are good at labeling, it might be worth your while to keep reading rather than skipping ahead—you might realize that you could benefit from beefing up your labeling skills, too.

HOW TO IMPROVE AT LABELING

Improving at emotional labeling is something anyone can do. The first step is building an emotional vocabulary, and the second step is practicing linking words to other people's emotional expressions. The third step involves linking vocabulary words to your own emotional states after you've already experienced them. The fourth step is intentionally labeling ongoing, current emotional experiences.

Step 1: Build an Emotional Vocabulary

The first step to labeling is increasing your **emotional vocabulary**. There are a lot of ways to do this. You could go through a dictionary and write down every word you see that refers to an emotion. You could listen for the emotion words that other people use in daily life, or that you hear in TV shows, movies, or podcasts. Or you could look at a list of words and their meanings. For example, Table 4.2 and Table 4.3 provide lists of emotional words arranged into families and a brief description of the types of expressions that tend to go along with each emotion family (Campos et al., 2013). As you can see, these lists include words that represent mild, moderate, and intense versions of that general feeling. You might notice there are more words for negative emotions (Table 4.2) than for positive emotions. That is because negative emotions tend to arise in situations that could be life threatening, so being able to distinguish between them is useful for survival (Schrauf & Sanchez, 2004).

The intensity distinctions are useful because being precise in the terms you use conveys not only the variety of feelings but also how intense those feelings are. Accurate labeling of intensity is one way to validate yourself in terms of what you are feeling and to receive emotional validation from others.

For example, I once worked with a client I'll call Cameron. He was high in alexithymia, and he didn't use a lot of emotion words, but when he did they were all pretty mild in intensity. Even in situations where other people would have been raging mad, like when his fairly new car was crumpled in a parking lot and the perpetrator sped off without leaving a note, he said he was "irritated." He also felt like people didn't understand him, and he often felt disconnected from his own experiences. When Cameron started tuning into his emotions a bit more and recognizing that his feelings did, in fact, vary in intensity, he started to use a bigger variety of words to name his feelings and, as a result, he felt like people "got" him more readily.

As an opposite example, I have a friend who uses extreme emotion words for most feelings. She says she's "despairing" when she's sad and "horrified" when she's slightly anxious. People call her overly dramatic, and that makes sense because her words convey a strength of emotion that doesn't seem to be matched by the situation.

TABLE 4.2. Negative Emotion Families

Basic emotion	Mild terms	Moderate terms	Intense terms	Signs and behaviors
Surprise	Unexpected, catch off-guard, unforeseen	Abrupt, startled	Astonished, bewildered, shocked, ambushed, alarmed	Gasp, wide open mouth, oh!
Anger	Annoyed, frustrated, irritated, offended, impatient	Mad, aggravated, exasperated, indignant, riled up, ticked off	Rage, furious, vengeful, irate, seething, hostile	Aggression, arguing, blaming, staring, stern/harsh tone, clenching fists, feeling hot, increased heart rate
Fear	Alert, hesitant, watchful, cautious, uneasy, doubtful, apprehensive, edgy, insecure	Afraid, suspicious, anxious, nervous, worried, alarmed, shaky, wary, rattled, unsettled, jumpy	Shocked, terrorized, panicked, horrified, phobic, petrified, paralyzed, dread	Fight, flight, or freeze; avoidance; catastrophizing; difficulty concentrating; crying; racing heart; sweating; trembling; muscle tension

Sadness	Disappointed, disconnected, listless, low, blue	Mournful, weepy, grieving, gloomy, downtrodden, forlorn, sorrowful, drained, woeful	Despairing, bleak, despondent, depressed, hopeless, heartbroken, morose	Apathy, changes in eating, crying, fatigue, difficulty concentrating, irritability, sluggishness, sleep problems
Guilt	Hesitant, flushed, self-conscious, awkward, humble, reticent, abashed, sheepish	Regretful, remorseful, embarrassed, penitent, chagrined, ashamed	Humiliated, disgraced, mortified, dishonored, degraded, belittled	Crying, shaking, feeling the urge to hide, heart racing, blushing
Disgust	Dislike, distaste, a little sick, dissatisfaction	Hate, grossed out, aversion, loathe	Repulsed, detest, recoil from, abhor, repugnant	Making a "yuck" or "ew" sound, crinkling nose, choking, gagging, revulsion in mouth/throat/stomach, feeling sick
Jealousy	Suspicious, insecure, distrustful, protective	Envious, threatened, demanding	Possessive, resentful	Frustration, making hurtful comments, making threats, negative thinking

TABLE 4.3. Positive Emotion Families

Basic emotion	Mild terms	Moderate terms	Intense terms	Signs and behaviors
Amusement	Lighthearted, mirth, beguilement, tickled	Delighted, enjoyment, entertained	Hilarity, whoopee	Smiling, head bouncing, laughing, head tilts
Awe	Respect	Wonder, revere	Astonished, reverence, venerated, wonderstruck, starstruck	Parted lips, looking upward, silence and reverence
Contentment	Comfortable, satisfied, quiet	Snug, cozy, restful	Peaceful, at ease, serene, tranquil	Small smile, relaxed body posture, slow breathing
Gratitude	Acknowledging	Thankful, appreciative	Indebted, praiseful, beholden	Smiling, verbal appreciation, gentle touch

Interest	Intrigued, attentive, inquiring, awakened, drawn	Curious, focused, enticed, hooked, impressed, inspired	Fascinated, absorbed, engrossed, riveted, captivated, gripped, rapt	Forward leaning, raised eyebrows, pressing lips together, asking questions
Joy	Pleased, gratified	Cheerful, happy, glad, rejoice, gleeful, carefree	Excited, exulted, jubilant, elated, exhilarated, ecstasy, euphoric, radiant	Open-mouthed smile, bright eyes, laughing, approaching others, open
Love	Warm, liking, affection, attached	Tenderness, fondness, admire, treasure	Devoted, idolized, endearment, passion, savoring, cherish, revered, adore	Head tilted, closed eyes, physical touch, buying gifts, doing things for a loved one
Pride	Dignity, self-assured	Worthy, flattered, confident	Triumphant, honored, fulfilled	Slight smile, sitting up straight, strong posture, raised head

Now, this friend is in fact emotionally sensitive (see Chapter 1), and I suspect that people in her life don't actually recognize the strength of her feelings. She's admitted that she likes to use strong words so that people take her seriously. The problem is that a "boy who cried wolf" situation can occur. Because she uses intense emotion words all of the time, it's harder to tell when her feelings really are that strong, versus when she's just using language to amplify her feelings so that she feels heard. It is generally better to use words that reflect the level of intensity you are actually feeling, because doing so will help you recognize variations in your emotions, and it will help others validate your emotional experience.

Step 2: Practice Linking Words to Others' Emotional Expressions

Practicing how to link words to other people's emotional expressions isn't 100% necessary for learning how to label your own emotions, but it can be useful in getting more familiar with the emotion terms in Tables 4.2 and 4.3. The idea is to practice using different kinds of emotion words (i.e., in different families) with different intensities by identifying emotions in other people. Paying attention to others' emotions is often easier and less frustrating than attending to your own, and it can help you build your emotional vocabulary before turning your attention onto yourself.

There is a psychological bonus to practice labeling other people's expressions. People who struggle with labeling their own emotions also tend to struggle with accurately recognizing emotions in others (Samur et al., 2013). Increasing labeling can thus help you understand others, and it may improve your relationships.

Sit down with your lists of emotions in front of the TV. Turn on the news, a TV show, a film, or a sporting event. Or plop yourself down on a bench in a public place (a busy park, mall, office complex, bus, etc.). You just want to be in a place where there are people who are likely to be experiencing emotions, basically just a place where there are people.

Watch the people around you and see if you can figure out what they are feeling on the basis of their facial expressions and body language. Watch one person and see if you can label their feelings—do they seem mad, guilty, or sad? Is it mild, moderate, or intense? Pick a word that seems to fit. If you don't know the definitions of all the words on the list, that's fine—pick a word you do know. Or download a dictionary app on your phone and look up the words you don't know.

If you really want to challenge yourself, turn off the sound on a TV show or film so that you are forced to rely solely on the characters' expressions or body language to figure out their emotional states. Or watch something in another language (turn off the subtitles!) and listen to vocal inflections for cues. For the purposes of this exercise, it is not important to know whether you are right in labeling their emotions. If you're trying to label the feelings of someone you know, you can ask them how they are feeling ("Hey, it looks like maybe you are feeling grossed out, is that right?"). However, many people try to mask their emotions, or deny their emotions, so being accurate is actually not important at this stage (we'll talk more about emotional expressions and accuracy in Chapter 8). Right now, the goal is just to start to recognize that emotions come in different families and in different intensities, and there are words to go with each.

Step 3: Link Vocabulary Words to Past Emotional States

The third step in improving labeling skills is the most crucial: Attach a specific emotion word to your own experience (Edwards et al., 2018; Kennedy & Franklin, 2002).

A client of mine, Linda, is a person who needed to work on this step in particular. She had a pretty decent emotional vocabulary and could spit out definitions of words. She could also label expressions of emotions in others. But she didn't know how to attach labels to her own internal sensations.

There are two different ways to practice this skill: the word-to-feeling method and the feeling-to-word method. Both are useful. At first, it is best to think about previous emotional experiences. The word-to-feeling method is a self-reflective exercise to use after an emotional episode to help bridge the connection between emotion and label. First, pick any emotion that you think you've experienced. Stick with the overarching emotion family category when you start.

For example, when Linda did this activity in therapy, she picked "embarrassed." I asked her, "What does embarrassment feel like to you?" Linda acknowledged that she doesn't feel embarrassed very often, but when she does her face and ears feel hot. She said that she also generally smiles when she's embarrassed because she doesn't mind laughing at herself. Then she started to think about the feeling of embarrassment more closely, and she acknowledged, "I also get louder when I'm embarrassed, I think to cover my embarrassment!"

Thinking through the links between the emotion word and your prior experiences can help your brain create connections between the word and the feeling so you have an easier time attaching a word to the feeling when it arises.

The feeling-to-word method involves applying a word to a feeling. You can practice by thinking about a time when you felt off, or different than usual. Review the situation in your mind. Think about where you were, who you were with, and how the situation progressed. Once you've recalled the situation, look at the emotion lists in Tables 4.2 and 4.3 to see what word best fits your experience. Ask yourself, "Hmm, was I feeling something mild, moderate, or intense?" Then choose the column that best fits your emotional intensity to think about which emotion you might have been feeling. See if you can identify which families your feeling belonged to, and find a word or two that fits.

For example, Garrett, whom you met in Chapter 1, took his kids to play at a trampoline park. He filled out the "You can't sue us if your kid gets hurt" waiver, bought the kids the socks with the little grippy bottoms, and let them loose. He sat down on a bench and watched his kids jump. In therapy a few days later, I asked Garrett what he felt as he watched his kids jump. Unsurprisingly, he initially said he was "stressed." But at this point in therapy he'd acknowledged that he had other feelings in him, so he broke out the lists in Tables 4.2 and 4.3. He looked at words in the fear family and identified that he was feeling *wary*. He said that he'd read about the dangers of trampolines for small kids, and he didn't want his 4-year-old to get a concussion. We were able to talk about his wariness and give space for his feeling while also acknowledging that his kids had a blast (and ultimately did not get hurt).

Step 4: Label Emotions as They Arise

Practicing linking emotion words with physical and subjective feeling states after the fact can help you get to the final step: labeling while the situation transpires. This is a considerably harder skill because it involves recognizing that an emotion is taking place (i.e., awareness) and having enough mental resources to remember that labeling is helpful, as well as remembering the list of emotion words (or at least where to find a list of emotions).

LABELING AND EMOTIONAL COMPLEXITY

Labeling does not necessarily mean picking one and only one emotion. Many situations evoke more than one feeling. For example, a friend of mine recently took her 5-year-old daughter to tour their neighborhood elementary school on the same day that there was a school shooting at a different elementary school in the same city. She told me that she sat in her office crying about the school shooting while feeling a sense of despair. She also felt anger and frustration that the lawmakers "seem to care more about banning kids from attending drag shows instead of cracking down on gun misuse." She also felt anxiety about sending her kid to any school, because the world felt very unsafe. Her feelings were complex because they were a blend of several emotions (anger, fear, sadness, disgust).

Many feelings are complex and multifaceted, because situations are complex and multifaceted. Yet some people tend to believe that emotional responses are supposed to be pure, simple, and discrete (Veilleux, Chamberlain, et al., 2021). People who think that emotions are supposed to be simple tend to struggle more with their feelings (Veilleux, Pollert, et al., 2021; Veilleux, Warner, et al., 2021). Even though experiencing one emotion at a time might sound simpler and easier to deal with, one-at-a-time emotions aren't really how the world works. Trying to shove a complex feeling into a single word, or trying to push away the conflicting parts of a feeling, is a recipe for frustration and disappointment—which, ironically, is itself a blended and complex emotion!

It's better to allow feelings to be complex. Human beings are complicated, and our emotions are complicated, too. Being able to recognize more complex, blended emotions is associated with greater emotional intelligence (Lane et al., 1990; Lane & Smith, 2021). Remember, one situation can activate more than one value, too!

Blended or *complex* emotions also include *mixed* emotions, which involve feeling a negative and a positive feeling at the same time. For example, I did a lot of theater when I was in high school. I remember standing backstage before the first performance of *Cabaret* my senior year of high school, when I played landlady Fraulein Schneider. I was excited to feel the energy of the crowd and to hear the applause. The feeling of excitement was sent by my values of Variety, Curiosity, and Achievement. But I was also anxious. Would I remember the lines? Would I be able to sing those low notes? Would I have on-stage chemistry with the other actors? Would people like me???? Anxiety was triggered by my value of Belonging and by the potential threat of failing to Achieve. Both feelings make sense, and I certainly felt both quite strongly!

Mixed emotions are tricky because they can be difficult to make sense of. Think about saying goodbye to a good friend who is moving away for a kickass new job. You can feel happy for their good fortune and success but also sad that you will not be able to see them as often; this characterizes "bittersweet," which is a classic example of a mixed emotion (Larsen & McGraw, 2011; Larsen & Stastny, 2011). Graduations and other life transitions are often loaded with these bittersweet mixed emotions. A graduation represents success and accomplishment and often goes with feelings of pride and happiness. Yet graduations are also endings; they can be fraught with uncertainty about the future and sadness that a great time in life is coming to an end.

If you are someone who has struggled to allow complex, multi-faceted, or mixed emotions, what can you do about it? First, give yourself a break. You probably learned that emotions should be simple from caregivers, teachers, or friends, or even from the media. Mixed or complex emotions are not talked about nearly enough. But this is an instance where knowledge is power. Now that you know emotions can be complex or mixed, when you practice emotional labeling, allow yourself multiple answers!

REMINDERS AND PITFALLS

Labeling is incredibly valuable to achieving emotional health. As I said earlier, and this is worth reiterating here, if you are going to practice only one skill in this book, I would recommend putting forth effort toward labeling, which is kind of an emotional superpower.

There are some pitfalls to watch out for with labeling. First, remember that some people think they are good at labeling, but they aren't. You might check with people who are known for giving honest-but-kind feedback and ask them, "Do you hear me use specific words for distinct emotions? Do I use a variety of different emotion words?"

Second, accurate labeling can be tricky. For example, a client I once worked with, Lauren, said she was "sad" every time I asked her what she was feeling. Lauren didn't say general words, like "upset" or "bad"; instead, she said she was sad. One time, she had caught her girlfriend snooping through her stuff, and her girlfriend admitted that she'd read Lauren's private personal journal. I asked Lauren how she felt, and she said (predictably) that she felt "sad." I responded, "You know, if my partner read my journal without my permission, I'd be *mad*, because I'd feel like my privacy was violated." This conversation helped Lauren realize that although she did use a specific emotion word ("sad"), she was applying it too broadly. We did a version of the word-to-feeling exercise in addition to looking at the physical markers of each emotion (in Table 4.2), and she realized that she was both sad and angry in this situation.

It is possible, however, that one person's emotions are individually theirs. If Lauren had said she only felt sad in this situation after discussing it, that would have been OK, too. Just because I would be mad doesn't mean she would feel the same.

Third, it is possible to go overboard with labeling. In one clever study, researchers asked participants to imagine asking a friend to meet them at a coffee shop to provide emotional support, but the friend never showed up (Vine et al., 2019). The researchers asked half of the participants to "thoroughly scrutinize" their feelings, by using a lot of words, and to completely label all nuances of their feelings. The other half were asked to label, too, but they were asked to use as few words as possible to label their overall emotional response. Participants completed an emotion regulation planning task in which they generated what coping strategies they would use in this situation and indicated which one would be the most effective. They found that people who used only a few words for their feelings generated more and better ideas for problem-solving than the people who thoroughly scrutinized and overlabeled their feelings.

Getting too nuanced about labeling may not be productive. This makes sense to me. I once supervised a graduate student who was working with a client named Arooj. Arooj cared a lot about specificity and nuance. We once asked her to complete a values activity like the one in Chapter 3. She took several weeks to complete it. When she brought it in, she had detailed notes about why exactly she had chosen each value. Then, when her therapist started trying to get her to label her feelings, she struggled because she "couldn't choose" just one word to characterize her feelings, which were often complex and layered. Yet when she tried to use multiple words, she got lost in the definitions. Spending so much time and energy labeling creates a big messy jumble, and it's harder to figure out what to do next when there are too many words for a given experience. This is one of those times where you want to choose the middle road: Use enough words to describe your feelings, and don't avoid complex or mixed emotions. But don't go overboard, because then clarity gets lost.

SUMMARY POINTS

- Emotional labeling is a kind of coping superpower because it is an implicit regulation strategy (labeling changes feelings even outside of your awareness), it can help you figure out what regulation strategy to use, and it can help you identify what is valued.

- Because some people think they are good at labeling but aren't, practicing is probably a good idea for just about everyone.
- Learning to label involves developing a richer emotional vocabulary, practicing identifying specific emotions in others, and practicing linking emotion labels to your internal sensations.
- A given situation does not need to have just one emotion word; complex (multiple feelings at once) and mixed emotions (both positive and negative feelings at the same time) are common, too.
- Labeling is important, but it's not great to get too nuanced with labeling—being clear and specific is better than cataloguing every tiny detail!

CHAPTER 5

COPING AHEAD

Sports and cooking are both huge sources of enjoyment for many people. Some people love to watch (e.g., go to sporting events, watch baking or competition cooking shows), and others love to do (e.g., play sports, cook delicious foods in their kitchens). Whether as a participant or a viewer, you probably know that both cooking and sports involve protective gear. Soccer players need shin guards. Hockey players, football players, and cyclists need helmets. Chefs need oven mitts and an apron. Both athletes and kitchen aficionados need good-quality nonslip shoes.

The reason for the protective gear is pretty obvious: People need to protect their bodies against injury, heat, spills, and potential accidents. Although sports and cooking can be a lot of fun, they both involve risk of injury. Wearing protective gear doesn't take away the chance of getting smacked in the face by a wayward soccer ball or crashing into a fellow chef carrying a hot pan; however, wearing protective gear does acknowledge that these things may happen and thus reduces the likelihood of serious bodily harm.

Emotions are similar. Instead of physical protective gear, we need psychological protective gear in the form of **coping ahead** strategies. Just like shin guards and oven mitts don't take away the possibility of injury, coping ahead strategies don't take away the possibility—or inevitability—of encountering a stressful event. In fact, cultivating psychological padding helps people prepare for the eventuality of stress rather than having to react to it in the moment.

You touch a hot pan with your bare hands, you get burned. But when you use a resource like an oven mitt to prepare for the hot pan, you don't experience pain. This chapter is all about using psychological resources to cope ahead and reduce the likelihood of lasting emotional damage.

I fully acknowledge that the emotions-as-messages metaphor is the least clear for this particular chapter, which is why we are talking about sports and cooking instead. Coping ahead is about engaging in strategies that make emotions easier to deal with. What kinds of strategies make messages easier to deal with? Shoveling the front steps so there is a clear path to the mailbox? Purchasing a letter opener so you can open an envelope without getting a nasty paper cut? Ensuring access to the internet so an important email will load?

For this chapter, thinking about chefs and athletes is a bit more straightforward, for three reasons. First, both have protective gear that they use to prevent pain and injury. Second, both need to condition their bodies and minds. Athletes need to learn about kinesiology, and chefs need to learn about seasonings. They also need to practice by building strength and flexibility, learning the muscle memory for how to perform their skills without thinking. Third, I also like thinking about chefs and athletes because cooking and sports are activities that bring joy. Pain, injury, and emotional distress are possible, but athletes and chefs don't let the potential fear of injury keep them from engaging in these valued activities.

Sometimes, people think that "coping ahead" means anticipating distress and trying to circumvent any kind of negative feelings. For example, I fell down a dozen times while trying to learn how to snowboard, and thinking about my bruised hips contributed to me refusing to go back out. Voilà, problem solved—if I don't do the activity, I can't get hurt! But that's not what coping ahead is about. Coping ahead is about doing the things related to your values (see Chapter 3) even with the chances of bruising. It's about wearing padded shorts under the snow pants and maybe practicing some "how to fall safely" skills on a mat the week before heading to the slopes. Coping ahead skills involve wearing "protective gear" and conditioning the mind and body when you are not emotional to buffer you and prepare you for any emotions that might pop up.

EMOTIONAL CONDITIONING

Perhaps you are wondering how the concept of coping ahead connects to earlier chapters. The answer is that the first four chapters of this book were helping you develop emotional conditioning, which involves building knowledge and habits so that you can use them effectively, and with little effort, when you need to draw upon them during heightened emotional states.

Athletes rely on conditioning drills to build strength, flexibility, and endurance. They lift weights, run sprints, and stretch. Chefs need to practice using knives so they can cut quickly without slicing their fingers off. These conditioning drills are used to prepare for a game or before a big catering event. During the game itself the athlete needs to be able to use their conditioned muscles to return a serve (tennis), tackle a quarterback (football), land a trick (gymnastics), or go as fast as possible (running, swimming, speed skating). During the dinner rush, a chef needs to be able to use their conditioned skills to quickly but accurately sauté the vegetables or sear the meat. The body has to be trained ahead of time, or the performance suffers and the risk of injury increases. While performing, the athlete and the chef both unconsciously rely on the strength, flexibility, and endurance these conditioning drills have awarded them.

Emotions are similar. Learning about how emotions work is like learning the rules of a sport or about flavor profiles; the knowledge provides a framework on how and why the conditioning skills are helpful. Cultivating compassion for your level of emotional sensitivity (Chapter 1), practicing mindfulness to increase emotional awareness (Chapter 2), linking your emotions and your values (Chapter 3), and labeling your emotions (Chapter 4) are all emotional conditioning drills. That's why we talked about those skills first. When practiced regularly, these skills become habits, training your emotional mind to respond adaptively in moments of emotional distress. The benefit of habits is that they become automatic, so you don't have to think about them to use them. You can make good choices more effortlessly (Galla & Duckworth, 2015).

ARE THESE REALLY COPING STRATEGIES?

Now let's focus on how to put on emotional protective gear by discussing the actions to take when you are not emotional to shield against emotional distress.

Consider Kayla, a married mother of two with a full-time job. She felt overworked, stressed out, and mentally exhausted basically every day. It took her 5 months to figure out how to make time to see a therapist. Even then, she did therapy on her phone, in her car, during her lunch break. Kayla was barely functioning, and it was clear to her therapist that she was clinically depressed.

Kayla sought therapy to develop more coping strategies, which is a common goal many clients say they want out of therapy. Perhaps you picked up this book because you want some better, more effective, and healthier ways to cope with the overwhelming emotions that seem to crop up more often than you'd like.

Kayla's therapist introduced the idea of coping ahead, but Kayla grew impatient. What she wanted was more effective methods of handling stress and dealing with emotions that had already been generated. Don't get me wrong; it is crucially important to learn effective methods of navigating emotional messages that have already been received. We'll talk about those, too, in later chapters.

For now, though, there are a variety of important strategies to use before the emotion is even activated. These strategies do not feel like coping strategies, just like a chef putting her hair in a hairnet doesn't feel like she is cooking. One of the reasons these coping ahead strategies don't feel like actual coping is because, when used well, they are essentially invisible. The chef who has her hair in a hairnet may not recognize that her hair would have caught fire when setting the bananas foster aflame. When disaster is averted, we forget that we actually did something preventative. Emotions work the same way. When coping ahead strategies are used wisely, emotions are less intense and feel easier to manage. Because it can be hard to recognize when efforts result in the absence of negative outcomes, a clearer understanding of how these coping ahead strategies benefit you might help motivate you to try them.

STRESS AND THE NEGATIVITY BIAS

To understand the effects of coping ahead strategies, we need to talk a little bit about the science of stress and coping. The first thing to understand is that *stress* and *stressors* are not the same thing. **Stress** is a subjectively experienced state of worry as well as physical and mental tension (Wheaton & Montazer, 2010). Stress occurs in response to **stressors**, which are the things in your life that you have to deal with. Stressors can be small, like trying to decide whether to kill a bug or usher it outside. Stressors can be moderate, like rushing to the laundromat to clean your clothes the day before a road trip, or waiting on the results of an HIV test. Stressors can also be severe, like dealing with the death of a loved one, not having a stable place to live, dealing with systematic oppression, or trying to figure out what to do about an unplanned pregnancy. Stressors are the things that pop up in life, and stress is the body's and mind's response to those things (Wheaton & Montazer, 2010).

The reason why the distinction between stressors and stress is important is because experiencing stressors does not automatically lead to stress. Two people can experience the same stressor but have very different subjective stress responses. For example, Kayla's friend Kyle had a situation similar to her own. They worked for the same company and were both married and had children of similar ages. Kayla felt burned out, overworked, and overwhelmed, but Kyle wasn't particularly stressed at all—Kyle was *resilient* (Klohnen, 1996).

Why are some people resilient and others vulnerable to stress? One reason is the **negativity bias**. The negativity bias is the tendency to give greater weight to negative, stressful, unpleasant information compared to positive information (Ito & Cacioppo, 2005; Vaish et al., 2008). To be clear, from an evolutionary perspective, it makes sense to focus on negative, threatening stimuli. We should attend more to an ice storm than a sunny day, or to a herd of stampeding buffalo than a swarm of butterflies. Ice storms and buffalo could, quite literally, kill a person! Positive information is life enhancing, but typically isn't life threatening. Our brains and bodies are hyperattuned to stressors that could threaten survival.

Yet, because the negativity bias can't tease apart which situations are and are not life threatening, negative information of all varieties stands out, weighs more heavily, and is harder to detach from (Rozin & Royzman, 2001). Positive information can be discounted and undervalued (Baumeister et al., 2001).

The negativity bias is at play for just about everyone, but some people do have a stronger negativity bias than others. Any guesses as to who might have a stronger negativity bias? If you guessed people with high threat sensitivity, you'd be right. People who have a high threat sensitivity are particularly likely to have a strong negativity bias and are more likely to experience subjective stress (Schneider, 2004). Some of this is biological, but some of it is about interpretation. For example, viewing stressors as threatening tends to produce a stronger physical stress response than viewing stressors as challenging (Jamieson et al., 2012). More resilient people tend to see the potential upsides of stress (e.g., for energizing the body for growth and to face challenges), whereas those with a stronger negativity bias tend to see stressors as threats.

Kayla, for example, had a strong negativity bias and was highly threat sensitive. She initially told her therapist that her boss never said anything nice at all about her work, but when Kayla brought in her written annual evaluation, the therapist saw several pieces of praise. In fact, from the therapist's lens, there was more positive feedback than negative! Yet Kayla had zeroed in on the 5% of comments that were critical because those were the comments that stung and felt stressful.

THE NEED FOR RESOURCES

Another contribution to resilience is resources. One prominent idea about stress is that when people lack the resources to adequately deal with stressors, they will feel heightened stress (Blascovich et al., 1999; Folkman et al., 1986). However, when people have the resources to manage stressors, they don't feel as stressed. Resilient people perceive themselves as having more resources and as able to use those resources to tackle the challenges that stressors set forth. This is a simple but powerful idea.

There are some people who seem to be able to multitask, turn the other cheek, and juggle work and home and friends without getting overwhelmed. You probably secretly (or maybe not so secretly) hate these people, because most of us do feel stressed and overwhelmed with all our responsibilities and obligations. Some people even try to look like they manage stressors easily by plastering a smile on their faces. They post filtered, cultivated pictures on social media that make it look like everything is fine. But then, in the privacy of their own homes, they break down (Rutherford, 2019).

But there are people who manage stressors well. Although it is tempting to see ourselves as deficient next to these resilient beasts of nature, it may be more productive to try to learn their tricks. What helps them experience less stress? Or, even if they feel the same amount of stress, what helps them bounce back from stress quickly? The answer is that they have resources.

Now, I'm not really referring to financial resources here, or to any kind of **privilege resource**. A privilege resource is an advantage or benefit granted to people who belong to a particular social group. Being White, straight, able-bodied—these are all resources that make life a bit easier but don't necessarily feel like advantages because they are often invisible. A person doesn't know they have this resource unless it is absent.

Financial resources are a type of privilege resource. People with less money do, in fact, experience significantly more stress than people who are financially well off (Cohen et al., 2006). Fears of getting evicted or not being able to buy food are incredibly stressful. It is also true that having the financial resources to throw money at problems can help reduce stressors. The suggestions to "take a vacation" or "hire a housecleaner" aren't viable solutions for people without vacation days or extra income.

One of the goals of this book is to provide scientifically informed suggestions that are feasible, and changing privilege resources is not easily feasible. Changing gender, race, disability, or financial status isn't practical. Instead, we'll focus on **psychological resources** associated with resilience.

Unfortunately, many of the psychological resources associated with higher resilience are personality traits. Personality traits are changeable (Allemand & Flückiger, 2017), but they don't change quickly. It can be hard to cultivate optimism, a sense of control or mastery over the environment, or high self-worth, or to develop a strong support system, which are the characteristics most closely associated with resilience (Taylor & Stanton, 2007).

What we need are resources that don't cost money, aren't long-standing personality traits or society-level factors, and can be obtained now to combat the effects of stressors on stress and to buffer against the negativity bias. What could those be? In the sections that follow, I discuss some of these.

RESOURCES FOR REDUCING EMOTIONAL VULNERABILITY

I began this chapter by talking about how adopting coping ahead strategies can reduce the negative impact of strong emotions. Coping ahead strategies are crucial because they give a person resources to feel more capable of handling stressors and reducing the negativity bias. They are armor and provide protection against negative emotions hurting quite so much. So, what are these magical strategies that can do so much?

Pleasure

The first resource is **pleasure**. I'm not alluding to sexual/physical pleasure here. The idea is to experience more pleasant, positive emotions, including contentment, gratitude, awe, amusement, joy, love, interest, and pride (all the emotions included in Table 4.3).

Why is pleasure important? Pleasure provides a buffer against stressors, so that when a negative event happens, it's more like dropping a drop of black paint into a swimming pool versus into a small cup. The paint won't really affect the color of the swimming pool, but it will cloud the liquid in the small cup immediately!

Pleasure helps balance the negativity bias. Think about a scale. In fact, when my daughter was a preschooler, she had a "monkey scale" designed to teach her numbers. The set came with ten little plastic toy monkeys and a set of numbers. The numbers differed in weight, so the number 8 on one side of the scale would become balanced when eight toy monkeys were placed on the other scale. The scale teaches kids that bigger numbers "weigh" more, just as negative experiences "weigh" more heavily than positive ones (Baumeister et al., 2001).

Balancing the Negativity Bias

If negative experiences weigh more, then how many positive experiences does it take to balance the emotional scale? If the negative weighs more heavily than the positive, how much more positive is needed to balance out the negative? A famous couples therapist once claimed that there is a magic ratio whereby a couple needs five positive interactions to balance out one negative interaction (Gottman, 1993). Other experts have suggested that the magic ratio is closer to 3-to-1 (Fredrickson & Losada, 2005), but there doesn't seem to be clear evidence that there even is a magic ratio at all, at least not a universal ratio (Friedman & Brown, 2018; Sabey et al., 2019). That's because not all negative information (i.e., stressors) or positive information is created equal. Some positive events are big deals and have stronger weight than others. For example, a wedding or the birth of a child weighs more than finding a dollar on the street. Yet some positive-on-paper events aren't exclusively positive—the birth of a child can be painful!

Also, a particular kernel of negative information can have a bigger effect on one person than on another. Think about two college seniors applying to college, Noah and Dulce. Neither is accepted to their top choice, but both get into four other good schools. Because there are four pieces of good news but only one piece of bad news, the four admissions should balance out the rejection. That was true for Noah, who shrugged off the rejection and happily accepted one of the other offers. But Dulce had her heart set on her top choice because she had dreamed about going to that school since she was a child. For her, the negative information weighed much more heavily because of how important it was to her, and the acceptance to lesser schools did not outweigh the crushing rejection she felt. In essence, we can't apply a simple mathematical formula to emotional events equally, let alone across people.

Even if there isn't a magical formula, it is still the case that experiencing more positive events and feelings can counteract the heavier weight of the negative events. People who have more positivity in their life tend to be more resilient and to have more life satisfaction and higher well-being (Diener, 1984).

Think about it. When you've had a great day, done fun things, and you are generally feeling good, stubbing your toe on the bathroom door is easy to get over. But when you've had a crappy day, and feel drained and stressed, stubbing your toe on the bathroom door not only feels more physically painful but also might be the tipping point into a storm of tears and eating an entire tub of ice cream. The first coping ahead solution is thus to intentionally engage in more pleasurable activities.

ENGAGING IN PLEASURABLE AND MEANINGFUL ACTIVITIES

A pleasant event is any activity that you could find pleasurable. There are long lists of potential activities you can find online if you don't have ideas of your own. A short list is provided in Exhibit 5.1. These pleasant events do not need to be big or expensive (e.g., taking that trip to Machu Picchu you've always dreamed of). They could cost money, like going to see a movie or getting a group of friends

EXHIBIT 5.1. Pleasant Activities

1. Take 10 deep breaths
2. Dance to a fun song
3. Take a 15 min walk
4. Swing on a swing
5. Paint a rock and leave it for someone to find
6. Dye your hair a bright color
7. Phone a faraway friend
8. Take a silly selfie
9. Stargaze
10. Put on a temporary tattoo
11. Build a sheet fort
12. Soak in a bathtub
13. Watch dogs romp at a dog park
14. Volunteer in the community
15. Walk around your room naked
16. Gather rocks or driftwood
17. Watch a comedy show (on TV or in person)
18. Try on new clothes
19. Pray
20. Jump on a trampoline
21. Sleep in
22. Play pickleball
23. Help other people solve their problems
24. Fold laundry
25. Sit and listen to the quiet

together to do an escape room. But there are also plenty of free pleasant activities, like taking a 10-minute walk in the sunshine, smiling at people you pass on the street, and standing outside a bakery and sniffing freshly baked bread.

Perhaps you look at the list in Exhibit 5.1 (or a longer list online) and say "Bah, these aren't pleasant activities!" To that I say, "They are to someone!" Yes, there are activities on every list that will be unattainable. If you have a broken leg, you can't play pickleball. Other activities might not be fun for you. Some people don't like baths. Atheists aren't likely to get anything out of praying. The trick is to not assume an activity will be unpleasant until you've tried it.

The other reason why these lists of pleasurable activities are not consistent across people is values. Activities that align with values tend to produce meaning or happiness, but not always both. For example, getting my work done on time is meaningful. It feeds my value of responsibility, but it's not always fun. Yet valued activities often do result in positive feelings, as we discussed in Chapter 3. The point here is that when you look at existing lists of pleasurable activities, or try to generate your own, you should think about activities that seem consistent with your values.

We met Kayla at the start of this chapter. Kayla was incredibly stressed and clinically depressed. When Kayla's therapist introduced the idea of pleasant activities—which is a scientifically backed treatment strategy to help improve depression (Kanter et al., 2010), Kayla kindly laughed in her therapist's virtual face. "I have no time for myself," Kayla said. "I get up; barely have time to shower; get the kids ready for school and day care; make everyone lunches; go to work, where I'm behind on every deliverable; race to pick the kids up from aftercare; heat up leftovers from the freezer; play with the kids; put them to bed; and then fall over tired. There's no room for literally anything else."

Then Kayla looked at the list of 330 pleasant events her therapist sent her. She came to the next session confused. She said, "There were some things on here I was expecting, like take a bath and play pickleball. Those are not going to happen, I don't have time for those. But . . . folding laundry? Smiling at a stranger? Those are pleasant activities? I already do those." Her therapist laughed knowingly.

One of the functions of a list like this is not only to help people generate new ideas for pleasurable activities but also to help them realize the things that they already do that might be pleasant and consistent with their values. The idea is to recognize the delight in small everyday activities. Kayla said, "I've just thought of folding laundry as a chore. But, when I think about it, laundry is time I get to myself to listen to a podcast, which feeds my value of Curiosity. And the soft, warm clothes feel nice on my hands. I like seeing a heap of crumpled fabric become organized, folded, and sorted; this feeds my values of Beauty and of Tradition. I'd never thought about what feels nice about laundry, but there's a reason I volunteer for laundry while my husband does the dishes!"

Kayla and her therapist talked about things she was already doing, and then they looked closely at the list for new things she could reasonably try. She said, "I won't find painting a rock pleasurable; that sounds stupid." Her therapist encouraged her to try it anyway, perhaps making it a craft activity with her kids. Kayla admitted a few weeks later that painting the rocks was fun. She said, "But the most fun thing was taking the kids to a path through the woods and trying to figure out where to put the rocks where hikers might see them." This fed Kayla's values of Curiosity and of Adventure. Over time, she tried more of the things on the list, first with her kids and then on her own. She started walking with a coworker during lunch a few times a week and calling her sister on the commute home from work. She realized that pleasurable activities didn't need to be activities per se, like a board game party or a pottery class, but could be small instances, small bursts of pleasure sprinkled into her day. She also benefited from thinking intentionally about how her activities—both new and old— fed her values. Even recognizing that things she didn't find pleasurable (making lunches for the kids, for example) fed her values of Duty and Belonging helped her see those activities as choices rather than obligations. When activities are consistent with your values, they add to your life force rather than drain it, and that perspective change can be incredibly powerful. Pleasurable activities, when engaged in regularly, are resources that can help buffer against stress.

Energy: Attending to Physical Health

The second category of coping ahead can be summarized as the **energy resource**. The easiest way to get energy is to think about whether the body is getting what it needs to function well. There are five main strategies in this category: (a) eating nourishing food, (b) trying to get enough sleep, (c) taking medications as prescribed, (d) limiting substance use, and (e) exercising.

All of these strategies focus on physical health. Perhaps it's obvious that the mind is housed in the brain, which is a part of your physical body, but it's a fact that people sometimes forget. Emotions are both physical and mental. When the body doesn't have sufficient energy, the energy it does have goes toward vital functions, like keeping the heart pumping, digestion, and walking around without falling over. There isn't enough energy left to cope with emotions gracefully or effectively.

EATING NOURISHING FOOD

I am not one to define what constitutes healthy eating, because I would happily subsist on a diet of chocolate cream pie and French fries if I could. That said, it is ideal to eat foods that fill you up and make your body feel energized. Protein, carbohydrates, vegetables, and fruit are all great. Bodies do well by eating foods of different colors and textures.

You want to eat enough food that you're full but not so much that you're bloated and stuffed. This is another one of those middle-ground concepts: When the body doesn't get enough food (and thus not enough energy), emotions are more intense and harder to manage

(Dicker-Oren et al., 2022). When the body gets a lot of food, people are tired and can't think as clearly (Hervé et al., 2024), suggesting that energy gets diverted to digestion, and then there's not as much energy left for navigating emotions.

Drinking water fits into this category as well. Water is a vital energy source, yet many people do not drink enough water. Or they have enough water but dehydrate their bodies with caffeine and alcohol. People tend to be crankier when they are dehydrated (Veilleux et al., 2020). I know I am!

Trying to Get Enough Sleep

Notice I said "trying" to get enough sleep, rather than "getting enough sleep." For many people, sleeping is a necessary but difficult task. Up to 30% of adults have one or more symptoms of insomnia (Roth, 2007) and that's not even accounting for other sleep disorders (e.g., sleep apnea, narcolepsy). The good news is that there are all kinds of strategies available to facilitate good sleep. For example, make sleep a priority—sleep is probably more important than watching 12 more videos on YouTube. *Sleep hygiene* is the term for creating the conditions and routines to facilitate "clean" sleep. Doing the same tasks each night (e.g., brush teeth, get into pajamas, read for 20 minutes) and setting an environment conducive to good sleep (e.g., blackout curtains, a white noise machine) are a part of sleep hygiene. You might need to experiment to figure out what helps you sleep. Some people might sleep better with a weighted blanket, and others benefit from a cooling pillow.

If you aren't getting enough good-quality sleep at night, then reach out for help. Cognitive behavioral therapy for insomnia is quite effective in helping people with insomnia learn to sleep better (Mitchell et al., 2012). Sleep is crucial for good emotional health (and physical health, too).

TAKING MEDICATIONS AS PRESCRIBED

If you've been prescribed medications, there is probably a good reason to take them. Yes, remembering to take meds can be hard, and there can be side effects to consider. But medications are often prescribed to help correct an imbalance in your hormones, neurotransmitters, or some other kind of biological function. Many medications also need to be taken consistently to work well, and inconsistencies can put the body into a tailspin. Taking medications as prescribed helps your body correct whatever imbalances are going on and thus gives you more bandwidth to tackle emotions.

LIMITING SUBSTANCE USE

Many people have a beer, cocktail, or glass of wine to unwind after a long day. Other people smoke a joint or do other drugs. Setting aside the legality of any particular substance, or the moral attitudes associated with substance use (Barata et al., 2019), there are good emotion-related reasons to cut back on substances. What are they?

First, although substances are often used in the context of positive emotions (e.g., champagne toasts at weddings, beer cheers at football games), substances can become a proxy coping strategy when people start to rely on them for their emotional effects. For example, when my grad school roommate Sarah came home and said, "Ugh, today was a doozy; I need a drink," I would snarkily respond, "Need? You NEED a drink?" Those words conveyed that she couldn't handle processing her crappy day without a drink. What she really meant was that she "wanted" a drink, but words matter. If she kept talking in a way that suggested she couldn't calm down without alcohol, she might have started to believe that she was incapable of dealing with her own feelings.

Second, substances change the brain's emotional circuitry. Each drug influences different neurotransmitters in the brain, and when the brain has jacked neurotransmitters, emotional triggers will influence it differently. It's true that sometimes emotions are dulled or numbed when on substances, which is partly why it is so hazardous to rely on substances for emotional health.

The main point here is that I'm not here to tell you to never have a drink or smoke a joint. I'll leave it to substance use medical experts to discuss how much is too much. From an emotional lens, though, it's learning to rely on substances that is the biggest emotional problem. Limiting them can help.

EXERCISING

I'm defining "exercise" here as any activity that involves moving your body, ideally at a moderate (or greater) level, at least 3 days a week. There are all kinds of ways to keep your body active, such as walking, running, swimming, playing sports, or doing workout videos on your phone. Exercise is a coping ahead strategy in a lot of ways. When people exercise more often, they have greater mind–body connections, which can help them automatically regulate emotions without even trying (Zhang et al., 2019). Also, exercising before encountering a stressor can make it easier to generate beneficial coping strategies (Bernstein & McNally, 2017). Exercise can improve heart rate variability, which is associated with better recovery from stressful events (Föhr et al., 2017). A little exercise can go a long way toward coping ahead.

Energy for Emotional Health

Attending to your food, sleep, medications, and substance use matter even when you are not feeling any kind of emotion or mood. Physical health can help build your armor and protect you from emotional vulnerability, because low mental and physical energy makes emotions stronger and longer. Can you think of a time when you were tired and then cried at work, or you were so hungry that you snapped at your sister? Yep. Attending to physical health increases resources, and so stressors are less likely to turn into stress.

Connect to Find Moments of Meaning

Although there are likely more than three categories of resources that are useful for coping ahead as psychological protective gear, there is one other crucial resource to discuss: **social connection**. Making an interpersonal connection by spending quality time with other human beings is a huge source of positive emotions for most people. Even more, feeling supported is a powerful protective resource. It can be like wearing an invisible but powerfully flexible emotional shield. Stressors are more likely to bounce off of the person who feels loved, cared for, and supported.

There is a reason I say "quality" time and not just "spending time with others." That is because spending time with others is not always rewarding. Sometimes, other people can be downright draining. People who are more introverted tend to find spending time with big groups of people more taxing, for example.

It's also possible to feel lonely in the presence of others! Think about being in a meeting, sharing a bench with someone on the bus, or sitting near someone at a basketball game. Those situations involve social proximity but may not feel like social connection. To be honest, watching TV while lounging on the couch with your partner isn't necessarily connecting, either.

This resource also isn't "spend time with supportive people." What's wrong with that, you might ask? Nothing, in theory. But it's dangerous to categorize people in your life as wholly supportive or non-supportive. The same person can be sometimes supportive and other times unsupportive—maybe even both within the same conversation!

Kayla, for example, had an intense relationship with her mother. Her mother called her daily and wanted to be heavily involved in her life. In that way, Kayla felt supported and cared for. But her mother also made snide remarks about her looks, her job, her husband, and her parenting choices. Friends and past therapists had told Kayla to distance herself from her toxic mother. Kayla recognized that her relationship with her mother was complicated, but she wanted to work with that complexity rather than circumvent it. She also recognized that sometimes she did feel supported—her mother gave her financial resources, bought her gifts, and they both loved five-course dinners. Those fancy dinners were particularly strong moments of connection. Other interactions felt like disconnection, to the point that Kayla learned to avoid telling her mom her biggest emotional concerns because she knew she'd end up feeling worse than if she'd just said nothing.

To really get the biggest benefit, you need to connect with other people in ways that feel personally meaningful. Remember that "fun" isn't always the same as "meaningful." Have you ever had a deep, serious conversation with someone, or cried in someone's arms? Those experiences aren't necessarily fun, but they can be meaningful. There are also brief, fun connections with others that don't feel profound, like laughing so hard that soda squirts out of your nose. Those moments have such joy (and make such good stories) that they are meaningful, too. The idea here is to add more moments of meaning and moments of connection into your daily life.

How do you do that? Well, connecting with others requires contact as the first step. Think about your daily interactions—who do you have contact with? Family members, friends, coworkers, the checkout clerk at the grocery store, they are all contacts. Virtual contacts can also count, like phone calls and FaceTime. It can be useful to think through a couple of recent days and about all the people you had contact with. Contact can be as small as bumping knees with someone on the train, sending a text emoji, or making eye contact across the room. Once you think about your points of contact, then think about whether these contacts felt like connections.

Kayla, who initially struggled with the pleasant activities schedule, also balked at connecting with others. She felt she had no bandwidth for anything else other than work, parenting, dealing with her mother, and, sometimes, sleeping. She admitted that she missed having friends, and she said that she and her husband cohabitated on barely overlapping schedules, which did not feel like quality time. Yet she was resistant to adding anything to her already-overflowing plate.

She started by thinking about moments when she did feel connection, like when she felt close to her kids during play time. But she also knew that although seeing her kids' joy was meaningful, it wasn't enough. Her kids weren't really supportive to her. She brainstormed ways to feel more moments of meaning. She started calling her family during her commute. On her twice-weekly walks with her coworker, she started opening up more about her frequent stress and was surprised to find her coworker felt similarly. She had thought that everyone had it more together than she did, and she was relieved to know that it wasn't just her. She also talked with her husband about having at least one night per week where they sat and talked rather than watching TV in parallel. Here as well, she was surprised to find that her husband was delighted with this idea, because he too had felt disconnected from her. They even started having more sex, which felt good both physically and emotionally to both of them. Kayla was amazed to find that even without adding more events to her social calendar, these small changes helped her feel more connected.

BARRIERS AND SOLUTIONS

Experiencing pleasure and positive affect, ensuring sufficient energy by attending to physical health, and having moments of connection are the psychological protective gear needed to cope ahead with emotion. These are resources that help people feel more in control of stressors, reduce how often stressors become stress, and buffer against the negativity bias. They are the psychological equivalent to the non-slip shoes, helmet (or hairnet), and gloves used by chefs and athletes.

The strategies discussed in this chapter all work because they make dealing with the inevitable negative affect easier to handle. They most certainly do not remove stressors—no strategy I'm aware of has that much power. But these do work to reduce the intensity and longevity of unpleasant feelings. That said, I recognize that building up these resources is not easy for many people, myself included. We differ in terms of which resources are more difficult to engage in, and why.

For example, I struggle when finding moments of connection. I have moments of connection with my husband and kids most days, and often with my colleagues or my students. But I often neglect my friendships because I am "too busy." Or I feel guilty scheduling time with friends when the repercussion is that my husband has to watch the kids even more than he already does.

There are barriers to the other resources, too. Eating enough-but-not-too-much nourishing food is hard if you don't cook, if you have no money, or if you aren't in tune with your body's sense of fullness. Sleep is a precious commodity that is disrupted by children (especially sick kids and tiny babies!), by storms, by "just one more episode" of a stellar streaming TV show, or by a thinking brain that doesn't seem to want to turn off. Medications can be hard to take if you don't have a doctor, if you're too busy to pick up the prescription, or if you can't swallow pills. Substances can be hard to limit when they are enjoyable and your body has gotten used to taking them. Exercise takes time and sometimes additional resources (e.g., a gym membership, a friend to play a sport with, other kinds of gear). It can be hard to feel motivated to do pleasant things when nothing seems appealing, and/or when the things that sound fun are inaccessible. It can feel daunting to prioritize moments of connection if you don't have fun, supportive people in your life!

These resources influence each other, too. Alcohol seems like it helps sleep because people fall asleep faster, but the sleep tends to be shorter and of worse quality. It can be hard to exercise when tired or hungry, and medication changes can influence hunger or tiredness. Substance use can impair relationships. Lack of physical energy reduces motivation to seek pleasure. If you struggle with any of these problems, take tiny steps. If you can't figure out how to take tiny steps, ask for help. Therapists can help.

The other reason why coping ahead strategies are difficult is that you can't just learn them and then forget about them. They require effort to build up and continued effort to maintain. For them to be effective, you have to keep doing them, because the stressors will keep coming! I wish I had a magic solution to overcoming the barriers to coping ahead activities, but I don't. You need to believe they are important and can help you buffer against stress, and then keep doing them long enough to find out if I'm right. The only good news I can give you is this: If you have been practicing the strategies covered in the first four chapters of this book, you may be developing some emotional conditioning, which may help you better commit to engaging in coping ahead.

PREPARING FOR EMOTIONAL DISTRESS

Earlier in this chapter, I talked about coping ahead strategies as both "protective gear" and "conditioning." Emotional conditioning and the protective gear skills work together. To build these emotional muscles, emotional conditioning skills (mindfulness, labeling, learning about how emotions work) should be practiced when you are not particularly emotional, and in multiple contexts. They can then be used in moments of heightened emotion.

The protective gear skills (pleasure, energy, and connection) are particularly useful in preparation for emotional events, like how athletes prepare for a game. Athletes are advised to sleep well, eat well, take their meds, and maybe cool it on the substances a day or two before a big game. The same goes for emotional events. One central difference between athletic performances and emotional events is that games for athletes are typically scheduled, whereas emotions can come out of nowhere, which means that regular and consistent attention to coping ahead can help you handle whatever emotions come your way.

Both emotional conditioning skills and protective gear skills can help you feel capable of seeing stressors as challenges instead of threats. Emotional conditioning skills generally prepare the body to be strong and emotionally healthy. Protective gear skills then give you the resources to respond to whatever emotional balls or grease spatters come flying at you with speed, grace, and dexterity.

SUMMARY POINTS

- Coping ahead strategies help buffer against the effects of stress and negative affect, just like chefs and athletes wear protective gear to protect against physical injuries.
- Stress is separate from stressors. Stressors are the things that need to be dealt with, and stress is the subjective response to stressors. Some people (e.g., those with a stronger negativity bias) are more vulnerable to stress than others.
- People with more resources are more resilient and less likely to experience stress, so coping ahead is all about increasing resources.
  - Engaging in pleasurable activities provides more positive affect, which can buffer against stressors.
  - Attending to physical health by eating nourishing food, trying to get enough sleep, taking medications as prescribed, limiting

substance use, and engaging in exercise can help give the body strength and energy to protect against stress.

– Connecting with others and feeling supported is a major psychological resource.

• There are often barriers to engaging in coping ahead behaviors, but viewing them as important and trying them even without an immediate effect can be truly helpful for emotional regulation.

• Emotional conditioning and coping ahead are like going to the gym to increase strength, flexibility, and balance. These are skills that make inevitable stressors less stressful!

CHAPTER 6

OPENING THE ENVELOPE

Throughout this book, I have talked about the idea that emotions are *messages*. We talked about how some people get more messages than others (Chapter 1; emotional sensitivity) and how it's important to watch the mailbox, but not too closely (Chapter 2; awareness). We talked about how emotional messages are intimately connected to values—your values are, in fact, what are sending the messages in the first place (Chapter 3; values), which is why knowing your values helps you understand why you're feeling the way you do. We talked about how learning how to identify which emotion you are experiencing (Chapter 4; emotional labeling) is an important emotional conditioning skill and noted that there are strategies you can use to protect your heart, mind, and body from difficult messages (Chapter 5; coping ahead).

It is now time to practice "opening the envelope"—actually looking at the message. Ironically, as you've lived your life while reading the previous chapters, you've probably received and opened lots of emotional messages. Messages show up whether we're ready for them or not!

The idea of opening the envelope is to take a systematic approach to exploring what the emotional message has to say. I've tried to make the point that emotions have a purpose, that they aren't here to harm us, but is that really true?

In this chapter, we're going to follow Elise's attempts to open the envelope. Elise is in her early 30s and about to get married. She was diagnosed with social anxiety disorder about 5 years ago. She felt relief at the diagnosis because it explained how she got tongue-tied and internally activated (heart pounding, sweaty, etc.) in pretty much any social interaction, unless she had a few alcoholic beverages ahead of time. Her anxiety was strong enough that she'd spent her undergraduate education sitting in the back of classes and not joining any activities, even ones she found interesting. Yet she'd met a man via online dating and was now preparing to move across the country to start a life with him. Her wedding was 2 weeks away, and her anxiety about people watching her walk down the aisle was, per her report, "out of control." How can Elise use opening the envelope to deal with her feelings?

NOT JUMPING TO REGULATE

Elise wanted to get rid of feelings she found overwhelming and painful. She wanted to regulate her feelings, and she wanted to learn the quickest, most effective method of wiping away her distress. Yet Elise was skipping over part of the process. She'd decided she didn't like her feelings and that she should try to reduce them. But regulation should not always be the goal. Many people jump to the desire to regulate because the emotion is uncomfortable, painful, or just plain icky. But sometimes uncomfortable, painful, or icky things are useful—like going to the dentist!

The goal of opening the envelope is to sloooooooooow down, examine the emotion, and decide what to do with the feeling. Changing the feeling—regulating—is one possible outcome. Using the feeling to help facilitate life goals is another outcome. Or a person can simply allow the emotional wave to crest and fall and learn what that feels like.

Mail is the same, right? When you get an email with a 2-for-1 milkshake coupon, you have to figure out whether it has any value to you before you decide what to do with it. If you're lactose intolerant, a milkshake coupon is probably not useful to you. But if you love milkshakes, the coupon can be used—you can call a friend to go out for milkshakes that very afternoon, or you can print the coupon out and stick it on your fridge and wait until the urge for a milkshake strikes.

IDENTIFICATION STAGE OF EMOTION REGULATION

In Chapter 2, we talked about the cycle of emotion generation, which refers to how emotions come about. But there is another cycle to learn about: the cycle of emotion *regulation* (see Figure 6.1; Gross, 2015).

Once a person is experiencing an emotion, they need to identify what they want to feel. Should the emotion be maintained (e.g., try to

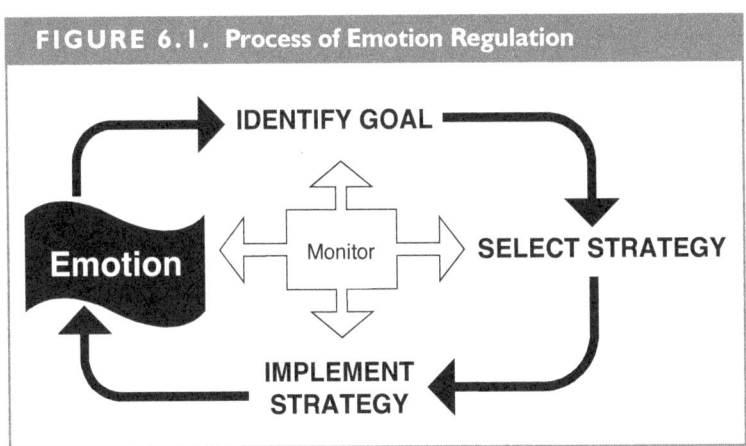

FIGURE 6.1. Process of Emotion Regulation

keep it at the same level), increased (e.g., up-regulate, to feel more of that feeling), or decreased (e.g., down-regulate, to feel less of that feeling)?

Identification is a critical part of emotion regulation, because if the ultimate decision is to not change the emotion, then the cycle stops, and no further action is needed. But if a goal to regulate is identified, then a person needs to choose a strategy for how to change the feeling. The strategy must be implemented. Throughout, the person has to monitor the cycle—is the goal the best goal? Is the strategy an effective one? Was the strategy implemented well?

All parts of the cycle are important, and we'll talk about choosing and implementing strategies in Chapter 7 and monitoring in Chapter 9. This chapter, though, is about determining whether or not a feeling needs to change. It sounds simple, right? Change bad feelings, maintain or increase positive ones. Easy-peasy!

Not so fast. In truth, identification of whether or not to change an emotion can happen almost instantaneously and without conscious thought or significant effort. Yet slowing down to understand the factors that play into these snap-second decisions can help you make more informed—and ultimately more effective—decisions around your feelings. Opening the envelope is all about breaking down the identification stage into its component parts.

STEPS OF OPENING THE ENVELOPE

Think about what it's like to open a physical envelope, or to click to open an email: First, you open the actual envelope (if it's a physical envelope, watch out for paper cuts!). Second, you skim or read the letter inside, and third, you decide what to do with the letter. Does the letter help you now (e.g., is there a birthday check in it that you can cash?) or will it help you later (e.g., is the postcard for a concert that you want to buy tickets for when they become available)? Or is the message junk mail that deserves to go straight into the recycling bin or the trash?

Opening the emotional envelope has similar steps. These five steps assume that there is an emotion already present:

1. Mindfully examine the emotion, assuming no malintent on the part of the sender.
2. Label the feeling.
3. Read the message: who it's from, the information provided, and the behavioral suggestions implied.
4. Consider what your goals are right now and in the long run to decide whether the emotion can be helpful to you.
5. Decide whether or not to regulate.

The Early Steps (1–2): Practicing Skills You Already Know

The first three steps of opening the envelope correspond to skills described in earlier chapters.

STEP 1: MINDFUL AWARENESS

The first step, in which you mindfully examine the emotion assuming no bad intent on the part of the sender, relates to emotional awareness (Chapter 2). You need to be aware, and ideally curious, about your emotional experience. The idea of "assume no malice" matters, too, and simply means to try to have awareness without judgment.

For example, Elise came to her therapy session acutely aware of her anxiety. Elise knew that she suffered from the Mail With Sticky Glue problem (Chapter 2), and she'd been hovering in a high level of anxiety for much of the prior week. Elise had trouble being curious or assuming no malintent, but she was at least acutely aware of her feelings.

STEP 2: LABEL THE EMOTION

Knowing what you are feeling *now* is crucial to setting an emotional goal, because without knowing what you currently feel, it will be hard to gauge the distance to what you want to feel (which will be in a later step). Say to yourself, "Hmmm, I'm feeling a bit off right now, what feeling is this?" (and revisit Chapter 4 if you need a refresher). Look at the words in Tables 4.2 and 4.3 to know if you are feeling hopeful, disgruntled, or calm. Once you've got the word, then rate the degree of what you're feeling, from 0 to 100.

Folks high on alexithymia who struggle with emotional aware-ness and labeling might need to hedge or even guess. For example, I've said to myself, "I might be hurt? I might be anxious? I might be sad? Which is it?" If you aren't feeling anything in particular right now, or can't find a specific word, just rate yourself from 0 to 100—how pleasant do you feel right now? Coming to a firm answer is helpful but not 100% necessary for opening the envelope.

Elise had developed strong emotional labeling skills by this point and was able to quickly label her own feeling as "extremely anxious," an 80 out of 100.

The Middle Step: Building on Past Knowledge

The next step builds on the previous skills but involves putting more effort into really thinking about what the emotional message is trying to say.

STEP 3: READ THE MESSAGE AND THE ACTION URGE

The purpose of this step is to understand what the emotional message actually is. In Chapter 4, we talked about recognizing the message of the emotion. Now, we'll go one step further to look at all three parts of an emotional message: (a) the sender, (b) the information, and (c) the implied action—what the sender wants you to do with that information.

Real messages are often the same way. For example, that postcard with a 2-for-1 milkshake coupon is telling you that the (a) ice cream shop (b) offers milkshakes, and for a limited time they are on sale, so (c) hurry up and come to this store ASAP and order some milkshakes! Unfortunately, understanding the message of postcards and email advertisements is much easier than deciphering emotional messages, unless you know where to look.

Figuring out the sender is crucial. Whether someone is trying to spam you and steal your identity, or send you a gift, the message comes from someone, either a person, a group of people, or an organization. The sender matters, because who sent the message can change how the message comes across. Getting a party invitation from a friend feels great, but getting a party invitation from a coworker you don't like is much less fun. Getting a milkshake coupon from Store A might be awesome, but you might not care at all about the same coupon from Store B.

Where do emotional messages come from? Emotional messages come from your values. That's the sender: your values. I'll repeat for emphasis: **Emotions are messages sent from your values.** One or more values can be found on the return address of the envelope or the "from" line of the email.

It's tempting to say that emotions come from other people, or are inherent to the situation, like when people say, "She made me so mad" or "He made me cry." These are understandable statements, because emotions often occur in the context of relationships, but other people can't "make" you feel anything. You feel hurt because your values remind you that you care about safety, and that other person tried to hurt you, take advantage of you, or threaten you. Other people can be crappy, and can try to push your buttons. But your feeling comes from your values, not from the other person.

In no way am I saying that you are to blame for your negative feelings of guilt, regret, shame, sadness, rage, or anxiety (or any of the other unpleasant feelings). Nor am I saying that abusive, neglectful, antagonistic, or narcissistic people are emotionally harmless. Far from it! Other people can be horribly toxic and emotionally damaging (see Chapter 8).

What I *am* saying is that no matter what anyone else does in the world, or does to you, your feelings are messages from your values and yours alone—you hurt where you care (Hayes, 2005). This matters because recognizing which value sent your feelings can help you be kinder to yourself by understanding that your emotions make sense.

To figure out which value or values sent the message and to decipher the information of the message and the implied action of the message, check out Table 6.1, which is similar to Table 4.1 but with a new column added to it.

For example, Elise easily recognized that she felt anxious. However, she struggled to understand the message without her therapist's help. (Many people struggle with reading the message at first, but it gets easier with practice!) She looked at Table 6.1 and read, "Anxiety means that something potentially threatening is looming in the future." She looked at her therapist and said, "Duh." Her therapist laughed and asked her what was threatening—which of her values were threatened by her forthcoming wedding? If the wedding was a disaster, what values would be hurting?

For Elise, the value most associated with anxiety was Safety. Research supports the notion that people who value Safety tend to want to feel more calm and relaxed and less anxious, but they actually feel anxious more often (Tamir et al., 2016)! Elise felt anxious even thinking about people watching her walk down the aisle.

The messages can come from any value. Surprise is about something new and unexpected, and surprise can have a positive spin,

TABLE 6.1. Action Tendencies of Unpleasant Emotions

Basic emotion	Message of the emotion	Action tendencies associated with the emotion
Surprise	Something new and unexpected is happening!	Allocate attention. Is this unexpected thing good or bad?
Anger	There has been an injustice; someone I care about has been wronged.	Correct the injustice (either by attacking or rejecting).
Fear[a]	Something threatening is nearby; I am in danger.	Withdraw or escape to protect yourself.
Anxiety[a]	Something potentially threatening is looming in the future.	Plan to avoid or circumvent the threat to protect yourself.
Sadness	I have lost or lack something I care about.	Take steps to heal (withdraw, seek support, mourn).
Guilt	I have done something morally wrong.	Make amends, strive to attain a moral standard.
Disgust	Something or someone harmful (physically or morally) is nearby.	Avoid or withdraw to protect yourself.
Jealousy	A valued relationship is being threatened, or someone has something I want.	Attack the threat, try to keep/ protect what is desired.

[a]Fear and anxiety are in reality in the same family of emotions because both are related to threats. But fear (which is often more visceral and physical) is about current threat, and anxiety (which is often more mental and cognitive) is about anticipated threat.

such as when sent by Intimacy ("Yay! My best friend showed up to surprise me for my birthday! We're going to have so much fun this weekend!"), or a negative spin, such as when sent by Achievement ("Crap. My best friend showed up to surprise me, but my house is a mess and now I'll be even more behind on this project."). It all depends on which value is highlighted!

The way to use Table 6.1 is to ask yourself a few questions. "What is the 'something' or 'someone' the message talks about?" Then ask, "Which of my values seem to be evident in this situation? If this situation went poorly, which of my values would be hurting?"

One additional piece of the message is the action urge that goes along with the message. Anxiety, for example, is an emotion that prompts withdrawal, escape, and avoidance. Elise felt this acutely—she was tempted to just ask her fiancé to elope so she wouldn't have to deal with the wedding at all.

The action urge can be a different way in to the emotional message. For example, some people (e.g., those high on alexithymia) tend to be more attentive to the physiological and action urge components of emotion (Lane & Smith, 2021). If that's you, then you can walk backward through the task and ask yourself, "What is it my urge to do right now? Which message is this most consistent with?" Anxiety wants you to retreat, sadness wants you to regroup and maybe get support, anger wants you to attack and correct the injustice, disgust wants you to create boundaries and get rid of threats, and guilt wants you to apologize and make amends. Understanding your urge can lead you toward your feelings.

Your urges may need deep exploration. Sometimes, the most obvious urges are urges based on secondary emotions, or **metaemotions**, which are feelings about feelings (Bailen et al., 2019). For example, I once worked with a client who experienced strong fits of rage. When I asked her what her urge was in one of these rageful moments, she said it was to "Run into the other room and slam the door." If you look at Table 6.1, you'll see that escape or avoidance tend to be associated with fear, anxiety, and disgust, not anger. When I showed her Table 6.1 and curiously asked her to explain, she became sheepish. She said, "Oooooh. My actual urge is to throw a plate at my boyfriend's head." She revealed that her urges to attack were so strong that she'd trained herself to quickly leave the situation because she was scared of her anger. Her anger was the primary emotion, and her metaemotion was fear—she was fearful of her own anger. It wasn't until we talked through it that she realized she was navigating a metaemotion.

Elise had a similar revelation when she really dug into her emotional message. Although her anxiety was sent by her Safety value, she felt angry about her anxiety because her value of Safety conflicted with her value of Intimacy. Her value of Intimacy wanted her to enjoy and fully experience her wedding, and that made her angry at her Safety value and her associated anxiety. Elise was surprised to realize that her feelings were more complex and nuanced than she'd originally thought, and that she had some metaemotions going on! She had not ever thought to explore the connection between her emotions and her values so deeply, and doing so helped her feel as though her emotions weren't as crazy as she'd previously thought.

Attending to the message of the emotion highlights the values, and thinking about values can make the emotions make more sense.

The Later Steps (Steps 4–5): Applying New Ideas

After reading the emotional message and figuring out who is sending it, the later steps involve figuring out what to do next.

STEP 4: IDENTIFY EMOTION GOALS

All of the steps in opening the envelope are important, but this step really gets to the crux of the matter. You have to think about your goals. This sounds easy, but there are three pieces to consider: (a) what do you *want* to feel, (b) can your current feeling be *useful* to you right now, and (c) can your emotion be useful to you *in the long run*?

Desired Emotions: What You Want to Feel

After considering how you already feel, then think about how you *want* to feel. If you're already feeling basically the same as you want to feel, the cycle ends; you don't move on to select a regulation strategy (see Figure 6.1), because no change is needed. But if what you're feeling right now is different than what you want to feel, then you've got an emotional *goal*. Much of the time, people have goals to feel more pleasant feelings and fewer unpleasant feelings. These are called **hedonic goals** (Tamir, 2016). "Hedonic" is a word that captures an emphasis on pleasure and good feelings.

For example, Elise reported hedonic goals. Recall that she reported rating the intensity of her anxiety at 80 out of 100. She said that she wanted to feel low (e.g., 0–20) anxiety. She also reported wanting to feel 70 or above on contentment and relaxation. Elise saw herself as an anxious person and was not particularly confident that she'd be able to make her anxiety decrease to the desired level, but she had a clear goal in mind.

The emotions people gravitate toward wanting are based in their cultural norms and values (Tsai, 2007). For example, people from individualistic cultures (e.g., those from Europe and the United States) tend to have values in the Self-Enhancement wedge of the values pie (see Chapter 3), like Authority, Esteem, Achievement, and Prosperity. These values are associated with seeking pride (Eid & Diener, 2001) and more high-arousal positive emotions, like excitement (Tsai, 2007). In turn, people from interdependent cultures (e.g., East Asia, South America) often have values in the Conservation wedge, like Belonging, Duty, Respect, and Obedience. These values emphasize group cohesion and harmony, and guilt is a more important emotion in these cultures (Eid & Diener, 2001). People from interdependent cultures also prefer to feel low-arousal positive emotions like calmness and relaxation because those emotions better serve cultural norms.

People also sometimes have goals to feel more negative emotions (e.g., anger, sadness, anxiety); these are called **contrahedonic goals** (Tamir, 2016). For example, in the TV show *Grace and Frankie*, one of the characters intentionally pursues her "yearly cry." She reserves a day and watches multiple sad animal movies (e.g., *Old Yeller*, *Marley & Me*) to cathartically experience and express sadness (Smolinski & Asher, 2019). Contrahedonic goals also include goals to feel less positive emotion, such as wanting to dampen your excitement about winning an award when your friend shows disappointment that they lost.

Why would people want to feel unpleasant emotions, when they are—by definition—unpleasant? Because sometimes negative emotions are useful (Southward et al., 2021). People want the warm and cozy, safe and supported hedonic goals—pleasant feelings are often like basking in a contentment bubble bath. Yet a *desired* emotion is not always the same as a *useful* emotion.

Useful Emotions: Helping the Current Moment

People set emotional goals because they think—whether accurately or erroneously, whether consciously or unconsciously—that their desired emotion will be useful to them. "Useful" and "desirable" are not always the same thing. How can emotions be useful?

A host of fascinating research on emotion motives has started to uncover the utility in all kinds of emotional states. Emotions are functional! They help people accomplish tasks, connect to others, understand themselves, and pursue meaning in life (Tamir, 2016).

Some emotions are both desirable and useful. For example, activated pleasant feelings, like happiness, joy, and excitement, tend to be associated with more creative behavior (Henderson et al., 2023; Schei, 2013). Pursuit of low-energy pleasant feelings, like relaxation and contentment, can buffer against depressive symptoms and declines in physical health due to aging (Hamm et al., 2021). Expressing (and feeling) gratitude increases relationship strength (Lambert et al., 2010). These are feelings that people tend to want to feel, and they are also useful.

Unpleasant emotions, which are rarely hedonically desirable, can be often useful. For example, negative emotions generally are associated with improved memory, because negative events stand out (Forgas, 2013). Specific negative emotions help with different kinds of tasks, as depicted in the excellent Pixar film *Inside Out* (Docter & Del Carmen, 2015). Disgust and fear help keep people safe, and anger helps people stand up for what's right and to correct a perceived injustice (Tamir, 2016). Sadness facilitates support and closeness—sadness can solidify bonds (Lench et al., 2016). Sadness is also associated with decreased gullibility—research has shown that people are better able to detect lying in others when they are sad compared with when they are happy (Forgas, 2013)!

To begin to start thinking about the ways in which emotions can be useful, look at the questions in Exhibit 6.1. These questions are geared toward helping you understand where your head happens to be in terms of your goals in life right now. What is most pressing? Are you working on a task that requires a certain level of performance, whether at work or school (or at home)? Are relationships particularly salient? Are you looking for understanding or familiarity (Tamir, 2016)?

Once you decide on what your current life goals might be, then you can revisit the usefulness of your current emotion and your desired emotion. For example, Elise wanted to feel low anxiety and high contentment. When her therapist asked her about the usefulness of low anxiety and high contentment, Elise said that these emotions would

---

EXHIBIT 6.1. Momentary Questions

When in an emotional situation, ask yourself what you are hoping for *right now*. Multiple options might be true, but which is *most* important to you *right now*?

- Do I have goals for *performance* right now? Am I doing a task? What kind of task?
- Do I have goals for *relationships* right now? Do I want to dominate someone, or connect with someone, or help someone?
- Do I have goals for *familiarity* right now? Do I want to feel familiar feelings that are comfortable and seem "like me"?
- Do I have goals for *knowledge* right now? Do I want to learn things about myself or the world? Do I want to grow?

---

feel good and would allow her to breathe easier. When her therapist asked Elise to link her current and desired emotions to her current life goals, Elise said that current life goal was to put on the perfect wedding free of complications. Her therapist gently asked her to think about her goals right now, rather than her goals for the wedding day. Elise pushed back, saying, "But my goal right now is to figure out all of the problems that could happen on my wedding day." Her therapist smiled. "OK, then. Which feeling is better at helping you think about all the problems you might encounter, relaxation or anxiety?"

This question sent Elise reeling, because the answer was "anxiety." Anxiety is a future-focused emotion that helps people plan for upcoming challenges. Her therapist asked her to think about what she wanted to prioritize on the wedding day itself. Elise said that she hoped that on her wedding day she'd be able to prioritize her relationship goals. She said she wanted to ignore the crowd and concentrate on her future husband and the vows they were planning to make to each other.

Her therapist smiled and said, "Your anxiety now is trying to help you make that vision happen." Elise was taken aback at first. She had not thought of her anxiety as anything but distracting or harmful. Elise responded with, "But when I feel anxious on my wedding day too, I won't get the wedding I want." Her therapist said, "Let's not assume what will happen in the future, but try to focus on the now. Your anxiety *now* is trying to help you." Elise replied, "But it's not helping me! My head is spinning around and I'm just seeing disaster, I'm not actually getting anywhere. I want to feel relaxed because I think I'll be able to think more clearly if I'm not so nervous. What if my anxiety is really trying to tell me I shouldn't be getting married at all?"

Her therapist smiled and said, "We can talk about that too. Is your anxiety trying to prepare you for the day, or for your long-term future? Your anxiety helping you feel familiar, isn't it? You're used to feeling anxious." Elise admitted this was true, but replied, "But I don't like that part of myself. Feeling anxious helps me feel like me, but what if I don't like me?" She started to cry.

Elise and her therapist had identified several important and tricky aspects related to emotional goals. First, the desired feeling (e.g., low anxiety, high contentment) is not always the same as the useful feeling, but it all depends on how "useful" is framed. Anxiety is intended to help people plan for challenges (Crum et al., 2020), but those intentions do not always result in clear planning. Second, and crucially, emotions serve not only short-term, right-now, immediate goals but also long-term emotional goals.

Useful Emotions: Helping You Be Who You Want to Be (Emotionally)
Consider your long-term emotional goals. What kinds of feelings do you want to have in the far-off future, if you were to become your ideal self? In the long run, who do you want to be emotionally?

Sometimes, emotions are useful in helping you achieve these long-term emotional goals, which means withstanding some discomfort now to reap the rewards later.

Long-term emotional goals are a new concept I've been studying with my graduate students. In our studies, we've identified 13 long-term emotional goals that people have described to us (Veilleux, Clift, et al., 2024). You can see these in question form in Exhibit 6.2. Over half of people reported strong hedonic goals: desires to feel frequent positive feelings (e.g., more cheerful, more grateful) and/or lower levels of unpleasant feelings, like anxiety, sadness, anger, guilt, and shame.

But there were other goals too. About half of the participants reported strong desires to refrain from wallowing in their emotional thoughts, with less self-judgment and less self-criticism. People indicated they wanted to be less emotionally sensitive, cultivate greater regulation and coping skills, and act on their emotions less frequently. They also reported emotional goals related to other people, such as being more empathic or compassionate toward others, generally wanting deeper emotional connections to others, and recognizing the desire to be more emotionally open or expressive with others. Others recognized a tendency to pay too much attention to other people and described wanting to set better emotional boundaries with others and/or learning to be more confident and less dependent on others. The answers conveyed how there are sets of goals that people in general tend to have for their emotional selves as well as how variable individuals can be in what they want emotionally.

None of these emotional goals are inherently bad. However, some are less common than others. When we've asked people to select their top three long-term emotional goals, the goal that people picked the least were goals to be more emotionally open to others (less than 6% picked that one as a top goal), wanting to understand their feelings (only 15% picked that one), and wanting to allow

EXHIBIT 6.2. Desired Long-Term Emotional Goals

INSTRUCTIONS: Indicate how much you desire to *someday* be a person with this emotional attribute. **Rating an item low doesn't mean that the item is unimportant to you, but that it is not a priority for you in terms of what you truly, deeply want for yourself emotionally.**

There is no time frame mentioned for any of these attributes. If you think it is crucial you achieve this someday, consider it as a desire even if you are not ready to work on it right now. **PLEASE BE HONEST WITH YOURSELF!** Really think about what is a priority for you! Write down the desire rating on the line next to each goal.

0	1	2	3	4	5	6
No desire	Low desire	Low-to-moderate desire	Moderate desire	Moderate-to-high desire	High desire	EXTREMELY STRONG desire

_____ 1. To be someone who allows my feelings to rise and fall naturally without trying to push them away.

_____ 2. To be someone who refrains from wallowing in negative thoughts.

_____ 3. To be someone who sets boundaries with others to safeguard my own heart, my own voice.

_____ 4. To be someone who frequently feels cheerful, happy, content, and grateful.

_____ 5. To be someone who avoids making rash decisions based on my feelings.

_____ 6. To be someone who is confident that what I think and feel matters, no matter what anyone else says.

EXHIBIT 6.2.	**Desired Long-Term Emotional Goals (*Continued*)**	

_____	7.	To be someone who identifies and acts on opportunities to express kindness to people in need of help.
_____	8.	To be someone who understands what I feel and why I feel the way I do.
_____	9.	To be someone who is not particularly sensitive and reactive to emotional triggers.
_____	10.	To be someone who develops and maintains strong emotional connections with others.
_____	11.	To be someone who has the skills to regulate extreme highs and lows.
_____	12.	To be someone who is emotionally open, so that my feelings are readable to others.
_____	13.	To be someone who feels low levels of anxiety, stress, sadness, anger, guilt and shame.

their feelings to rise and fall without pushing them away (only 10% picked that one; Veilleux, Clift, et al., 2024).

I find these results fascinating because people who express their feelings, understand their feelings, and allow their feelings tend to be more emotionally intelligent, generally feel happier, are upset less often, and are more satisfied with their lives. Yet even though expressing, understanding, and allowing are clearly advantageous emotional goals, they aren't priorities for most people!

When Elise was asked to pick which three emotional goals were most important to her, she initially reported goals to refrain from wallowing in negative thoughts and to feel low levels of anxiety, stress, and other negative emotions. The third one was hardest for her. She initially said she wanted to be less emotionally open, but her therapist pointed out that Elise's emotions were actually not usually visible in session, or in the waiting room. This made Elise think that perhaps understanding her emotions (and their functions) might be a better long-term emotional goal. Her therapist agreed.

MATCHING UP GOALS

Emotional goal setting is complicated because all three pieces matter: (a) What do you want to feel; (b) what would be helpful to your momentary goals at this moment in time, and how is the current feeling helping or hindering your immediate goals; and (c) how might feeling the feeling now help contribute to your long-term goals?

Sometimes these three elements coincide beautifully. For example, Morgan was a mother of three in the midst of a combative divorce. She was facing a court date related to custody of her children. She reported that the last time she had gone to court she'd been so anxious about being in the same room as her ex—who had been physically violent with her and with her daughter—that she had been unable to think clearly. She'd stumbled with her words, and the judge hadn't taken her seriously. She reported feeling 98 out of 100 on an anxiety scale, but she wanted to be about 40—enough to make her look focused and serious, but not so much that she couldn't think straight. She'd had the goals of speaking clearly and advocating for herself in the moment, which also coincided with her long-term goals of being less reactive to her feelings and better at emotion regulation. In this instance, high anxiety was not helpful to her goals, nor was it what she wanted to feel. For Morgan, there was synergy among what she wanted to feel, her momentary goals, and her long-term goals.

For Elise, however, matching up her goals was much less clear. When she thought about the upcoming event, she wanted to feel less anxious. She also thought that being anxious at her wedding wouldn't be helpful to either her short-term or long-term goals.

However, remember that Elise was primarily focused on her anxiety now (in the days prior to the wedding). She certainly did not want to feel anxious before the wedding. But she couldn't deny that her anxiety might be trying to help her plan and prepare. She also remembered her long-term goal about trying to understand herself better. She kept the option open that perhaps her anxiety had some information to offer.

When what you want to feel, what is useful to you in the moment, and what is useful to you in the long run coincide, the decision of what to do is simple. Much of the time, though, the decision is more complicated than that, particularly if—like in Elise's case—you allow for possibilities that could happen even if they aren't certain.

STEP 5: DECIDE WHETHER OR NOT TO REGULATE

The final step of opening the envelope is about deciding what to do with the envelope. Do you act on the message right away? Do you file the message away as information but do nothing else (e.g., like I file my quarterly retirement account statements), or do you actively save the message to use for later, like posting the milkshake postcard on the fridge to remind you to go use that coupon when the weather warms up? Or do you throw it out?

There are choices to make with emotional messages, too. You can choose to change your feeling (or aim to experience a less intense version of the same feeling), enact the action urge of the feeling by doing what the emotion wants you to do, acknowledge the message and do nothing, or save the emotion to deal with later.

The decision should be fairly easy when your momentary goals, your long-term goals, and what you want to feel all coincide. Sometimes, the choice is to use the emotion to enact the action tendency the emotion suggests. For example, let us consider art teacher Sarah, who needs to complete a set of lessons. She (1) wants to feel pleasant and joyful. In addition, high-arousal positive affect is especially good for creative tasks (Henderson et al., 2023) and so would be (2) useful for working on the project, which is her most pressing momentary life goal. Finally, Sarah (3) wants to be someone who experiences pleasure regularly and who has good regulation skills—and remember (see Chapter 5) that pleasant activities are a type of coping ahead that contributes to good regulation. Sarah's desires and goals align, and thus the choice to maintain or use the pleasant joyful feelings is clear.

Alternatively, sometimes the clear choice is to regulate. For example, Morgan wanted to regulate her anxiety because it was unwanted and inconsistent with all of her goals. If regulation is the decision, then you have to decide how to regulate—turn to the next chapter for more on that!

Sometimes, though, the choice isn't clear. When desired feelings, useful-for-momentary-goals feelings, and maybe-useful-for-long-term-goals feelings are different from one another, then choices need to be made about which to listen to.

Earlier in the chapter, I made the point that *not all emotions need to be regulated*. Remember that emotions are meant to help, not hurt. Sometimes, feeling the emotion can help you in the moment, like when anger can help you confront someone or correct an injustice. Sometimes, the emotion in the moment just hurts, but allowing that emotion to be there can help you in the long term—like by realizing that emotions aren't permanent and that you can indeed withstand a difficult feeling. In essence, sometimes feeling the feeling has no purpose in the moment of time but feeling it helps you become the person you want to be.

Research suggests that people who can tune in to their long-term goals during emotional moments tend to have better outcomes (Veilleux, Clift, et al., 2024). Being able to consider long-term emotional goals is associated with feeling overall more positive affect and less negative affect, as well as having greater life satisfaction. People who consider their long-term emotional goals also tend to be happier with who they are emotionally!

Elise found these arguments compelling. She felt too sensitive and reactive to her emotions, and she didn't want to be anxious forever. Her therapist told her that every time she felt anxious and tried to regulate, she was telling herself, "You can't handle this, it's too much." But her therapist also said, "Elise, I think you *can* handle these feelings. The only way out is through. Maybe if you feel these feelings now, in the weeks before your wedding, and you explore your feelings a little, they won't affect you so much in the long run."

Elise decided that she could try to feel her feelings now, but she wanted to plan for regulating later. She and her therapist made a plan for some regulation strategies that she could use on the day of her wedding to help her focus on her husband-to-be (see Chapter 7 for more on regulation strategies), including deep breathing to reduce the physiological activation that often comes with anxiety and intentionally sharing her feelings of anxiety with her family (see Chapter 8 for a discussion on emotional expression). They even came up with a script of what Elise could say if her worst fears came to be—if she tripped or threw up while walking down the aisle.

Then, in the weeks before the wedding, Elise focused on her long-term goal to understand herself and her feelings better. She set aside time to tune in to her emotions, and when anxiety popped up, she told herself "Thanks, values, for trying to protect me and keep me safe." She explored her feelings and the connections between her feelings and her values, and she let the anxiety wash over her like a wave, without trying to push her anxiety away.

At first, Elise felt the pull to distract herself, or to let her anxiety help her withdraw and escape to safety. But she just let herself feel, and it was uncomfortable at first. After a few days, though, she noticed her overall sense of anxiety was lower, even though she didn't do anything to cope. She acted in ways consistent with her long-term goals, and doing so eventually helped her short-term and long-term goals align.

Revisiting the Process

Opening the envelope involves really looking at the emotion and what it's trying to tell you so that you can make an informed decision about what to do with it. In reality, these steps can take place in a split second, and they aren't as drawn out as they are here. But while learning to read the message and deciding what to do with it, you may need to take the time to really consider each step in turn. With practice, the steps can become habitual, and you can do them without thinking.

WAYS TO NOT OPEN THE ENVELOPE EFFECTIVELY

Opening the envelope involves identifying whether an emotion needs to change. There are a couple of ways in which this process can go awry. The two most common are: (a) throwing the message away without looking at it (otherwise known as avoidance) and (b) hanging on to a message longer than you need it (otherwise known as rumination or repetitive negative thinking).

Throwing the Envelope Away Without Reading It

Opening the envelope is a complicated process that involves quite a few steps. It may often seem easier to just throw the envelope away without looking at it—which is essentially treating the emotional message as junk mail.

Virtually everyone I know (including myself) has done this at one time or another. If you've ever found a negative emotion undesirable and/or unpleasant, it makes sense that you'd want to avoid experiencing it again. Feeling bad literally feels bad. It is perfectly logical why you wouldn't want to feel the same sort of bad again. If you see an email subject line for a company that scammed you, why read the message when you could just delete the email and not waste energy or time on it?

The more formal name of this approach is **avoidance-based coping**, or *disengagement emotion regulation*, and it involves trying to push away, escape from, or circumvent emotions. For example, consider Becca, who drove to a party but saw her ex's car on the street and then drove home instead of having to face the ex at the party. Or, perhaps Becca got to the party early but quickly left out the back door after seeing the ex arrive with a new date. Trying to avoid thoughts about the situation can occur, too, like if Becca went to bed early when efforts to stop thinking about the ex didn't work.

Any version of "We're not going to talk or even think about that upsetting situation" is an example of throwing the emotional envelope away. The problem with avoidance is that, although it does work to push the message away for a short period of time, the message will just come back again. Remember, emotions are messages sent from your values, so your values are going to keep sending you more messages until you read them. Your values want you to get the message.

There is a fantastic children's book called *There's No Such Thing as a Dragon* (Kent, 1975/2009) that beautifully conveys the problems with avoidance. In the story, a kid named Billy wakes up to find a small kitten-sized dragon on his bed. He asks his mother about it, and she says, "There's no such thing as a dragon!" The dragon starts to grow bigger, and even though Billy keeps telling his mother about the dragon, she continues to tell him that dragons don't exist. The dragon gets bigger and bigger until it takes over the entire house. Billy eventually firmly tells his mother that there IS, in fact, a dragon. As soon as he says this, the dragon starts to shrink until it's again the size of a house cat. Billy's mom acknowledges that the tiny dragon isn't so bad and asks why it had to get so big. Billy thoughtfully says, "I think it just wanted to be noticed."

Feelings are similar. Do you want the dragon? No! But pushing feelings away, ignoring the message, failing to open the envelope just makes the dragon grow bigger. The dragon wants to be noticed, and it will keep growing until you notice it. You can circumvent, suppress, or avoid emotions by pushing them out of your awareness, but because the emotional message wants to be received, the result is that you're just going to get more and more messages until you pay attention to them. The solution is to at least open the envelope to figure out what the emotion has to say before you toss it out. An emotional message is not a pipe bomb or a letter laced with anthrax—the message itself won't hurt you, and you'll save yourself a lot of hassle in the long run by receiving the message when you get it.

Hanging On to an Envelope

The other thing that many people do with their emotional messages is hang on to them when they aren't actually helpful. Metaphorically, this is like tucking a postcard from a mortgage refinancing company under your pillow when you don't even own a house, or marking an email as unread so that it stays at the top of your inbox. Hanging on to a message is a metaphor for getting stuck in an emotion, latching on to it and continuing to read the message even when it is not practically helpful (or desirable).

Latching onto feelings isn't something people usually do on purpose. Instead, what happens is that the mind continues to revisit emotional images (e.g., the mental picture of the dead deer on the sidewalk) from recent emotional situations (e.g., the screaming match you had with your spouse in front of your toddler) or feared hypothetical situations (e.g., thinking about a family member dying in a plane crash). The emotion gets reactivated. Remember that thinking and interpreting (i.e., appraisal) are core to how feelings are generated in the first place (revisit Chapter 2 if you've forgotten this)! When the mind keeps thinking, the heart keeps feeling.

The thought processes that underlie hanging on to an envelope are rumination, worry, and obsessive thinking. All of these processes include repeatedly thinking about negatively tinged things, where the thoughts feel intrusive and uncontrollable (Ehring & Watkins, 2008). There are a few distinctions between these terms, such that rumination typically involves thinking about the past, worry involves thinking about the future, and obsessions are often image based and tend to be inconsistent with a person's self-view (e.g., obsessive images of dying by ingesting too many germs; Wahl et al., 2011). But all of these kinds of thoughts tend to be negative and pessimistic in tone, repetitive and hard to detach from, and they don't tend to solve any problems.

Rumination and worry can seem helpful (Watkins, 2016). Morgan, for example, engaged in significant rumination about her prior court date. She kept replaying the events of the day in her mind because she wanted to figure it out. She asked herself what she could have done differently, why she acted the way she did, why her lawyers acted the way they did. She wanted to understand, and the desire to understand is often rational and helpful. From an emotional messages standpoint, **rumination** is asking, "Why am *I* the person who got this message and not someone else? Better hold onto it to be able to understand things better."

Worry is similar but tends to be about planning for future events. Worry is about thinking about "what if" this or that bad thing might happen, and then ideally taking steps to avoid any of those bad things. For example, Elise worried about her wedding. She worried that she would trip on her wedding gown, fall on her face, and then bleed all over her expensive dress. She worried that her face would flush. She worried that she would puke. Mostly, though, she worried that people would think, "Why did he pick *her*? She isn't pretty enough, smart enough, or good enough for him." Her mind went through a whirlwind of awful possibilities. Worry is "What if this postcard is a sign? What if this is a warning for the future? Better hold onto it to be prepared for an uncertain future!"

"Why?" and "What if?" are the core questions that under-lie rumination and worry. To be fair, "why" and "what if" are very useful questions for a high school English paper. Why did Hamlet give his big soliloquy? What if Ophelia had lived? But they are less useful questions for emotions. "Why" and "what if" questions are traps. They tend to focus people narrowly on abstract, global, nega-tive kinds of possibilities, which are usually self-critical judgments. For example, when Morgan asked herself, "Why couldn't I just *talk*? Why did I freeze?," her mind responded "Because I'm an incapable loser."

We will revisit notions of when to save emotional envelopes for later in Chapter 9. For now, try asking yourself, "Can I throw this out now?" Remember, messages are from your values. Have faith in your values; they'll resend the message when you need it. In the meantime, let go of messages that you don't need any more, or that you might never actually need at all.

ASSUMING THE BEST OF VALUES

Despite the best intentions, your values might occasionally send you messages that aren't desirable, useful now, or useful later.

It may be tempting to call these type of messages junk mail—unsolicited mail that you didn't ask for, and you don't want, and that doesn't seem helpful. Yet calling the messages "junk mail" assumes that your values are trying to scam you, spam you, or get you to buy something. With actual mail, that might be the case, because the people sending you that junk mail are looking after their own best interests rather than your own. The store sending you that milkshake coupon is sending the coupon to benefit them—to drive business into the store.

Emotional messages are a bit different because the messages are sent from your values, from you, from what you think of as important. That's why emotions are not junk mail. Now, it is also the case that some emotional messages are undesirable, unwanted, and unhelpful. These messages are designed to be helpful, but that doesn't always translate into actual helpfulness. Just last week, my husband tried to be helpful by filling my water bottle for me. Sounds nice, right? Except he closed the lid so tightly that I couldn't open it on my own. He wanted to be helpful, but the result was not helpful. Values are the same way. Sometimes the message isn't actually helpful.

Why would your own values send an unhelpful message? We'll get back to this question in Chapter 9, but the short answer is that what's important isn't always what the moment calls for. Your values, and what you think is important, have been built and shaped through your past experiences, and sometimes they call out warnings when there is not actually any danger.

Instead of calling unhelpful emotional messages "junk mail," find a new name for them. I call them "try mail" because they are trying to be helpful, and this phrase sounds kind of like "tree mail," which is the term used in the reality show *Survivor* for how contestants get messages about clues or upcoming challenges. But you call them whatever you like.

It's impossible to know for sure that a message—whether emotional or otherwise—is "try mail" without looking at it. For example, a few days ago I got an envelope addressed to me in what looked like handwritten cursive font. Did I think it was probably garbage? Yes, but I dug deep for some curiosity and said to myself, "Let's be curious to see if there is anything fun, interesting, or useful in here." I opened the envelope. It was a form letter—also printed in cursive and made to read like it was personal—trying to get me to sell my car. I have no desire to sell my car. This message wasn't helpful to me. I tossed it right into the recycling bin. But I didn't know until I opened it. You have to open the envelope.

SUMMARY POINTS

- This chapter focused on identifying whether or not an emotion should be regulated, which is the first step of the emotion regulation cycle.
- Setting emotional goals—thinking about how you want to feel, what feelings would be useful right now, and what feelings would be useful in the long run—is a big part of this step.
- Hedonic goals are ones that increase positive and decrease negative emotions, whereas contrahedonic goals increase negative and decrease positive emotions.

There are five steps of opening the envelope:

1. Mindfully attend to your emotions (i.e., show emotional awareness).
2. Label the feeling and the amount of the feeling (e.g., 0–100).
3. Look at the message of the emotion—which value is sending it, what is the information the value is trying to tell you, and what does the emotion want you to do?
4. Consider emotional goals in terms of desired emotions (e.g., what you want to feel), what emotions would help you with

your goals of the moment, and what emotions might help you become you want to be in the long run.

5. Decide whether to regulate, act on the emotion (e.g., enact the action urge of the emotion), or do nothing and let the emotion rise and fall.

Two common ways in which people commonly fail to open the envelope are understandable but are ultimately not helpful for emotional health:

- Throwing the envelope away without reading it (e.g., avoidance)
- Hanging on to the envelope longer than needed (e.g., rumination, worry, obsessive thinking)

Remember to assume the best of values—they want to help!

CHAPTER 7

ACTIVELY REGULATING EMOTIONS

Back in the early 2000s, a show called *MadTV* did a sketch that has become infamous in therapist circles (Campbell et al., 2001). It's called "Stop It." (Note: I highly recommend you stop reading right now and go watch it online if you can!). In the sketch, Bob Newhart plays a therapist who has a client come to him for help in dealing with claustrophobia (i.e., a fear of small spaces). He tells the client, "Stop it!" The sketch is hilarious, largely because the therapist is blunt and abrupt (and charges only $5!), but it also rings uncomfortably true. When people are truly struggling, drowning in their emotions and sometimes engaging in behaviors that might have real negative consequences (e.g., binge eating, drugs, risky sex, drunk driving, avoiding people, self-injury, considering suicide), they either think "Why can't I just *stop*?" or someone else tells them "Well, just don't do that anymore," as if it's that simple.

Just stopping strong and overwhelming emotions, or refraining from acting impulsively in response to emotions (Carver & Johnson, 2018), is not simple at all. And assuming that "If I just had more willpower, I'd be OK," is also based on misguided folklore. Willpower is not the solution. Instead, it is important to learn how to manage feelings and behaviors by figuring out alternative options—ones that help reduce emotional pain without the negative consequences.

Indeed, the most common reason people typically give me for seeking therapy is the desire for coping skills. Regardless of the diagnosis, or even when a person doesn't meet criteria for any diagnosis, the underlying idea is "I have feelings and thoughts I don't know how to deal with, and they're destroying me. HELP."

This chapter is about cultivating a set of **emotion regulation strategies** that you can use in response to emotions. Once you have decided that yes, an emotion needs to be altered, dampened, regulated, or changed in some way, then you need to figure out what to do and how to do it. What, generally, will your strategy be, and what specific tactic will you use to achieve your emotional goals?

This is the chapter on what most people think of as coping skills. However, I prefer the term "emotion regulation" because it's broader and includes all emotions, including down-regulating emotions that you deem unhelpful to you (i.e., coping), and up-regulating emotions that are helpful to you.

It is also worth noting that many of the concepts discussed earlier in this book also operate to intentionally shift emotions, but in a less obvious way. Emotional labeling (Chapter 4) helps regulate emotions even if it doesn't feel like regulating. Regular mindfulness practice (Chapter 2) is helpful for coping ahead (Chapter 5), which can help you circumvent the need to regulate. Finally, articulating both your values (Chapter 3) and how values are the senders of your emotional messages (Chapter 6) can give you a deeper understanding of your emotions, which also tends to make emotions seem friendlier and less like a disease trying to attack you.

What strategies can you intentionally use to modulate your emotions? That's what this chapter is all about.

REVISITING EMOTION GENERATION AND REGULATION

Before we get into the specific strategies, it is worth revisiting how emotion and emotion regulation unfold. Remember back in Chapter 2, when we talked about the processes by which emotions come about? There's some kind of emotional trigger (whether internal, like a memory or a concern about the future, or external, like someone cutting you off in traffic), then a person attends to an aspect of that trigger, interprets what they pay attention to (what emotion scientists call *appraisal*), and then the emotional response is generated (Gross, 1998b).

Then, in Chapter 6, I told you about the cycle of emotion regulation (see Figure 6.1). After an emotional response is generated, a person needs to identify whether the emotion should be changed based on their desired feelings and goals for the moment, as well as their goals for future. If the result is "Yes, the emotion needs to change," then they must select a strategy (or, as we will discuss later in this chapter, multiple strategies; Ford et al., 2019), implement it well, and then monitor whether the strategy is having the desired effect—whether the strategy works (Gross, 2015).

These processes are in constant motion. Potential emotional triggers are everywhere. As a person walks around in the world, they encounter all kinds of situations that could be emotional, depending on the person's values, sensitivities, and levels of awareness, all of which are based on their own idiosyncratic life experiences.

For example, one of the undergraduate students taking my senior-level emotion seminar came to my office hours. We started talking about her reactions to the course, and she said that she's often sitting there in class thinking about how the material applies to her brother. She said she's often having personal reactions to the material during class. For her, the class content triggers an emotional response, but it doesn't for everyone.

Mostly important for this chapter is that, although the strategies we will talk about certainly can be used after an emotion has been generated, they can also be used earlier (i.e., during the trigger situation, attention, and appraisal stages, not only at the response stage).

In fact, experts disagree on whether it's even possible to separate the processes that generate emotion from the processes that regulate emotion (Campos et al., 2004; Gross & Barrett, 2011; Gross et al., 2011). If a person can change an emotion even before it's fully erupted—like telling a delivery driver to bring the message to a different address—is that even regulation? My perspective is that any intentional—whether conscious or unconscious/automatic—strategy to alter the trajectory of the emotion, at any stage of the generation process, counts as emotion regulation (Gross et al., 2011).

There are a couple of reasons why revisiting the cycles of **emotion generation** and regulation are important. First, the strategies used to regulate emotions generally fall into one of four categories, based on the cycle of emotion generation:

1. Strategies for changing the trigger, or altering the situation
2. Strategies for controlling or shifting attention
3. Ways to change the interpretation or appraisal of the situation
4. Direct ways to dampen the subjective feeling itself

I'm going to highlight one or two scientifically backed strategies in each section that are important tools for any emotion regulation toolbox.

Second, there are all kinds of ways that people struggle with emotion regulation and coping (this is often called **emotion dysregulation;** Gratz & Roemer, 2004) that are relevant to the cycles of emotion generation and regulation. Having a small regulation toolbox is one pathway to emotion dysregulation, because it's hard to regulate well when a person has limited strategies at their disposal. In his memoir, *Friends* actor Matthew Perry (2022) repeatedly discusses his two strategies for dealing with his feelings: (a) making people laugh and (b) substances (alcohol mostly, but not exclusively). That's it.

Two strategies. Two is usually not enough for all of the ways that emotions can pop up in a person's life.

A second pathway to emotion dysregulation could be called **underregulation** (Tice & Bratslavsky, 2000). Underregulation is a failure to regulate in situations where regulation would be helpful, or not regulating *enough*. If a person tries a strategy for a minute and gives up before seeing how the strategy unfolds, that's not regulating *enough*.

A third pathway to emotion dysregulation has been dubbed **misregulation** (Tice & Bratslavsky, 2000). We'll get into this one more in Chapter 9 but, in short, misregulation involves picking strategies that aren't likely to work, either because the strategy itself isn't great, or—and this one is more likely—the strategy isn't well matched to the situation.

A fourth pathway to emotion dysregulation is a failure of implementation (Gross et al., 2019). This occurs when a helpful strategy is selected that fits the situation at hand, but it doesn't "work" because the person doesn't use it well. Emotion regulation strategies need to be implemented with high quality, or they won't actually change the emotion at all (Southward et al., 2021)!

What all this means is that you can benefit from learning and practicing a variety of strategies and trying them early in the generation process, as well as after an emotion has erupted. We'll cover several of the best strategies according to science, but this isn't an exhaustive list. There are a lot of strategies out there that can address emotions, and many of them take practice and attention to do well.

One final note. There is actually an entire set of additional strategies that we are going to cover in Chapter 8—the strategies related to how other people can be incorporated into the emotion regulation process. This chapter focuses on strategies that can be done alone, without others. Shall we get to it?

1. CHANGING THE TRIGGER

One of the most basic emotion regulation strategies is trying to change the emotional trigger. This overarching method actually involves two slightly different versions, one involving proactively selecting into (or out of) a situation, and the second trying to change the situation you're already in. The latter generally goes by the name **problem-solving** because it recognizes that emotions sometimes stem from problems that can be fixed, solved, or changed (Aldao et al., 2010; Naragon-Gainey et al., 2017).

The thing about emotional messages is that unlike typical mail that shows up at a static physical mailbox—like the one at the end of your driveway—emotional messages have the capacity to follow you around anywhere. Seen through this lens, emotional messages are more like text messages on your phone, which you probably carry around everywhere (if you're like most people I know in the modern age).

Although you might think that changing the trigger means trying to avoid getting a message in the first place, this isn't about nailing your mailbox shut or deleting the email application from your phone. Instead, it's about changing the situation so that your values don't get triggered. If the message is from your bank informing you of an overdraft, a proactive approach is watching your account balance so you never get the overdraft in the first place. A problem-solving approach is getting the message and then quickly moving money from savings (or borrowing it from your parents) to cover the overdraft.

For a more emotionally salient example, I know that I tend to feel anxious when faced with uncertainty (which, per our discussion in Chapter 4, makes perfect sense—anxiety is about future-focused uncertain threats). In fact, my stress nightmare, which I have when I'm feeling particularly overwhelmed, is about me desperately packing and trying to catch a plane but feeling unsure that I'll make it on time. When I have this nightmare, I know I need to think about changing the trigger—by trying to proactively select myself into situations that will be pleasant, rejuvenating, and fulfilling, and/or engaging in some problem-solving to reduce how many stressors I have floating around at that moment.

Proactive Selection

Proactive selection is a particularly good strategy for people who struggle with classic coping (Webb et al., 2018). Why? Because it takes the choice away. There is a myth that good emotion regulation, or good self-control (which is very much related to emotion regulation; Tice & Bratslavsky, 2000) involves **willpower**—a mystical force needed to push away a crappy feeling or resist the temptation to do something you think you shouldn't do.

Yet people with good self-control and emotion regulation don't necessarily have more willpower. In fact, several studies have shown that people with high self-control do not have higher will-power, but instead are better at avoiding temptation situations in the first place (Ent et al., 2015). There are good reasons to suggest that someone who is trying to cut back on drinking should not keep alcohol in the house!

One caveat for proactive selection is that there is a fine line between proactively selecting into situations and avoidance—which often involves proactively selecting out of situations that are deemed threatening. The person with posttraumatic stress disorder who avoids going to the grocery store during the day because there are too many people, or the person with social anxiety who avoids auditioning for the school play (even though they really want to act) are examples of intentionally trying to circumvent triggers that are avoidant in nature.

A few good examples of proactive selection are carrying sunscreen or a water bottle around at all times so you won't be caught without them. Or, I used to get irritated when I received emails from my students asking me how to do things, so now I post "How to Do X" documents and I provide example papers so that I don't have to feel irritated.

Problem-Solving

Being able to fix a situation or alter a trigger that starts an emotion generation cycle can certainly reduce unwanted emotions. In general, people who engage in more problem-solving tend to have fewer symptoms of psychopathology (Aldao et al., 2010; Naragon-Gainey et al., 2017).

There are some therapy approaches dedicated to helping people learn problem-solving skills, and these approaches do seem to work in decreasing distress. In problem-solving therapy, people learn to identify and define problems, understand the nature of the problem, set specific and measurable goals, generate a variety of solutions, choose the best options, implement the selected strategy, and evaluate whether or not the strategy helped the person meet their goal. Problem-solving is a skill that can be learned!

There are a few caveats about problem-solving. First, not all problems are solvable. Grief, for example, is typically not a problem that can be solved. It's not possible to fix the death of a loved one. Unsolvable problems are often related to other people. When other people are toxic, or abusive, or creating havoc, there is no way to fix them, especially if those people don't want to change. I see this quite a bit in women escaping domestic violence situations who get trapped into ruminating about interactions they or their children had with their ex. We can't control what other people do. The idea is to solve problems when they can be solved and use other approaches when problems aren't solvable.

Second, problem-solving is more beneficial for people who have labeled and processed their feelings (Baker & Berenbaum,

2007). The idea is that jumping to problem-solving without actually considering the emotion may be counterproductive. There is a reason why this book covers emotional awareness, labeling, and opening the envelope before considering problem-solving as an option.

Summary

In general, changing the trigger tends to decrease negative emotions (Lennarz et al., 2019) and increase positive emotions (Baker & Berenbaum, 2007). Why? Likely in part because proactive selection and problem-solving both involve *agency*, which is the sense of control a person feels over their life. An agentic person feels capable of getting things done, making beneficial choices, and sensing that their words and actions matter.

2. DOS AND DON'TS OF DISTRACTION

Distraction is an incredibly common emotion regulation strategy that involves shifting attention. Distraction is "I'm feeling bad right now, so I just need to focus on something else." Watching TV, talking to a friend about unemotional topics, and burying yourself in work are all potential distraction techniques to move attention away from the emotional trigger onto a safer target.

There are a few important questions about distraction viewed through a scientific lens: (a) does distraction actually work and (b) even if distraction works, is distraction a good idea, or is it more of a problematic strategy? The answer to (a) is clear—distraction can be effective. Shifting attention away from an emotional trigger onto something else can reduce negative emotions (Strauss et al., 2016) and increase pleasant emotions (Volkaert et al., 2020). Distraction takes some of the sting out of an emotional message by simply not attending to it for awhile. The answer to (b) is far less clear. Distraction is likely a good idea sometimes, but it isn't good all the time. Why? Because distraction can be used as an avoidance strategy. When a person tries to distract themself from a painful emotion now because they never want to feel the emotion, then distraction is avoidance. Remember how we talked about how avoidance is "throwing away the envelope"? Avoidance-based distraction is intentionally turning away from the envelope and hoping it gets thrown out or misplaced.

Remember that the intention of emotional messages is to be helpful. Avoidance-based distraction as a go-to strategy means never getting those helpful messages. In fact, research has demonstrated that people who use distraction and believe that emotions should be avoided have poorer outcomes than people who use distraction but generally have the attitude that emotions are useful (Wolgast & Lundh, 2017). That is why this section is called "The Dos and Don'ts of Distraction." Distraction can be used strategically, with the knowledge that emotions are generally useful but may not be right now.

Pitfalls of Distraction (Don'ts)

I sometimes call distraction the "gateway drug" to avoidance. Distraction helps people shift their attention away from emotionally evocative stimuli (or a strong emotional response) and thus can provide emotional relief. But when distraction is pursued with the mindset of "I can't think about that," then it becomes a vehicle for **thought suppression**. Thought suppression is the tendency to try to inhibit or push away thoughts, typically thoughts about emotional triggers (or about the emotions themselves). The rationale behind thought suppression is logical: If paying attention to thoughts results in emotional pain, then pushing away the thoughts (e.g., by distracting yourself with other activities) will make the emotional pain go away.

Thought suppression, however, doesn't work. Paradoxically, to successfully avoid something, you actually have to pay more attention to it to ensure it doesn't come creeping back into your consciousness. A famous psychological study, commonly referred to as the "white bear study" (Wegner et al., 1987), showed that people who were asked to not think about a white bear actually thought about the white bear more often. Why would trying not to think about something result in a person thinking about that thing more frequently, and with more intensity, than just letting the thought run wild?

An example might help. Pretend you are guarding a medieval castle. One day, you catch a spy from a nearby kingdom who is trying to sneak into the castle. You are under direct orders to not kill anyone, so you banish the spy, telling them to never again come near the castle. But because you don't trust them, you have to remain even more vigilant—you have to monitor and keep close watch on the spy to make sure the spy doesn't come back.

Another distraction "don't" is relying on substances or other activities that change your brain chemistry (e.g., sex, gambling), because these activities will hijack your brain's reward centers. That's not to say you can never drink or smoke weed as a distraction from feelings. However, drugs directly affect attentional systems, which means they can work too well. Alcohol, for example, creates a kind of nearsighted focus on the present moment (Steele & Josephs, 1990). When drunk, it's easy to attend to the now and forget the past or the future, which makes alcohol a dangerous tool for distraction— alcohol is very good at helping distract people from their feelings. But then the brain has a harder time using distraction effectively on its own.

To summarize: Don't use distraction as a way to avoid the emotion permanently, and don't overly rely on substances or other brain-rewarding activities as distractions. The idea of distraction is to get your mind off the emotional trigger so that you can get a better handle on yourself, and to regain your footing, not to ignore the message entirely.

Using Distraction Wisely (Dos)

Distraction can be used wisely. It is particularly beneficial when emotions are intense (Sheppes et al., 2011). Strong emotions tend to narrow attention onto the emotion (Friedman & Förster, 2010). When emotions are intense, thoughts are loud and emotion laden, but not clear, balanced, or holistic (Veilleux et al., 2022). When emotions are high, distracting yourself until the emotion comes down a little bit can be advantageous in that it gives you time to regain some mental clarity.

How can you use distraction wisely? There are a few crucial tips. First, it is better to focus on something (e.g., try to really immerse yourself in that TV show) than to try to not focus on your feelings or the emotional stimuli (McRae et al., 2012). Why? Because of the thought suppression ideas discussed in the "Pitfalls of Distraction (Don'ts)" section. Trying to not think about something increases awareness of that unwanted topic because part of your mind has to monitor whether you're thinking about it or not. So, trying to focus on something more pleasant is simpler for your brain and actually more effective in changing emotions.

Distraction is best used as a strategy to temporarily shift attention away from an emotional stimulus to allow strong emotions to subside a bit. Distraction is the "set aside the envelope to look at later" strategy, but remembering to pick it up later is important. I find that it's useful to think of distraction as a kind of strategic delay. **Strategic delay** is the adaptive form of **procrastination**. As you likely know (because most people procrastinate at one time or another), procrastination involves voluntarily putting off or delaying an important activity, even though the delay comes with discomfort and other negative consequences (Klingsieck, 2013).

Procrastination is most often discussed in a school context, like putting off working on a big assignment until the night before it is due, or not studying until the morning of an exam. But of course, procrastination can be used in all kinds of areas—waiting to do taxes until the 14th of April, or waiting to clean the house until 20 minutes before your family arrives. The thing about procrastination is that it's got negative consequences: Saving things for the last minute is stressful and rarely results in quality work. Some people think of procrastination as "screwing over your future self." The procrastinating person thinks, "This activity seems hard or awful, I'll put it off until later, I'll be able to deal with it better later" (Sirois & Pychyl, 2013).

Strategic delay shares many features with procrastination but doesn't have the negative consequences. With strategic delay, the delay is intentional and helpful. Sometimes people are in fact able to do a better job later on! For example, if you are sick or hungover, you will probably not write a very good term paper. In these instances, it may be strategic to delay—not to delay forever, or to delay until the last minute, but to strategically wait until the mind can focus, process the emotion, or effectively use other kinds of strategies (e.g., problem-solving, shifting thoughts). Strategic delays are temporary, not permanent. When you can think of distraction as a "Let me focus on this other thing right now, but I'll get back to you later" strategy, then distraction can work well.

To summarize: Do intentionally try to immerse yourself in a fun, pleasant activity (rather than trying to avoid your feelings). Do use distraction to shift your attention and allow the unpleasant feeling to decrease and, ideally, more pleasant feelings to rise. But remember to *go back to the emotion*. Whether you distract yourself by throwing yourself into a work project, singing karaoke with a friend, or going to the gym, turn toward the distraction, but remember to turn back to process your feelings later.

3. SHIFTING THOUGHTS

Of all of the emotion regulation strategies commonly described in therapy manuals or studied in scientific research, shifting thoughts—sometimes called **cognitive reappraisal** or **cognitive reframing**—has received the most scientific support. Thinking about the situation from a different angle is a widely popular and extremely successful strategy for both increasing positive feelings and decreasing negative feelings (Clark, 2022).

There are actually several different ways to shift thoughts in emotional situations. We'll review two of the most common ones—**reinterpretation** and **distancing**—here. They help a person shift thoughts in different ways. Both are useful strategies to have in an emotion regulation toolbox.

Reinterpretation

Trying to reinterpret or *reappraise* a situation is the classic example of shifting thoughts. It's so crucial that this strategy is at the heart of most cognitive behavioral therapies (Clark, 2022). The idea stems from appraisal theories of emotion, which we talked about in Chapter 2. Appraisal or interpretation of an emotional trigger is a crucial part of the emotion generation process, because how the situation is interpreted relates to whether an emotion occurs at all, and which emotion is felt.

For example, when situations are interpreted as irrelevant or unimportant, no emotions emerge. When a situation is interpreted as important and negative, when outcomes are deemed certain and the situation is perceived as being caused by other people, anger is the likely feeling (Frijda et al., 1989). However, when the situation is interpreted as important and negative, familiar, unexpected, and/or about someone else, the emotion is likely to be sadness.

The idea is that the interpretation shapes the emotion, so a different interpretation creates a different emotion. Many research studies have demonstrated how this works. In one study, participants were shown emotionally evocative images and asked to think about the images in a way that decreased their emotional response (Lieberman et al., 2011). For example, if a person looked at an image of a woman in a hospital bed hooked up to an IV, a reappraisal might be "She's just sleeping and getting fluids after having a baby, she'll be going home soon."

When applied to the self, the steps typically involve trying to understand what the interpretation was, including any automatic, negative thoughts. Our thoughts become automatic and habitual when we think the same kinds of thoughts over time and across situations. For example, some people blame themselves (e.g., "This is all my fault"). Some people look only at the negative, such as by saying "This coffee is too hot," which ignores the fact that the taste is also sweet. Some people overgeneralize (e.g., "I will always feel this way"). Some people interpret situations on the basis of what they think should have happened (e.g., "I should have said . . ."). There are so many ways to interpret a situation!

Reinterpretation is about examining your interpretation of the situation and then generating alternative interpretations. People who have only a surface level of reinterpretation tend to say that this strategy is just about thinking positively, or finding the silver lining. I want to be crystal clear here—reinterpretation is not just about thinking positively. In fact, there are serious hazards to the "good vibes only" mentality (Goodman, 2022). Ignoring the unpleasant emotional messages and looking only at the positive emotional messages isn't listening to what your values have to say.

Reinterpretation could involve seeing the positive aspects of a situation (because it's far easier to attend to the negative aspects . . . remember that pesky negativity bias?), but there are other ways to reinterpret (see Exhibit 7.1). Thinking about whether the current circumstances could be viewed differently is another way—even another negative way. For example, consider a woman named Christin, who bought a plane ticket and flew across the country to visit her sister, Melissa. The visit was a surprise, and when Christin got there Melissa wasn't actually thrilled to see her. Christin's initial

---

EXHIBIT 7.1. Tips for Shifting Thought

Reinterpretation

For reinterpretation, try asking yourself these questions:

- How am I interpreting this situation? Am I seeing it as wholly negative, catastrophic (a big deal), or as my fault? What are my thoughts about what I think is going to happen next?
- Pick a trusted friend or family member. How would they interpret the situation? Would it be different? How so?
- Then try asking yourself these questions, and try to pay attention to your own resistance to considering alternative explanations:
  - Is it possible that the consequences of this situation could be better than I originally thought?
  - What might I not know about the circumstances of the situation? Are there circumstances that I might not have considered?
  - Are there people (myself, someone else) who have the skills to deal with the situation effectively, and might that change things?
  - Might other people feel similarly to me? Is this situation understandable?

Distancing

For distancing, try these two ideas:

- Repeat the thought in third person rather than in first person, using your name instead of "I."
- Add some words to get distance from the thought:
  - "I'm thinking that . . ."
  - "I'm having the thought that . . ."
  - "I'm recognizing that I'm having the thought that . . ."

---

reaction was to feel extremely sad and guilty that her surprise wasn't welcomed, and she had a lot of self-blame ("I should have called first, I messed this up").

When she tried reinterpretation using one of the questions in Exhibit 7.1 to think about how one of her friends might have felt, Christin thought, "Huh. My friend would have been *pissed* that her sister wasn't willing to change her schedule and accommodate someone who flew across the country as a *gift*." Reinterpreting the situation helped Christin feel better about being sad, because she realized that sadness just meant she was feeling a loss of appreciation. She actually preferred to feel sad rather than angry.

Reinterpretation is hard to do well. If you want more extensive guidance, consider buying a cognitive behavioral therapy workbook; virtually all of them will have steps for cognitive reframing.

Distancing

A different way of shifting thoughts is to try to create distance between yourself and your thoughts. This technique is sometimes called **defusion** (Harris, 2006) because, in moments of high distress, thoughts and feelings can become fused together, and the idea is to take a step back to be able to gain perspective. Distancing differs from cognitive reframing because distancing involves changing the relationship to the thought, rather than trying to change the thought itself.

For example, Russell is prone to what he calls "shame spirals," in which he will be spending time with his wife and two young children, and his wife will ask him why he neglected to do a task she asked him to do (e.g., make peanut butter and jelly sandwiches for the kids' lunch, pick up toilet paper on the way home from work). He will think thoughts like "I can never do anything right. She's going to leave me and take the kids because I can't do these simple little things she asks of me." These thoughts blossom into feeling ashamed, and then he tells himself he wouldn't feel this way if he just did the things his wife asked for, and the cycle goes round and round.

Cognitive reframing would be about changing the thought, like "I didn't do *this* right, but I can do other things right. I surprised her by getting her a gift she loved on her birthday last week." Distancing involves not changing the thought itself but the distance. There are at least two ways to do this, both of which can be effective.

The first way is talking about yourself from a third-person perspective. So, Russell would think, "Russell is thinking that he can never do anything right. He's thinking that his wife is going to leave him and take the kids." It's the same thought, just shifted from the first person to the third person. Why does this work? Studies have shown that when people write journal entries in the third person, compared with the first person, they gain better abilities to reason about their problems (Grossman et al., 2021) because these techniques create distance and perspective (Kross et al., 2014). If you've ever thought that other people's problems seem easier to solve than your own, this technique might be helpful to you, because doing this makes your problems seem outside of yourself and thus easier to see clearly.

The second tactic for distancing involves labeling the thoughts as thoughts and adding words to the sentence to specifically identify the thought as a thought rather than as a truth (Assaz et al., 2018). Examples of how to do this are provided in Exhibit 7.1. Russell, for example, could say, "I'm having the thought that I can never do anything right. I'm realizing I'm having the thought that I am afraid my wife is going to leave me. I'm noticing that I'm judging myself for not following instructions."

Distancing tries to help create space between you and your thoughts. Rather than assuming the thought represents a fundamental truth about you, these cognitive shifting strategies help highlight that they are pieces of information floating through your mind.

Caveats and Barriers

There are several barriers to using cognitive reinterpretation and distancing successfully. First, my experience is that many people try these techniques and quickly decide they don't work, particularly cognitive reinterpretation. Yet it may be that the strategy didn't work because it's hard to do well, which is different from assuming the strategy itself is ineffective. In fact, cognitive reinterpretation is a skill that has to be practiced. Coming up with alternative interpretations in the moment is difficult. I've had some clients who truly were unable to generate any alternative thoughts because they couldn't see any other possible way to view the situation.

Cognitive reinterpretation is especially hard to use when emotions are intense because that is when cognitive resources are lowest (Ford & Troy, 2019; Sheppes et al., 2011). When emotions are high, cognitive distancing is quite a bit easier (Orvell et al., 2021). Simply remembering to try a cognitive shifting strategy is a barrier in and of itself, but rephrasing the thought in third person or adding "I'm thinking that" involves much less mental effort (Moser et al. 2017).

It is also the case that cognitive reinterpretation can feel invalidating and result in a person feeling inauthentic. For example, Caitlin, a Mexican American woman, feels angry and hurt when someone overhears her speaking Spanish and yells "Go back to your country!" Does she really want to come up with another interpretation of that situation? Thinking "They didn't really mean to be racist," or "Maybe they were just having a bad day," or "I bet a Spanish-speaking person insulted them last week" just detracts from the situation. Not all emotions or situations should be reinterpreted.

4. DAMPENING THE RESPONSE

So far, we've talked about strategies to change the emotional trigger, change where attention is allocated, and shift appraisals/thoughts, which are all strategies that can be used to alter the trajectory of an emotion before it fully erupts. The other three strategy types are referred to as "antecedent strategies" because they can be used during the process of emotion generation (Gross, 1998a), although of course they are often used after the fact, too. This final strategy type, however, is about trying to dampen the emotional response directly. There are three major techniques I suggest here: (a) targeting the physical components of emotion (i.e., changing physiology), (b) opposite action, and (c) mental grounding.

All three of these techniques act directly on the components of emotion, which we talked about in Chapter 1. The idea is that changing physiology, acting opposite to the action urge of the emotion, and engaging in grounding can help lower emotional intensity and provide more choices to prevent people from acting impulsively on their feelings.

Targeting the Physical Components of Emotion

Many emotions involve physiological changes, because one of the functions of emotion is to prepare the body for action. Whether amping up activation (anxiety, anger) or reducing activation (sadness, loneliness), the body is intimately involved in emotions. This response-focused strategy thus involves changing the physiology of the body to change the subjective experience of the emotion.

The strategy often suggested is deep breathing, or paced breathing, which reduces physiological activation and is thus especially useful for high-activation feelings, such as anxiety, stress, and anger (Jerath et al., 2015). The regular practice of deep breathing is likely a coping ahead strategy (see Chapter 5), because practicing deep breathing reduces overall levels of stress and negative affect (Perciavalle et al., 2017). Progressive muscle relaxation, which involves systematically tensing and then loosening muscle groups in the body (e.g., starting with the foot muscles and moving all the way up to the neck), can also help with shifting the physiological component of emotion.

There are other ways to change up the physiological workings of the body, too. Many emotions feel "hot," and so using temperature changes can be really helpful (Linehan, 2015). For example, my oldest kid is quite emotionally sensitive and gets angry very easily, and he tends to act out on that anger, like snatching what he wants from his sister, or sometimes pushing her. Sometimes, when he has the urge to act on his anger, he will say, "Mom, I'm having a hot feeling, can I have an ice cube?" Sucking on an ice cube, or holding an ice cube in his hand, can physically cool him off, which also reduces the intensity of the feeling.

More active tactics can fit here, too. In Chapter 5, we talked about exercise as a coping ahead strategy. Exercise can also be used here as a way to burn off some of the energy that emotions can generate. I know several people who strap on some running shoes and go for a several-mile-long run when they feel intense emotions. Exercise-generated endorphins can counteract unpleasant feelings, and even for those of us who don't necessarily like to exercise (ahem, I put myself in this category), the relief and "ahhhhhh" of completing a workout can shift an emotional response.

Opposite Action

Opposite action is a skill from dialectical behavior therapy (Linehan, 1993; 2015). The idea is to act opposite to the action urge of the emotion as a way to change the emotional response. For example, anger is an emotion associated with muscle tension and physical strength, where the urge is to attack/criticize others. An opposite action response would involve finding a loose, relaxed physical posture and intentionally trying to be grateful to others (Sauer-Zavala et al., 2019).

This strategy acts on the expression (e.g., body language) and action urge components of emotion, as well as the physiological responses to the emotion (e.g., internal muscle tension).

For another example, sadness is an emotion with a heavy, slow physical posture. The action urge is to cry and retreat into yourself, often withdrawing from others to find comfort. Acting opposite would be to do jumping jacks, smile and say hello to strangers, and plan to do pleasant activities.

I find that opposite action is the most effective when it involves a sense of silliness, which can facilitate perspective change. So, when someone is angry (tense, jerky movements), I suggest acting like a melting pile of goo. When someone is sad (heavy, slow moments), I suggest doing the can-can. Even holding a pencil (or your finger, if you can't find a pencil) between your teeth can shift the muscles of the face into a real smile, which makes cartoons seem funnier (Strack et al. 1988). There is some contention in the scientific community as to whether changing body posture or facial expressions truly changes emotional experience (Coles et al., 2019), but I'm generally on team "If it can work for you, try it!"

Mental Grounding

Grounding techniques are often taught to help people stay in the present moment and refrain from acting on action urges. The idea is that people, when emotional, are often drowning in the emotion. When people are drowning, they are flailing around, trying to survive. People who feel that they are drowning in their emotions tend to be overly attentive to their feelings and are often stuck thinking about the past or future (e.g., rumination or worry). Drowning can also involve fusion between action and feeling, such as when a person feels compelled to act on the emotion. This is what happens to my older kid when he's angry—he feels compelled to lash out.

Grounding techniques help people anchor themselves to the present moment. In truth, many of the strategies in the "Targeting the Physical Components of Emotion" section (e.g., do deep breathing, hold an ice cube) are also considered grounding strategies. What I mean specifically here, though, is that there are ways to tether your mind to the present moment by giving yourself something to think about that is not the emotional trigger or the emotional response.

The two grounding exercises I give most frequently to clients are "5-4-3-2-1" and the "Describe Your Environment" skills (see Exhibit 7.2). The 5-4-3-2-1 exercise involves marshaling your senses to think about 5 things you can see, 4 things you can touch, 3 things

---

EXHIBIT 7.2. Grounding Techniques

5-4-3-2-1

To use this strategy, you want to use your senses to identify 5 things you can see, 4 things you can touch, 3 things you can hear, 2 things you can smell, and 1 thing you can taste.

Example: "I see a yellow bowl, a microwave, a coffee cup, a fork, and a lunch bag. I can touch my coffee cup, this computer, my phone, and my hair. I can hear birds chirping, a lawnmower, and my keys as I type . . ."

Describe Your Environment

To use this strategy, just start describing things you see in your environment. Describe the shapes and colors of the objects you see, trying to avoid using "like" or "dislike" words and sticking to objective descriptions.

Example: "I see a silver cart with a black microwave on the second shelf. The microwave is plugged in and shows the time. On top of the microwave is a round turquoise plate. On the top shelf is a hot pink tray, and on the tray is a plastic baggie with a yellow bowl sitting on it, another turquoise plate stacked on the bowl, and then another yellow bowl on top of the plate. Next to that is a mug . . ." Note that I *stopped* myself from saying "The cart is starting to look gross, there are crumbs on the plate that I forgot to clean because I'm disgusting." Just describe.

---

you can hear, 2 things you can smell, and 1 thing you can taste. Describe Your Environment involves using your eyes and mouth as you describe (out loud) what you can see, identifying the shapes and colors of objects in your sphere of awareness and trying to avoid making judgments about what you see.

I personally prefer the Describe Your Environment strategy because I can't always smell or taste anything! But both are useful for the same reason: They get a person into the current environment, into the moment, and using multiple senses. Talking out loud is particularly helpful because it's hard to think and talk at the same time, so speaking out loud can reduce the noise inside your head.

Grounding techniques share some overlap with distraction techniques because both actually do aim to alter attention. Distraction, however, is about immersing your attention into something else, while grounding is a mindfulness-adjacent technique that aims to anchor or ground you in the present, giving you more agency to decide what to do next. Practicing mindfulness regularly when not emotional, as a coping ahead emotional conditioning strategy (Chapter 5), can help you make grounding more effective during the emotional moments when it's needed most.

POLYREGULATION

The set of strategies described in this chapter provide a variety of ways someone could intentionally regulate their emotions. There are a lot of options!

When we talked about the cycle of emotion regulation earlier in this chapter, we noted that once a person identifies an emotion to regulate, they then select a strategy, implement it, and monitor to see whether or not it works. Of course, whether a strategy works depends entirely on the goal (see Chapter 6), and it's worth reminding you that strategies aimed at facilitating long-term growth may not be able to be immediately judged as working or failing.

One problem with the way I've described the emotion regulation cycle thus far is that you might believe that a person must select only one strategy at a time. Yet that's not actually how regulation works. People actually can—and do—use multiple strategies at once. This is called **polyregulation** (Ford et al., 2019), and it's actually pretty common (Hartmann et al., 2024; Ladis et al., 2023).

The concept of polyregulation is still fairly new, but it certainly makes intuitive sense that strategies can be combined. For example, problem-solving may involve thinking of the situation from multiple angles, thus combining the changing-the-trigger strategy with the shifting-thoughts strategy. Strategies could also be sequenced. For example, my graduate students and I coined the phrase "thinking threshold" to denote the idea that people can't think clearly during extremely intense emotions. On a scale from 0 (*no distress*) to 100 (*extreme distress*; see Chapter 1 for emotional charting), most people say that when their feelings are stronger than a 70 or 80 their thinking is impaired. Each person can have their own thinking threshold (Veilleux et al., 2022). The idea is that when the emotion is above the thinking threshold, it is helpful to do something behavioral—such as using a dampening-the-response or distraction technique. Then, when the emotion comes back down below that thinking threshold and mental effort can be appropriately harnessed, you can either solve the problem or use cognitive reinterpretation.

BELIEFS ABOUT EMOTION CONTROLLABILITY

We've reviewed quite a few emotion regulation strategies in this chapter, all of which can be effective in modulating emotions. They typically need to be practiced to be implemented well, and seeing a therapist can be helpful for getting feedback on whether you are implementing the strategies with high quality and/or how to potentially enact them better.

There are two additional pieces that we haven't talked about, which relate to whether or not emotion regulation will be effective: whether you believe that emotions can change and whether you believe that you can change your emotions (Ford & Gross, 2019). The first is a belief in the property of emotions, and the second is a belief (or lack thereof) in your own abilities. These are related, because people who think that emotions can't change are also likely to believe that they themselves can't change emotions (e.g., how can you change something that is itself unchangeable?). However, I've worked with clients who think that emotions are changeable for other people, but they have no confidence in their own regulation skills.

Beliefs about the changeability of emotions are incredibly important. Think about actual mail that you get, whether email or physical mail. Do you believe that you can control which kinds of catalogs you get? Or do you believe that you have any control over what you do with those catalogs when they show up at your door?

People who think that emotions are uncontrollable tend to use fewer and less effective emotion regulation strategies, and they have more symptoms of anxiety and depression (Kneeland, Dovidio, et al., 2016). Beliefs about emotion aren't necessarily consistent over time, either. In moments when people find emotions more uncontrollable, they tend to use more avoidance-based regulation strategies (De Castella et al., 2018; Veilleux, Warner, et al., 2023). Believing that emotions are uncontrollable results in throwing away the emotional envelope without looking at it (Kneeland, Nolan-Hoeksma, et al., 2016).

Evidence suggests that controllability beliefs matter for all of the strategies suggested here. Believing that problems can be solved results in more active coping and use of problem-solving. Believing that you can handle the emotion eventually (even if not right now) results in using distraction more wisely. Believing that thoughts can be shifted and that changing thoughts can indeed alter emotions results in more (and better) use of cognitive reappraisal. Believing that you can change your body's physical chemistry results in better use of dampening responses.

Many people lack confidence in their abilities to modulate and shift their emotions, or in just letting the emotion unfold without regulating. If this is you, what can you do? Can beliefs about emotion change? Yes, they can!

Although not directly described as providing methods for increasing self-confidence in managing emotions, this entire book has been focused on helping you understand your emotions more, fear your feelings less, and realize just how many things you can do to manage your emotions. Learning labeling strategies, practicing mindfulness, engaging in coping ahead practices, and opening the envelope are all methods intended to target your beliefs.

This chapter has been about actions—things you can do to cope with strong emotions. Doing things differently is the best way to change beliefs. Try the strategies described in this book, and then ask yourself whether you do, in fact, have the power to change your emotions. I know you do, but you may have to learn that for yourself.

SUMMARY POINTS

- Once you are already experiencing an emotion, what can you do about it when you decide that you want to regulate? Select a strategy, implement it well, and monitor to see whether the strategy is helping you meet your emotional goal.
- Changing-the-trigger strategies include proactive situation selection and problem-solving.

- Distraction is a useful strategy for shifting attention, but it should involve engaging with an alternative target and should not be used as an avoidance tactic.
- Reinterpretation (i.e., changing thoughts about a situation) and mental distancing (i.e., changing your relationship to the thought) are both effective thinking-based strategies.
- Responses to emotions can be dampened by changing physiology, acting opposite to the urge of the emotion, and using grounding to anchor you in the present moment.
- Polyregulation is combining strategies, either simultaneously or in sequence.
- Believing that emotions can be modulated and that you have the skills to change emotions is crucial for success in intentional emotion regulation.

CHAPTER 8

EXPRESSING AND SHARING EMOTIONS

Movies and television shows are full of examples of characters trying to hide their feelings from other people. My personal favorite is *Zoey's Extraordinary Playlist*, which aired on NBC from 2020 to 2021 (Blackman, 2020–2021). Zoey is a computer programmer in San Francisco. When her beloved father gets sick with a progressive neurological disease, Zoey schedules a magnetic resonance imaging scan to see if she might be at risk too. During the scan, there is an earthquake, after which she develops a kind of emotional super-power: She can "hear" the feelings of people around her in song (it's a musical!). Even when other people try to mask or hide their feelings, Zoey hears their innermost desires and woes.

The show raises some interesting questions: Why do we try to hide our feelings from others so often? What are the pros and cons of expressing (and, for Zoey, how does she handle being on the receiving end of emotions that people don't want to share)? Also, as a therapist—how do I get this superpower for myself?!?!

Emotional expression is a tricky topic, because emotions are inherently social. Not all emotions occur when one is around other people, but most emotions are about relationships (Lazarus, 2006). These include relationships we have but don't want, relationships we want but don't have, relationships that are solid, relationships that feel rocky, and relationships with ourselves.

The social nature of emotions is why expression is a core component of the emotional experience (see Chapter 1). Remember that one of the central functions of emotions is to communicate with others (refer back to Chapter 3 for a discussion of the functions of emotions). From an emotional message standpoint, emotional expressions are broadcast announcements. Emotions are messages sent to you, from your values. Your values try to help you clue in to what's important. At the same time, the message is also intended to be broadcast to your surroundings. The emotional message wants you to receive it, but it also wants people near you to know that you're getting the message.

Think about a kid at a grocery store, looking at fruit. The distracted parent is in the next aisle, examining cans of soup, and hasn't realized the kid stayed in the produce area. When the kid trips on a banana peel and hits her head,[1] she is in pain, and she's scared because her dad isn't nearby. Her value of Safety is threatened. The loudspeaker might say, "Hurt and crying child in Aisle 1! If your child is wearing a green shirt and purple leggings, go find her!" The kid receives the message of the emotion, but it's the broadcast (e.g., the expression) that notifies her dad that his kid needs his help.

Emotional messages were designed to be broadcast. An email about and for you also is blind copied (bcc'd) to everyone in your vicinity. If we think about it this way, it actually makes a lot of sense why many people learn to lean on **expressive suppression**, which is the scientific term for hiding or masking feelings. Why? Because who wants their personal, private business broadcast to everyone? If an emotional message is meant for me, and was sent from my values,

---

[1]Although I have never seen anyone actually trip on a banana peel, cartoons certainly suggest that this is a real potential hazard!!

there is certainly no need for other people to nose their way into my problems!

I worked with a client I'll call Freddie. Freddie suffered from prolonged grief after his husband, Juventino, accidentally drowned. Freddie was referred to therapy by his boss, who recognized that Freddie wasn't performing as well at work as he used to. Freddie was definitely depressed—he was uninterested in things he used to do, and sometimes he actively avoided activities he used to like because he couldn't bear doing them without his husband. What really struck me about Freddie, though, was his unwillingness to share his feelings with anyone in his life. He and his husband were pretty social people, and many people were touched by Juventino's death, but Freddie did not want to talk about Juventino or about his grief with their friends. He relied heavily on expressive suppression in his daily life, trying to come across as cool and collected. By masking his emotional expression, and not intentionally verbally sharing his feelings with others, he became more and more isolated. Not only did he not fully process his grief, he also didn't get the commiseration and support he could have gotten from his friends and family had he allowed that broadcast to get out.

In this chapter, we delve into why emotions are meant to be expressed, with the recognition that sometimes those emotional broadcasts can be minefields. This is the trickiest part of emotional expression: getting the benefits of expression while minimizing some of the problems that can occur when other people don't respond to your emotional expressions in the way that you'd like.

TYPES OF EMOTIONAL EXPRESSION

Because emotions occur in the context of relationships, emotional expressions are particularly salient for couples. In my experience doing couples therapy, communication around emotion is the subject most couples seek help with, just like Jeremy and Danielle did. Jeremy, a White man who grew up in California with hippie parents, was a professor of sociology. His wife, Danielle, was a Black woman of Nigerian descent who grew up in Minneapolis. Both were in their 60s, had been married for over 20 years, and reported a being in a rut in their marriage. Danielle had retired from a long career as a librarian one year earlier, and she'd been pressuring Jeremy to retire, too, so they could travel the world together. However, Jeremy loved his job and had no interest in retiring. They had been getting into fights, and both of them felt as though the other was not listening.

Jeremy and Danielle expressed emotions very differently from one another. In many ways, they went against gender norms related to emotional expression. For example, women tend to express more emotions in general (Kring & Gordon, 1998) and are socialized into caretaking roles from a young age (Rochat, 2023); thus they tend to exhibit more empathic, "vulnerable" emotions, such as anxiety and sadness. Men, on the other hand, are discouraged from expressing anxiety and sadness, which are interpreted as "weak" and "sissy" feelings (Fischer & LaFrance, 2015). Yet, with this couple, Jeremy was empathic and cried easily; he was highly emotionally sensitive and expressive. He was prone to anxiety, and he'd had several depressive episodes throughout his life. Danielle, however, identified as alexithymic and rarely expressed emotion outwardly. She tended to see the world through a more logical lens, and she believed that she was probably autistic, though she'd never been tested.

Danielle and Jeremy, like everyone, have multiple ways to express their feelings. I am defining **emotional expression** here as any way in which the emotion comes from inside the mind and body to the outside (i.e., an emotional broadcast). There are two basic types of emotional broadcasts. Because emotions are social, expression often involves **emotional sharing**—the type of broadcast in which feelings are made obvious to one or more others, through words, tone of voice, or body language. The *Broadcaster* is the person who has feelings to express. The *Receiver* is the observer who takes in the Broadcaster's message. Multiple Receivers are also possible, if a Broadcaster sends the message out in a public setting (e.g., angrily shouting on the bus) or to multiple friends at once (e.g., crying over a breakup with two friends and a bottle of wine). We'll spend most of this chapter talking about emotional sharing.

The second type of emotional expression is the solo broadcast, which is expression without sharing, simply bringing feelings from the inside to the outside with no one else around. Let's talk about that first.

Expression Without Sharing

When I think about expressing without sharing, my first thought goes to people crying alone, which is quite common (Bylsma, Vingerhoets, et al., 2008). Jeremy used solo crying as a central form of expression, often on the way home from work or late in the night, after Danielle had fallen asleep. Some people tend to think of expressing feelings alone as cathartic, with the idea of releasing the emotion from the body (Bylsma, Vingerhoets, et al., 2008). *Frozen* princess Elsa singing "Let It Go" on a mountaintop while building an ice castle using her magical snow powers (Buck & Lee, 2013) is a classic example of expressing without sharing. Other forms of cathartic expression could include letting loose a primal scream, or exercising vigorously (e.g., hitting a punching bag, going on a long run).

One valuable form of expression without sharing is *journaling*. Danielle did this. She set aside time every Sunday afternoon to write. Sometimes she wrote about her reactions to the events of the week, sometimes she delved into the family drama of her past, and sometimes she wrote to help her sift through the thoughts and feelings underlying her most recent paintings. The specific topic doesn't matter. What does matter is that the writing is intentionally deep and emotional. Exhibit 8.1 provides an example of the types of prompts given to participants in the original expressive writing studies conducted by Pennebaker (1997), which I recommend you try for yourself.

The benefits of expressive writing are truly astounding. The studies found that compared with people who wrote about mundane,

---

EXHIBIT 8.1. Expressive Writing Prompts

Set aside 20–30 minutes per day for 3 days in a row. Set a timer if you'd like. You can write on a computer (e.g., typing) or freehand, with a pen or pencil and paper.

1. Write about your very deepest thoughts and feelings. You can write about any difficult or emotionally disturbing events you're going through, or that you've experienced in the past. Stressful or traumatic experiences can be tied in, too. Really let go and explore your deepest thoughts and feelings. Feel free to write about your relationships with others. You could write about how your thoughts and feelings may be linked to your past, who you are now, or who you want to be in the future.
2. You can write about the same issue each day, or about a new issue. That doesn't matter.
3. Don't worry about spelling or grammar, or about form or style, or sentence structure. This is just for you.
4. Keep writing for at least 20 minutes. If you run out of things to say, repeat what you've already said. Just keep writing.

A note: Many people feel a bit sad or down after doing this task, particularly on the first day. However, the mood will lift after a bit. Don't let the immediate down feeling stop you from writing on the second and third days. Remember that this activity is designed to help you in the long run—feeling a bit of pain now allows for growth and less pain later!

---

unemotional topics (e.g., daily tasks and activities), people who engaged in expressive, emotional writing had better mental health, better physical health (Pennebaker, 1997), and stronger relationships (Slatcher & Pennebaker, 2006). These positive outcomes persisted over time, even though the people in the expressive writing group tended to feel significant distress during and right after writing. Remember in Chapter 6, when we talked about the trade-off that can sometimes occur between what people want to feel, or what is helpful in the short term, and what is helpful in the long run? Expressive writing hurts in the short term, because writing about truly deep and serious experiences, including traumas, grief and death, and loneliness, is painful. However, there are remarkable long-term benefits of expressing feelings to yourself, without ever showing them to anyone.

Interestingly, it's not the "releasing" that is psychologically helpful (Baikie & Wilhelm, 2005). Instead, when people express their feelings in writing, they start to label their feelings (revisit Chapter 4 for a reminder about how great labeling is). People who engage in several days of expressive writing get the most benefit from it and start using more positive emotion words (e.g., "joy," "relief," "relaxation," "contentment"), along with a moderate amount of negative emotion words, as well as words that convey meaning-making (e.g., "understanding," "because," "reason"; Pennebaker, 1997). When people create a narrative understanding of their life events, including difficult, stressful, or traumatic incidents, healing happens.

Expression without sharing is about broadcasting the emotion to yourself, and that's not super helpful on its own—you also need to listen to your own broadcast. Said differently, "letting feelings out" helps the most when there are reflection and understanding accompanies the expression. When you tune in to your own emotions by recognizing them, labeling them, and processing what they mean to you, your emotional health can improve.

Emotional Sharing

Emotional sharing is about letting someone else access your emotional broadcasts. There are two main channels, so to speak, of emotional sharing. The first is the verbal channel—when emotions are clearly verbally articulated, like an all-points bulletin emotional broadcast. For example, a few days after their beloved cat died at the vet, Jeremy said, "I'm sad we didn't get to say goodbye." Danielle, as the Receiver, touched Jeremy's arm and said, "I'm sad too," and then they hugged and cried together.

The other channel is the nonverbal emotional channel. Facial expressions, tone of voice, *vocal bursts* (brief, nonword utterances, e.g., growls, sighs, "oooh"s, yelps; Simon-Thomas et al., 2009), body language, the intensity of the words selected, speed of speech, and loudness of speech are all ways that people broadcast their feelings. These nonverbal methods of broadcasting are very effective forms of communication—nonverbal signals can convey a person's emotional state faster and more efficiently than words (Izard, 2010).

As a species, human beings are exceptional at receiving emotional broadcasts from the nonverbal channel. You can see the love two people share by observing beaming eyes, gentle touch, and a soft smile, just as you can immediately sense anger from a furrowed brow, raised eyes, and a tense physical stance. Babies and toddlers who don't have language are masters at nonverbal broadcasts, smiling and gurgling to show joy and crying to show hunger or the need for a diaper change. Even the tone of written text on social media can convey emotion. For example, one study found that people who were depressed didn't explicitly discuss their depressed mood on Facebook, but trained coders were able to pick up symptoms of depression from the way they phrased their messages (Bazarova et al., 2017).

People who are highly emotionally sensitive, like Jeremy, often broadcast on the nonverbal channel. For example, every day when

Jeremy came home from work, Danielle would ask, "How was your day?" and he would reply, "A day like any other," regardless of what had happened that day. His words weren't a clue to how he was feeling, but his body language was. When he came through the door whistling, stopped to get the mail on his way in, or wiggled his eyebrows at Danielle, he was generally in a good mood. But when he took his shoes off immediately upon coming through the door, or sighed deeply, Danielle knew he wasn't feeling so great. It took her time to learn his emotional broadcast "tells," but they were far more helpful to her in sensing his mood than his words were. This is an example of a crossed signal—when the broadcast coming from the verbal channel does not match the broadcast from the nonverbal channel.

Think about the typical methods you use to share your emotions. Do you state your feelings directly, with clear verbal labels? Do you show your feelings nonverbally, in the form of how much effort you put into your hair that day, or how quickly you are walking, or your posture, or your tone of voice? Which channels do you rely on, or which channels do you try to shut down? Do you send crossed signals—different broadcasts on different channels? When someone asks you, "How are you?" do you say, "I'm fine!" even when you are anything but fine? If you aren't sure of your broadcast tendencies, this is a good opportunity to ask someone close to you how (or if) can they tell when you're all up in your feelings.

PROS AND CONS OF EXPRESSIVE SUPPRESSION AND EMOTIONAL SHARING

One of the central functions of emotions is to facilitate communication with others (Izard, 2010), and communicating about positive emotions tends to be much simpler. Most people tend to be fine with broadcasting excitement, amusement, interest, and joy (or any other positive feeling; Gross & John, 1995). These pleasant feelings tend to be warmly received, and they can feel contagious (Hatfield et al., 1993). Sure, there are times and situations in which sharing positive emotions may be a poor idea (e.g., sharing pride at getting a job offer with a friend who has just been fired), but in general sharing positive feelings creates bonds, helps with impression management, and can inspire others (Sels et al., 2021).

But there are all kinds of ways in which broadcasting and receiving can go wrong, and these occur more commonly when sharing unpleasant or distressing feelings. For example, crossed-signal broadcasts can be confusing; which channel should the Receiver listen to? Sometimes, nonverbal broadcasts feel strong to the Broadcaster, but the signal is actually too weak for a Receiver to pick up. Or, a particular Receiver might be oblivious and doesn't notice—or actively ignores—obvious broadcasts. Emotional sharing can be a minefield!! This is why people often try to stop those broadcasts from going out by hiding or masking their negative feelings from others (i.e., expressive suppression). Babies and little kids don't really use expressive suppression; they don't know how. But as kids get older, they learn how to mask their feelings, in part because of societal expectations that being mature and grown-up means getting control of those "irrational" feelings (e.g., "There's no crying in baseball!" or "Big Girls Don't Cry," or a hundred other examples). I suspect every adult has masked their feelings at least once. I know I have!

However, there are real downsides to blocking those emotional broadcasts and significant advantages of intentionally and openly sharing. But, if we're being honest, there are also advantages to sometimes hiding emotional expressions, and some clear disadvantages to sharing emotions, too. Table 8.1 provides an overview of the pros and cons of both suppressing and sharing emotions, and the next sections unpack the benefits and pitfalls in detail.

TABLE 8.1. Pros and Cons of Sharing and Suppressing

Action	Pros	Cons
Sharing emotions with others	• You get a sounding board • Reduces distress about distress • You get validation and support • Outsourcing problem-solving • You get out of emotional tunnel vision • Increases insight • Facilitates development and maintenance of relationships	• Invalidation and negative feedback from others (e.g., "unprofessional") • Can harm relationships (e.g., blaming, criticism) • Problematic interpersonal regulation (venting/corumination, excessive reassurance seeking) • Perception that one is a burden
Expressive suppression (masking feelings from others)	• Can reduce distress • Useful in some situations (e.g., when being the Receiver, when not socially appropriate, with toxic people) • The ability to suppress, when used flexibly, increases emotional control	• Habitual use associated with increased negative emotions and symptoms of psychopathology • Effortful, takes resources • Doesn't really work • Harms relationships when people aren't authentic; can anyone be known without being vulnerable?

Cons of Expressive Suppression

The cons of expressive suppression are substantial: Habitually masking or blocking emotional broadcasts is associated with poor mental health outcomes. Hundreds of studies have shown that people who use expressive suppression frequently tend to have more symptoms of anxiety and depression (Aldao et al., 2010; Naragon-Gainey et al., 2017), less happiness (Fernandes & Tone, 2021), lower overall well-being (Haga et al., 2009), and poorer social relationships (Chervonsky & Hunt, 2017). Why is expressive suppression so bad?

The first reason is that expressive suppression tends to prolong negative emotions (Brans et al., 2013). Masking one's feelings doesn't usually make the feelings go away. Remember that emotions are intended to be expressed, which means that attempts to mask or block the broadcast takes physical and mental effort. Using effort for suppression results in greater internal physiological reactivity to emotions (Tyra et al., 2024). If the emotional broadcast is blocked, it just turns inward and builds up inside of you.

The second reason why expressive suppression isn't great as a go-to regulation strategy is that hiding feelings results in poorer relationships. People who suppress the expression of their feelings are not known. I can't even count the number of times I've encountered a therapy client who feels lonely and disconnected and masks their real feelings. They have a public side and a private side, and the private side is kept hidden behind an "Everything's fine" mask. Is it even possible to feel loved and accepted and truly connected to another person if only part of the self is known, when only the public side is visible? No. We need to share the private side to feel truly connected. This is why people in Western countries who habitually use expressive suppression are rated as less likable (Gross & John, 2003).

Notice that part about Western countries? One of the most interesting insights from cross-cultural research on emotional expression is that people from collectivist cultures (e.g., East Asian countries,

India, and many South American and African countries), which value social harmony, loyalty, and the needs of the community, don't show the same kinds of negative outcomes from expressive suppression as people from individualistic cultures (e.g., the United States, Canada, and much of Western Europe), which put more emphasis on individual rights and achievements (Soto et al., 2011). For example, if Ilana from Canada masks her feelings, she may feel inauthentic and like she's unable to show her true self. These kinds of interpretations are likely to contribute to her feeling disconnected and perhaps even depressed. Yet if Gita from India masks her feelings, she may feel proud of herself for her ability to attend to the well-being of her family.

An individual's norms about whether emotions should be shared or hidden are shaped not only by broader cultural or country contexts but also by family. For example, Jeremy's hippie parents expressed a lot of joy, but also sadness, so Jeremy learned that expressing those emotions was normal. In couples therapy, Danielle revealed that she'd been more emotionally expressive as a kid, but her parents had made fun of her meltdowns, telling her she was a "baby" and that she needed to "get herself together." She'd learned to shut down her emotional broadcasts. Understanding this helped both of them recognize that their habits were rooted in cultural expectations (Perel, 2001) and provided a pathway forward. Jeremy explained to Danielle that when she didn't express her feelings, he didn't feel like he could express his own feelings. He also told her that he felt disconnected. She hadn't realized that her use of expressive suppression—which was not an effort to block him out but an adaptive reaction to her upbringing—was one of the factors contributing to their marital stuckness.

Pros of Expressive Suppression

If expressive suppression is so bad for mental and emotional health, why do people keep doing it? There are many reasons why people hide their feelings from others! The most notable are that people don't want their private, internal, vulnerable information broadcast outwardly. Some people believe that expressing emotions is a sign of weakness (Laghai & Joseph, 2000). Some people don't want to burden others with their feelings. Some believe that expressing negative feelings will leave them vulnerable to attacks from others.

It is also the case that expressive suppression can serve as a dampening-the-response (see Chapter 7) emotion regulation strategy (Webb et al., 2012). When people have an emotion they don't want, blocking the broadcast can sometimes help them gain control of themselves. I have certainly experienced this myself. When I'm upset, if someone notices nonverbal signals of emotion, like my eyes are starting to water or my face is red, and they ask me to share my feelings verbally, I will invariably break down and start crying. But, if I can successfully stop the broadcast and pretend like everything is OK, I can refocus on something else (e.g., use distraction; see Chapter 7) and retain a sense of control.

There is a time and a place for expressive suppression. In fact, it's advantageous for a person to be able to share sometimes and suppress or mask emotions at other times—this multipronged ability is called **expressive flexibility.** Research studies have shown that people who can intentionally enhance their expression (i.e., express more) and intentionally suppress it (i.e., express less) in a contextually sensitive way tend to have more adaptive responses to stress (Westphal et al., 2010) and higher life satisfaction (Chen et al., 2018).

When is expressive suppression advantageous? I've posed this question to students in my classes, and they've supplied some thoughtful answers.

One student said that it's probably helpful to use expressive suppression when you are supposed to be the Receiver of someone else's emotional broadcast. When your task is to listen to someone else's emotions, it might benefit the relationship for you to mask your own feelings to give their broadcast some airspace.

A few other students suggested that there may be times when broadcasting is inconsistent with social norms. For example, laughing at a funeral is thought to be in poor taste (unless, of course, the service is intended to spark joyful memories). Breaking down crying during a job interview may be viewed as a red flag by a hiring manager. These might be reasonable times to use expressive suppression.

There also are people who are just bad at receiving. Some people just act like jerks in response to other people's emotions. Victims of domestic violence and children of volatile parents (e.g., parents who overused alcohol or drugs) often learn to use expressive suppression as a defense strategy. When a Broadcaster is demeaned, criticized, and blamed, expressive suppression can help protect that person from further harm.

The take-home point here is that expressive suppression should not be used all the time, but having the ability to suppress is useful. Why? Because when people know they can suppress expressing their emotions, they feel more agentic and have greater perceptions of emotional control (Ford & Gross, 2019). In general, people who think they are more capable of regulation tend to use expressive suppression more strategically (Geisler & Schröder-Abé, 2015).

Cons of Emotional Sharing

People turn to expressive suppression because they fear that expressing their emotions will have negative consequences. Unfortunately, sometimes these fears are true. There can be real hazards to broadcasting feelings. Two of these feel particularly bad for the Broadcaster (invalidation and blaming), and two actually feel pretty good for the Broadcaster but have long-term negative repercussions (venting and excessive reassurance seeking).

INVALIDATION AND BLAMING

The most obvious con of emotional sharing is the possibility of emotional invalidation. **Emotional invalidation, which we first talked about in Chapter 1, is when a Broadcaster perceives that the Receiver thinks that their emotions are incorrect, inappropriate, or wrong** (Zielinski & Veilleux, 2018). Note that it's about the Broadcaster's perception; a Broadcaster can feel invalidated even if the Receiver did not intend to belittle the Broadcaster's feelings. In fact, sometimes Receivers accidentally stumble into invalidation with well-meaning intentions. For example, phrases like "Just try to see the silver lining," or my personal pet peeve response to grief, "He's in a better place now," are meant be supportive. Yet to the Broadcaster, it can feel like the Receiver is saying, "Stop feeling this way. Get over these bad feelings that you're infecting me with. Be happy. NOW!"

When a Receiver doesn't treat the Broadcaster's feelings with care, it feels horrible. Upsetting emotions are bad enough, but then to have those emotions invalidated by others? The momentary pain is worse, the Broadcaster's trust in the Receiver goes down, the relationship gets shakier, and the Broadcaster will be less likely to share in the future.

Jeremy frequently felt invalidated by Danielle. Earlier in their relationship, Jeremy's habit was to come home and share his daily stress with his wife. Danielle tried to be a good Receiver and listen to him, but over time she started to realize he was saying basically the same thing every day, and she started to tune him out. She peeked at her watch, or she mentally checked out, daydreaming or planning her next painting. Her intention wasn't to be invalidating, but Jeremy noticed her inattention and assumed she just didn't care.

A related con of emotional sharing is blaming, which can occur in response to invalidation. Blaming involves attributing the generation of emotion to another person. Statements like "You made me sad," or "You don't care about me or my feelings" are blaming statements. Blaming, along with criticism and contempt (which involves attacking a person's character, not just their actions), are part of what famed couples therapist John Gottman calls "The Four Horsemen of the Apocalypse" (see Gottman & Silver, 2015). Gottman identified blaming, contempt, defensiveness, and stonewalling as the four problematic communication strategies that predict divorce. Many couples therapies aim to decrease the use of these communication styles.

Blaming and contempt are problematic because, although they do involve emotional sharing, they don't involve the Broadcaster owning or taking responsibility for their own feelings. Jeremy was particularly prone to blaming. He said things like, "If you would only set down your painting, I wouldn't be so angry" or, even worse, "You're ignoring me on purpose to make me feel sad." In response, Danielle stonewalled him by saying nothing and leaving the room. Her nonresponse incited him even further, and he'd lash out at her for allegedly causing his strong emotional response. When emotional expression involves blaming, it's the equivalent of saying, "You're the reason I'm getting this emotional message." Now, it may be that the Broadcaster's emotions are in fact related to the actions of the Receiver. But remember that it is the Broadcaster's values sending the messages (see Chapter 6), after attending to and interpreting the actions of the Receiver (see the discussion of the cycle of emotion generation in Chapter 2). It may seem like actions directly cause emotions, but they don't.

VENTING AND EXCESSIVE REASSURANCE SEEKING

The other major cons of emotional expression, venting and excessive reassurance seeking, are cons in the long run but can actually feel really good in the short term (refer back to Chapter 6 for the discussion of long- and short-term trade-offs). Venting and reassurance seeking are **interpersonal emotion regulation** strategies—methods of trying to regulate emotions via other people (Zaki & Williams, 2013). **Venting** is about airing out emotions, similar to the catharsis people often seek from expression without sharing. I often hear friends say "I need to vent," and they launch into an emotional tale of woe. **Reassurance seeking** often accompanies venting because a Broadcaster wants to know that their feelings aren't crazy, their reactions make sense, and that someone is in their corner. These were go-to interpersonal regulation strategies for Jeremy. He wanted Danielle to listen to him recount his stressors and tell him everything would be OK.

Perhaps you are wondering why venting and reassurance seeking are in the "cons" category. Isn't getting the emotions out a good thing? After all, we vent the steam above a kitchen stove because if we didn't, the house might burn down. The steam needs a place to go, to be let out. Isn't that true of emotions, too? And isn't getting social support and reassurance from friends good too, both for the Sharer and for solidifying relationship bonds?

There are two reasons why venting and excessive reassurance seeking are problematic. The first is that these strategies tend to prolong upsetting feelings (Tice & Bratslavsky, 2000). Venting invites **corumination**, which is rumination with a partner. When people vent, they aren't usually looking for processing, understanding, or meaning-making (Rose, 2021). They unconsciously seek commiseration—for someone to join them in their misery (i.e., co-misery).

Because Danielle never really jumped onto the corumination train when Jeremy vented at her, Jeremy found a friend who would. For example, Jeremy told his friend the story of a contentious faculty meeting two weeks ago, and his friend said, "How *dare* she have said that during the faculty meeting? Doesn't she know the rules?" Jeremy responded with "She clearly doesn't, because she said the same thing this week!" This example points out the central elements of venting: complaining about other people (and/or detailing an ongoing situation) without a lot of clear emotional labeling but plenty of nonverbal expression.

Venting and corumination can feel validating. Jeremy aired or vented his frustration by storytelling, and his Receiver friend ended up feeling a similar righteous indignation. These shared feelings can seem like bonding, and the Broadcaster often gets the reassurance they seek. But the negative emotion persists for longer than it would without the venting/corumination. Even more problematically, there is typically no resolution or problem-solving in these kinds of conversations. Growth comes from processing feelings, not airing them.

The second problem with venting and excessive reassurance seeking is that relying on them as go-to methods of managing emotions is associated with poorer mental health outcomes (Dixon-Gordon et al., 2018; Evraire & Dozois, 2011; Joiner & Metalsky, 2001). Why? Because overuse of reassurance seeking and venting are related to perceptions of low controllability (Khosravani et al., 2020), which we talked about in Chapter 7. If someone doesn't trust their own thoughts or feel in control of their emotions, they may have a hard time providing themselves reassurance or processing the feelings on their own (e.g., via journaling). They then seek help from others. Commiserating and getting soothed by others provides temporary relief, but the uncontrollable, self-critical, and "What if I *am* crazy?" thoughts creep back in and can't be squashed without someone else to squash them (Osborne & Williams, 2013).

There is nothing inherently wrong with wanting to share an emotional experience with someone else, or even with seeking (and getting) emotional reassurance. In fact, these are some of the real advantages of emotional broadcasts. But venting and excessive reassurance seeking are harmful to long-term emotional health, so the trick is to find ways to share without venting and limit the reassurance seeking, and find ways to provide reassurance to yourself, too.

Pros of Emotional Sharing

There are huge benefits of emotional sharing, for both the Broad-caster's emotions and the relationship between the Broadcaster and the Receiver. Jeremy and Danielle found this to be the case. When they both learned to share their feelings directly, and ask for what they wanted, they each found their own emotions easier to deal with, and their relationship was stronger for it. How does this work?

Benefit for Broadcaster

This chapter is technically about emotional expression, but it is also about interpersonal emotion regulation, in which, as described earlier, the presence of another person can make emotion regulation easier and/or more effective. There are several benefits to the Broadcaster consistent with interpersonal emotion regulation that come from sharing feelings.

Sounding Board. When the Broadcaster talks out loud about their emotional experiences and doesn't really care who the Receiver is or what they say, the Broadcaster can get the sounding-board benefit. The sounding-board benefit occurs when the Broadcaster hears them-self talk and they work through their own emotional situations, like expressive writing, but out loud and with another person nearby (Zaki & Williams, 2013).

When I first introduced the sounding-board concept to Jeremy and Danielle, Jeremy immediately perked up and said, "I do this!" He said that when he griped out loud, he wanted Danielle to serve as a sounding board. Danielle wrinkled her nose and said, "But it seems like you want me to be involved in the conversation, it doesn't seem—sorry, Honey, real talk here—that you're actually processing your gripes." Danielle was right—Jeremy was venting. If, instead, he didn't care what her response was and just talked for the sake of talking things through, that would be sounding-board sharing.

Reducing Distress About Distress. Some of the pros to emotional sharing are direct counterpoints to the cons of expressive suppression, namely, where expressive suppression tends to prolong feelings, expressing feelings tends to reduce the overall intensity and length of distress. This may sound counterintuitive, because I've heard people say that they're afraid that if they express their feelings, the feelings will get stronger. There is some truth to this—attending to and processing emotions does intensify feelings temporarily (Baikie & Wilhelm, 2005). But then the emotional wave crests and falls, and the result is an overall shorter emotional experience. It's kind of like the "ripping the Band-Aid off" idea—when you do it quickly, the pain is more intense but shorter lived, whereas pulling it off slowly avoids the burst of pain, but the pain lasts longer.

Expressing primary emotions is particularly helpful in shortening the overall length of emotions. That's because when primary emotions are broadcast, the likelihood of metaemotions (which you may recall from Chapter 6 are emotions about emotions) decreases. For example, Jeremy wanted to raise a controversial issue in a faculty meeting, but he was worried about saying the wrong thing. Afterward, he was angry at himself for feeling worried. He thought to himself, "You're not a real man. You didn't speak up. You shouldn't feel nervous in a department you've worked in for 20 years!" But, if Jeremy had expressed his primary feeling by saying, "I've got something to say, but I'm a bit anxious to voice it," he would have used the labeling superpower (see Chapter 4), circumvented the metaemotion of anger, and likely received validation from his colleagues (see next section), which would result in the whole emotional event resolving much faster.

Getting Validation and Support. What most people want when they share emotions are **validation** and support (Liu et al., 2021). People want to hear that their emotions are understandable, they want to know that others have felt the same way, and they want to be soothed (Hofmann et al., 2016). When a Receiver says something like, "Oh, man, that's rough" or "I felt just like that last week!" the Broadcaster gets help with dampening the response (see Chapter 7).

Validation and support feel fantastic to receive, but there is a paradox. When broadcasting, people are reticent about sharing their emotions with others, but the same people are often quite validating of other people's emotions when in the Receiver role.

I feel the validation paradox deeply. When I have feelings to share, I sometimes think, "I don't need to dump my own stuff on other people." Yet, when I'm the Receiver, whether as a friend, a teacher, a mentor, a supervisor, or a therapist, I'm never thinking, "This person's feelings are a burden to me." Perhaps my training as a therapist and my intellectual interest in emotions make me atypical, but I think many people want to be there for their friends, they want to be known as someone who can be turned to for help. So why do we assume that other people don't want to receive, when we often do?

I don't have a firm answer here, but I strongly suspect that one potential reason is the beast of self-criticism. We humans are far more judgmental and critical of ourselves than we are of our friends (Neff, 2003). Because we hate our own feelings, we expect that others will hate them, too. Yet other people can be very kind and gracious when given the chance.

Jeremy encountered this when he inadvertently teared up during a happy hour the day after his cat, Fezzik, died. He tried to suppress his feelings, but he remembered that we'd talked in couples therapy about the benefits of expression. Instead, he simply said, "I'm sorry, everyone; I'm having a rough day and feeling sad because my cat died." His colleagues surprised him with how validating they were—they asked to see pictures of Fezzik, commiserated with him about how hard pet deaths can be, and went to get him a Kleenex. Jeremy found out firsthand that when he took the risk and allowed his emotional broadcasts to go out, his feelings were validated, and although he was still sad, the sting of his sadness diminished.

Outsourcing Problem-Solving. Outsourcing problem-solving is essentially getting help with changing the trigger (see Chapter 7). When emotions are strong, logical thinking is often impaired (Veilleux et al., 2022). In these situations, it makes sense to turn to someone whose thinking is clearer.

I am part of a Facebook group with about 500 academic women who have children about the same age. It's a very niche group, and incredibly emotionally supportive even though most of us have never met in real life. Almost every day, someone posts about an emotional event or stressor, sometimes related to children ("My kid keeps having poop accidents in his underwear and it's gross"), sometimes related to work ("I'm so mad my boss is trying to block my promotion!") and sometimes related to other kinds of relationships ("My mother-in-law is visiting and she keeps trying to tell my daughter to lose weight, and I might throttle her if she doesn't shut up. Help?!?!"). Much of the time, the post is related to advice: What would these other like-minded women do in this situation? Sharing feelings with someone else (or 500 someone elses!) can elicit great social modeling because people who've been there can give you ideas you wouldn't have generated on your own (Hofmann et al., 2016). Getting information on how other people have successfully dealt with similar situations can prompt hope and motivation to tackle tricky problems.

Getting Out of the Tunnel. Especially for emotionally sensitive folks who experience strong emotions (see Chapter 1), emotions can wreak havoc with attention (see Chapter 2), creating a kind of emotional tunnel vision so that it's hard to see anything besides the emotion (Gable & Harmon-Jones, 2010). In an emotional tunnel vision situation, the multiple pathways a person took to get into the tunnel and—perhaps even more important—the multiple pathways for getting out are obscured. The Receiver can help the Broadcaster out of the tunnel by assisting with thinking-based regulation strategies, namely shifting thoughts and distraction (see Chapter 7).

Have you ever called a friend and shared your feelings and said, "But I don't really want to think any more about this right now. Tell me what's going on with you."? The Receiver can crack jokes, entertain the Broadcaster, or just shift the focus over to themselves, which can help regulate distress (Battaglini et al., 2023).

The other way the Receiver helps the Broadcaster out of the emotional tunnel is by facilitating perspective-taking by helping the Broadcaster reframe or reappraise the situation (Battaglini et al., 2023; Liu et al., 2021). In fact, sometimes simply asking questions can help jump-start the Broadcaster's own reflective processes.

For example, Danielle identified as alexithymic (see Chapter 2) and struggled to understand, label, and share her emotions. When I suggested that Danielle narrate her emotional responses out loud to Jeremy, she resisted at first. She said, "I wouldn't even know what to say." Because Jeremy was invested in finding out more about Danielle's internal experiences, he was able to prompt her by asking her questions. On one occasion, Danielle appeared grumpy, and Jeremy asked her to share how she was feeling. She said, "I'm not feeling anything!" Jeremy said, "All right, walk me through what you've done in the last few hours." Danielle started talking about how earlier that afternoon she had to wash her painting clothes twice because the washer hadn't done a good job the first time, and she'd had less time to paint as a result. As she was talking, she stopped herself short. "Oh," she said. "I was *frustrated*." She then said, "I could have put on different clothes and painted anyway, but I got stuck thinking I had to wear *those* clothes. How silly of me." She laughed at herself. Jeremy facilitated perspective-taking even further when he said, "I know that was frustrating, but I'm so impressed you were able to regroup and keep going, and that you made something so lovely in a shorter amount of time!"

This example shows how sharing emotions can help prompt labeling and reappraisal and that interpersonal emotional sharing can include multiple strategies at once. In fact, people typically want validation and caring, but it's perspective-taking that actually helps the most (Pauw et al., 2019). Why not get both? When the Receiver can help soothe hurt feelings (Hofmann et al., 2016) and help the Broadcaster see the situation from a different angle, both short-term relief and long-term growth can occur.

BENEFIT TO RELATIONSHIPS

One of the most profound benefits of sharing emotions—particularly vulnerable emotions, like sadness, grief, regret, embarrassment, and anxiety—is in forging social bonds and increasing the strength of already-existing relationships (Niven, 2017; Shariff & Tracey, 2011). This is particularly true for people who have strong interpersonal values in their Top Tier (Intimacy, Belonging, Caring, etc.; see Chapter 3).

There is a common misconception that the Receiver needs to be part of one's circle of trust before emotions can be shared. In fact, when I discuss the benefits of expression with clients or students, they agree 100% that having close friends (or a therapist) to share emotions with is beneficial. But they think that trust and closeness must be earned first.

It actually works the other way around. Sharing vulnerable emotions is how we develop close relationships (Kennedy-Moore & Watson, 2001). Think about your close friends. You probably started to feel closer to them when they shared their feelings with you. Likewise, your friends feel closer to you when you share with them. That's because there are real benefits to emotional broadcasting for the Receiver (Niven, 2017). It can feel like a gift to be let in to someone else's emotional life. As a therapist, I am often struck by how much closer I feel to clients after they broadcast feelings to me in session and how grateful I am that they took the risk to be vulnerable with me. I feel helpful being able to sit with someone in their pain, providing validation and helping them regulate their emotions. I feel similarly when I'm gifted the emotional broadcasts of my students, my friends, and my children—like their feelings are a song I didn't set out to hear, but listening to that song together gives us a shared experience that links us together.

Don't get me wrong: I recognize that being emotionally open is scary! Emotions are core to who we are (remember that emotions are messages from values!), and sharing that core self with someone else can feel like a risk. But the risk can be worth it. When you share your feelings with someone else, you are sharing an important part of yourself. It is sharing this vulnerability that creates and maintains bonds, which is one of the most important benefits of emotional sharing with others.

INTEGRATING PROS AND CONS: TIPS FOR SUCCESSFUL SHARING

Expressive suppression as a go-to strategy is problematic, and the ability to express emotions is extremely beneficial. But are there times to suppress? Yes. Are there risks to expression? Yes!

So what is the take-home point? The ultimate goal is to get the benefits of sharing and the benefits of suppression by using emotional broadcasts strategically and flexibly. How on earth can you do that?!?!

Recognizing your own tendencies and habits is a good first step. What did your family and cultural groups expect in terms of what emotions are acceptable to express? Are you someone who masks your feelings, or who gets dinged for being emotionally cold (i.e., low emotional sensitivity or alexithymic)? If so, you might learn to broadcast more.

Are you someone who is an open book and shows every emotion, or maybe you try to amplify your emotions to get people to pay attention to you, like Jeremy? Are you in a relationship or cultural environment where expressing emotions isn't working for you? You might benefit from some additional skills around suppression, to learn a bit more emotional control. Or perhaps you aren't on either extreme but just want to be more flexible and strategic in your emotional expression.

No matter your starting place, most people could benefit from adopting some tips for successful sharing, starting with knowing what you want. Knowing what you want can help you select who to share with and what medium to share in, and to synchronize your broadcast channels. These tips can maximize the likelihood that you'll get the most benefit from your emotional broadcast.

Knowing What You Want

The first thing to consider as the Broadcaster is what you hope to get from sharing your feelings, while recognizing that you might want different things at different times. Be honest with yourself about what you want in each emotional sharing situation. Do you want to work through your feelings yourself, with a sounding board? Do you want validation and support? Do you want advice for how to solve a problem, or do you want to be distracted? Do you need help getting perspective on the situation because you've got emotional tunnel vision?

Knowing what you want makes it easier to get what you want. Remember that a combination of goals tends to be the most effective.

Seeking support and gaining perspective have the best outcomes (Behfar et al., 2020)!

Consider the Receiver(s)

Part of the reason why expressing emotions to others is complicated is that the choice of whom to express feelings to matters. Different Receivers have different skills, and the idea is to seek the Receivers who will be able to give you what you want. For example, my friend Katie is great at validation. My Facebook group is my go-to for problem-solving. My husband is my sounding board. I certainly don't always have the time and space to find the best Receiver when I have emotions to express, but thinking about who I'm with can definitely shape whether I let the broadcasts go out or whether I try to block the signal.

I've asked my students how they figure out who good Receivers for different kinds of goals are. They've said they learn through trial and error. One savvy student said that she likes to share less intense emotional information first to see how the Receiver responds, and if the response is favorable, then that shows the person can probably handle deeper or more personal feelings the next time.

An advantage of the trial-and-error method is that it can also reveal the Receivers with the tendency to invalidate, belittle, or discount emotions. These are people to consider avoiding emotional conversations with, and people to use expressive suppression with. Now, we're all capable of being poor Receivers on a bad day, when we are distracted or self-focused. Receiving is also a skill that can be learned, and some Receivers can be prompted to change their invalidating ways; it's not fair to assume that just because a Receiver was unhelpful or invalidating once that they will always be that way. But when a Receiver has shown a pattern of poor responses, don't give them the privilege of your emotional broadcasts.

There are cultural aspects to consider here too. It might not be fair, but Receivers often have different implicit standards for different Broadcasters' feelings on the basis of cultural norms. For example, when women express anger they are more likely to be labeled as having angry personality traits (e.g., called "a bitch"; Brescoll & Uhlmann, 2008), and this effect is amplified for Black women because of the stereotype of the "angry Black woman" (Walley-Jean, 2009).

Taking the time to think about the receiving skills and cultural expectations of people you encounter is a type of coping-ahead strategy (see Chapter 5) that can help you maximize the pros and minimize the cons of emotional expression.

Asking for What You Want

We've already discussed how the biggest con of emotional sharing is the risk of invalidation. When invalidation is unintentional—when the Receiver is not trying to discount feelings, but the Broadcaster doesn't feel heard, understood, or accepted—there is typically a mismatch between what the Broadcaster wants and what the Receiver thinks is best. This mismatch can be circumvented by the Broadcaster telling the Receiver what they want. Look at Exhibit 8.2 for some sample scripts.

A 2-minute spoof video called "It's Not the Nail" (Headley, 2013) conveys this mismatch beautifully. In the video, a woman with a nail in her forehead tries to get validation from her partner. He quickly jumps to telling her to remove the nail to solve her problem. She fires back that he is not listening, and she just wants some support. Begrudgingly, he provides caring by saying, "That must be so hard for you," and she melts, saying, "It is. Thank you."

The situation in the video is hilarious in part because it mimics what often occurs when the Receiver tries to fix the situation (i.e., outsourcing problem-solving), but the Broadcaster really just wants

EXHIBIT 8.2 Asking for What You Want

When sharing emotions with others, consider using one of these lines to ask for what you want from the interaction! This will increase the likelihood you'll get what you want.

- Sounding Board:
    - "I don't need a response from you, I'm just talking to work things out for myself."
- Outsourcing Problem-Solving:
    - "I want you to help me figure out what to do to make this situation better."
- Validation and Support:
    - "I just want you to give me a hug right now."
    - "I need for you to tell me things will be OK."
    - "I need you to just listen and tell me that this sucks."
- Normalization:
    - "I want to know if my feelings are completely out of control. Can you tell me if you'd feel similarly in my shoes?"
- Distraction:
    - "Thinking about this is pulling me into a tailspin. Can you distract me by telling me a story?"
- Perspective Taking:
    - "Is there another way to view this situation?"
    - "What can you see as an observer that I'm having trouble seeing because I'm stuck in the mud?"

Remember, though, that when the goals are validation and support the best outcomes come from getting support and letting the Receiver gently challenge you to see things from a different perspective!

to be heard, loved, and listened to (i.e., validation and support). This was often the dynamic with Danielle and Jeremy, but not in the gender-normative way that the video shows. In their relationship, Jeremy was the one wanting validation and caring, whereas Danielle tended to jump into logical problem-solving. Jeremy had called Danielle a "robot" because she seemed unfazed and unemotional much of the time. When she learned to adopt more verbal and physical validation skills during their conversations, Jeremy felt much more secure in the relationship.

Consider the Medium

Communication differs between an in-person conversation; a video call, like FaceTime or Zoom; an audio-only phone call; a text message; and an email. Remember, emotions convey messages faster and more efficiently on the nonverbal channel (Keltner et al., 2019), but some of those nonverbal signals will be lost or dampened when the medium changes. For example, a video chat uses facial expressions and tone of voice but may miss other body language. A phone call or voice memo has voice fluctuations but misses facial expressions. Text messages, emails, and social media posts could use memes and emojis, but they lack the nonverbal signals that phone, voice, and video can convey.

The central point here is that to share emotions successfully in technology-mediated ways (or with old-fashioned pen pal letters!), the Broadcaster needs to lean on the verbal channel because there are fewer nonverbal cues for the Receiver to pick up.

Synergize

Earlier in this chapter, we discussed mismatches between the verbal and nonverbal channels. This most often occurs when a person denies feelings verbally—"Nothing's wrong!"—but there are clear nonverbal distress broadcasts. A mismatch could also involve an emotional statement (e.g., "I'm sad!") said in a neutral or perky way.

Emotional sharing works best when the verbal statement of emotion matches the nonverbal aspects. This synergy is easier for the Receiver to interpret because there aren't two conflicting signals. Most often this means accurately conveying emotions verbally (but without blaming). For example, when Jeremy learned to say "I feel sad and unheard when you check your watch," Danielle knew to give him her full attention. Synergy can work in the other direction, too: Some people could benefit from amplifying their nonverbal signals so their verbal feelings are taken more seriously. Danielle did this and found that not only was Jeremy less disparaging of her, she also felt more in tune with her internal world.

Combining strategies is particularly effective. Synergizing the broadcast channels, asking for what you want, and strategically choosing your Receivers can make emotional sharing smoother—you can get the benefits of expression and minimize the potential damage.

CONCLUSION

I started this chapter by talking about *Zoey's Extraordinary Playlist*, a show in which a woman gets to hear and see other people's emotions in the form of songs. Ironically, Zoey initially relied on expressive suppression as her go-to regulation strategy. But, as the show progressed, she realized that receiving other people's emotional messages was a gift, not a curse. She got to know people's authentic, real selves. And eventually she started to share her feelings more, too.

Emotional expression is confusing because it's both a component of emotion and a regulation strategy. Expressions are built into the emotional experience because emotions are supposed to facilitate communication and forge relationships. Broadcasting emotions (whether to yourself, e.g., via expressive writing, or to others, e.g., with emotional sharing) can help with regulation. When we process our feelings, and obtain understanding, connection, and validation, our distressing emotions start to fade.

It is also the case that emotions are at the heart of relationship ruptures, breakups, and misunderstandings. You can see why expression is toward the end of the book, instead of the beginning, right?

The main lesson to walk away with is the one Zoey learned: Sharing and expressing emotions is a vital skill. Listening to other people's emotions is a vital skill, too. Learning to be both an effective Broadcaster and Receiver can give you the tools to be able to express flexibly.

SUMMARY POINTS

- Emotions are meant to be expressed, and they can be shared with others (intentionally or unintentionally).
- Engaging in expressive writing (e.g., focused journaling) can help people make sense of their feelings. Expressive writing is associated with better physical and mental health.
- There are pros and cons to intentionally sharing emotions and to intentionally trying to mask emotion (i.e., expressive suppression).
  - Cons of expressive suppression: Masking feelings is associated with worse mental health, and hiding feelings tends to actually prolong those feelings.
  - Pros of expressive suppression: Sometimes suppression can dampen the emotion, and sometimes suppression can help relationships (e.g., when suppression serves the other person).
  - Cons of emotional sharing: Other people can be invalidating, blaming is related to relationship disruption, venting seems helpful but prolongs the negative emotions, and excessive reassurance seeking is associated with low emotional control.

- Pros of emotional sharing: Expressing emotions to others reduces distress about distress, creates insight, and deepens relationships. Notably, humans tend to be more receptive to other people's feelings than we think others will be to ours, so maybe we could take a chance and share?

- To successfully share emotions with others, think about the goals for the interaction, the selection of the Receiver, and the medium (e.g., in person, phone, text). Asking for what you want can help you maximize the benefits you get from emotional expression.

- Synergize your nonverbal and verbal broadcasts to clarify the message.

CHAPTER 9

PUTTING ALL THE PIECES TOGETHER FLEXIBLY

Isabel initially was excited to soak in the lessons of this book. She was in her early 30s, had a master's degree in business, and was earning good money at a job she mostly enjoyed. She knew that on the surface, everything looked fine. In fact, she made sure that she was the "right" amount of chipper and perky to be well liked but stoic enough to be taken seriously. She had good friends, a nice car, and was building the capital to afford the down payment on a house.

Yet she sought therapy because things did not feel fine on the inside. She drank heavily on the weekends to feel numb, and she regularly skipped meals to feel a sense of control about her body. She was also desperately lonely but, paradoxically, afraid of commitment. She dated both men and women, but when a partner wanted to get closer to her she found an excuse to move on.

Isabel pursued therapy to try to get a sense of control over a life that felt like it was spiraling out of control. Her picture-perfect exterior felt more and more like a sham hiding a crumbling, weak interior. When her therapist suggested she learn more about emotions, Isabel was game. She'd always been a good student, and she gained a deeper appreciation of the complexity of emotions through her learning. She identified her level of emotional sensitivity (Chapter 1) and started increasing awareness of her emotions (Chapter 2). She completed a values clarification activity (Chapter 3). She struggled to enact the two secret superpowers of emotional labeling (Chapter 4) and coping ahead (Chapter 5), although she understood the purpose of buffering against future stressors. She was resistant to the idea of opening the envelope at first (Chapter 6), but considering goals was appealing to her, and she thought closely about her long-term emotional goals as well as her immediate goals, which were most often related to emotional relief. She happily built up her emotion regulation toolbox (Chapter 7), and she was interested in the benefits of using emotional expression to improve relationships (Chapter 8).

After doing all of that, she felt much more knowledgeable about emotions, and she'd started to feel a bit better. She was drinking less, and eating more, and as a result she was sleeping better and feeling stronger. She had started to explore how her values related to her commitment issues and her feelings of panic when another person started to get close to her. Yet she still felt like something was missing.

Isabel asked her therapist, "Is this it?"

Her therapist smiled and pointed out that achieving emotional health is a task we all have to keep working on—it's not as if learning the lessons in this book immediately fixes the problem. Emotions aren't a chipped tooth or a broken chair. We have to keep remembering to listen to what our emotions are telling us, and to try to be kind to our values for sending us these messages, even when we don't want them. Learning to regulate, modulate, and shape our emotional experiences also takes practice to make the strategies easily accessible and usable.

But, her therapist added, "There's also one more critical piece now that you've got all the building blocks. Now you have to learn how to be *flexible*."

What does it mean to be flexible when dealing with emotional messages? That's what this final chapter is all about.

DEFINING EMOTION REGULATION FLEXIBILITY

In the earlier days of research on emotion regulation and coping, flexibility wasn't a major topic of discussion. Instead, most scientists focused on figuring out the best and worst regulation and coping strategies.

This early research established many of the findings I've shared with you so far. For example, people who regularly mask their emotions tend to have weaker social relationships (Chervonsky & Hunt, 2017) and more symptoms of anxiety and depression (Aldao et al., 2010; Naragon-Gainey et al., 2017). Avoidance-based strategies (Bresin, 2020; Chawla & Ostafin, 2007) and strategies that keep people stuck in their emotions (e.g., rumination and worry; Ehring & Watkins, 2008; Segerstrom et al., 2000) were identified as bad or maladaptive. On the flip side, strategies like cognitive reinterpretation and obtaining social support were touted as adaptive, useful, and good (Clark, 2022; Naragon-Gainey et al., 2017).

The problem is that this early research didn't take context into account. There are no always-good strategies and always-bad strategies. Instead, *the strategy needs to fit the situation* (Aldao et al., 2015; Bonanno & Burton, 2013; Cheng, 2001, 2003; Crum et al., 2020). For example, worry can be helpful sometimes, because worry can help people take steps to protect themselves (Sweeny & Dooley, 2017). For example, worrying about sunburn or skin cancer can prompt people to wear sunscreen, which does protect against sun damage. Yet worrying frequently, or in situations that don't allow for actions (e.g., worrying after sun exposure that maybe skin cancer is imminent) can be overwhelming and debilitating.

The idea is that all the regulation tools are useful to have in a well-stocked toolbox. But just because a hammer is a good tool to own doesn't mean it's the best tool for all situations. Trying to hammer a screw into a wall is much less effective than using a screwdriver. The tool needs to fit the job at hand.

More recently, the emphasis has shifted from thinking about strategies as good or bad to thinking about building **emotion regulation flexibility** (Aldao et al., 2015; Bonanno & Burton, 2013). With emotion regulation flexibility, a person has enough tools in their toolbox to be able to adapt to the situation at hand and select a strategy that addresses the needs of the moment.

The concept of emotion regulation flexibility is intuitively appealing for many people. Including Isabel. When Isabel heard about the concept of emotion regulation flexibility, she immediately gravitated to it. She recognized that sometimes it was harder for her to push herself to express her feelings, and she noted times when problem-solving wasn't working. She wanted to be flexible, but she didn't know how to make flexibility happen.

Experts suggest that there are three main components of emotion regulation flexibility: (a) context sensitivity, (b) breadth of repertoire, and (c) monitoring and feedback (Bonanno & Burton, 2013). Let us review each of these components in turn and then talk about how to build up those components.

CONTEXT SENSITIVITY

If the task is to pick the strategy that best fits the situation (Wenzel et al., 2019), then defining the important features of situations becomes crucial. What features of a situation should a person be particularly sensitive to?

This is a deceptively difficult question, because there are a lot of ways to think about contexts or situations. Think about the situation you are in right now, reading this book. You could think about your location. Are you at home, or work, on the bus, or sitting at the airport? You could think about social contexts. Are you alone, are there strangers walking by, or are you lying in bed with a snoring partner next to you?

People do all kinds of activities throughout their days, which is another kind of context: reading, doing homework, talking on the phone, running on a trail, attending a concert, driving in traffic, getting the kids ready for school, or millions of other things. All of these reflect physical or environmental contexts that could be relevant for emotion regulation.

Psychological and physiological contexts matter, too. A person experiencing an emotion could be hungry or full, tired or rested, drunk or sober. They could be feeling supported or in the middle of an interpersonal conflict. Situations can have many different kinds of psychological features (Funder, 2016; Rauthmann et al., 2014). For example, does the situation require duty or responsibility? Is clear and logical thinking necessary? Is anyone being threatened? Are there opportunities for closeness and intimacy? Is there lying involved? People who are better able to identify psychological features of situations seem to have better flexibility (Cheng, 2003).

I wish I could say there are clear answers to which features of situations are most crucial to pay attention to. However, research on emotion regulation flexibility is still fairly new, and I suspect that we'll know more in a decade than we know now. It also may be the case that the relevance of situational factors differs across people. After all, people prioritize different values (Schwartz, 2012) and differ in their long- and short-term goals for emotions (Veilleux, Clift, et al., 2024), so it would make sense that the importance of contextual features might be idiosyncratic to some degree. We do know that people who seem to be able to identify more features of situations (e.g., recognition of resources, understanding the social parameters) seem to be better off (Cheng, 2003), which suggests that simply trying to tune in to the features of situations might be a useful training activity to strengthen the skills underlying flexibility.

There are a few contextual features we know are important when considering which emotion regulation strategy to select.

First, the *intensity* of the emotion matters. Some emotions are stronger than others, and stronger emotions may require more than one strategy (e.g., polyregulation; Ford et al., 2019) or strategies that are particularly well suited for strong emotions. For example, as discussed in Chapter 7, grounding (Linehan, 2015) is especially useful when emotions are strong because it helps people anchor to the present moment and act with intention rather than on impulse (Linehan, 2015; Veilleux et al., 2022).

Second, the *controllability* of the situation matters. When problems are solvable, solve them! Cognitive reappraisal is particularly good for unsolvable problems (Troy et al., 2013). When a problem is unsolvable (e.g., grief), it can be easy to dwell on it (i.e., ruminate) or engage in self-blame or self-criticism. Using cognitive reappraisal in these situations can help provide perspective or relief.

However, there are also uncontrollable situations in which cognitive reappraisal is likely ineffective, or perhaps even harmful. For example, think about a person who was the victim of sexist or ableist comments. Sexism or ableism may be solvable by society in the long run, but they are unsolvable in moments of time for individuals (Ford & Troy, 2019). Is using cognitive reappraisal valuable in this situation? Maybe, but saying "Oh, they really didn't mean it, they must have said that by accident" could be considered a form of self-invalidation. Reappraisal may be harmful if it is used to invalidate real experiences of distress.

Third, *social context* definitely matters. There are some strategies that are hard to use when other people are around, or the conflict is ongoing, and other strategies (e.g., asking for a hug) that are hard to use when alone. Who is around can definitely shape what the situation looks like, and what strategies are possible, because emotion regulation efforts also have an effect on the people nearby. For example, in Chapter 8 we talked about expressive flexibility (Westphal et al., 2010) and the value of being able to both show feelings and mask them, depending on the situation. In some interpersonal contexts (e.g., with a boss in a meeting), expressing emotion may result in a reprimand or a disparaging remark, whereas in another context (e.g., with a friend), expressing emotion may result in empathy and commiseration. Relatedly, other people can be really valuable for helping distract you when you really need to down-regulate quickly, whereas distraction is less necessary (and less valuable) in situations where you might have time to process feelings (Pauw et al., 2019).

Isabel had not thought much about context sensitivity before learning about emotion regulation flexibility. When she started thinking about it, she realized that she had different rules for herself when alone, when with people in her inner circle (her mother and her two closest friends), and when around anyone else. She despised feeling or showing emotions with most people, preferring others to see her as competent, easygoing, and positive. She masked her negative emotions most of the time, but she felt comfortable both allowing and expressing emotions with those in her inner circle.

Isabel realized that she wasn't particularly attentive to other kinds of contexts. She hadn't thought about controllability or about emotional intensity. Nor had she thought about how physical resources played a role in how she navigated her emotions until she started working on coping-ahead skills. She started thinking about all the nuances of her life, about how sometimes she might need to shift her strategy when trying to help other people with their emotions, like when she felt responsible for pushing her own emotions away to soothe her agitated boss. She also started thinking about her issues with commitment and how feeling trapped in a relationship might be a context she was ignoring but that probably influenced her emotional responses.

The idea of context sensitivity—that different strategies might be needed in different contexts—is intuitively appealing but hard to put into practice. One simple method is to ask yourself questions about different kinds of contexts, to see if you're attending to different elements. Possible questions are listed in Exhibit 9.1.

For instance, ask yourself, is this situation under my control, or are other people in control? Is this novel or familiar? Am I tired or hungry? How important is this situation—how much does this situation ignite my values? By revisiting these questions in different kinds of situations you may start to tune in to the different physical

---

EXHIBIT 9.1. Context Sensitivity Prompts

These are questions you can ask yourself to start tuning in to different situational contexts. Remember, you want to think about the current, momentary situation—not an unfolding multistage drama. This is the scene, not the overall show.

- Is the situation controllable? Am I controlling the situation, or is someone else controlling it?
- How important is this situation to me?
- How intense is the emotion right now? (Label the feeling, then rate from 0 to 100.)
- Is this situation new, or familiar?
- Do I have any specific obligations or duties in this situation?
- Is anyone (me or anyone else) being threatened?
- Is anyone (me or anyone else) lying?
- Are there opportunities for closeness and intimacy in this situation?
- Is clear thinking needed?
  - If yes, am I able to think clearly right now? Or is my mind scattered in many directions?
- Is there a problem to solve, and is it solvable?
  - If yes, do I feel capable of solving the problem?
- How hungry am I?
- How tired am I?
- Am I drinking, drunk, or on drugs? Am I hungover?

---

and psychological contexts that influence both your emotions and the choices you make to manage them.

Breadth of Repertoire

Having a broad repertoire to pull from is also important for emotion regulation flexibility. You need to have a big toolbox to be able to pull the ideal tool for the job! Many of the other chapters in this book are about building your repertoire. We reviewed many specific regulation strategies in Chapter 7, but other chapters are relevant, too. Emotional labeling (Chapter 4) is an important technique because it's an implicit or unconscious emotion regulation strategy (Torre & Lieberman, 2018). Coping ahead (Chapter 5) is like keeping your house in good shape so that you don't even need your toolbox as often. Expression (Chapter 8) is both a component of emotion and a way to regulate. Even things that don't feel like regulation strategies, such as emotional awareness and skills for reading the message of the emotion (Chapters 2 and 6), are actually tools to cultivate, too.

The reason why a broad and varied repertoire is useful is that it's hard to know ahead of time what tool will be needed. The same is true for home renovation projects. Some tools are used pretty regularly (hammer, screwdriver, hex wrench), and others are more specialized tools that aren't needed all the time. For example, a brass minihammer might not be needed often, but it's super helpful when you need to hammer nails in tight places. (Bonus: It can be used as a nutcracker!) There are all kinds of tools like this, which are annoying to lug around when you use them only once or twice a year but great to have on hand when the situation calls for them.

Something I haven't mentioned yet is that experts think that there are differences between emotion regulation *strategies* and **emotion regulation** *tactics* (Gross et al., 2019). The strategy is the overall approach to managing emotions (e.g., distraction, reappraisal, problem-solving). The tactic is the specific way in which the strategy is enacted. For example, Isabel often used distraction to avoid thinking about her life spiraling out of control, but she did this in a variety of different ways. She used different distraction tactics. Some tactics, like spending extra time on work, had benefits, such as praise from her boss and feeding her value of Achievement. Other tactics, such as binge drinking, were effective at getting her mind off her feelings and helping her feel looser but had negative consequences, such as hangovers and poor sleep.

A flexible regulator has a broad set of strategies and multiple tactics within each strategy domain. This is akin to having multiple types of screwdrivers—a flathead, a Phillips head, and some of the more unusual ones, too (e.g., spanner, Pozidriv, square or Robertson). Each is a different specific type of the same general tool, just as specific emotion regulation tactics are different unique varieties of an overall strategy. Table 9.1 lists some possible tactics within each strategy domain, with the recognition that there are many, many options for tactics!

For example, Isabel benefited from thinking about broadening her repertoire of both strategies and tactics. She liked distraction, but she recognized that spending all of her time working hurt her pursuit of other values (e.g., Intimacy, Beauty), and she knew that binge drinking multiple times per week wasn't helpful to her long-term mental or physical health. She learned to add other distraction tactics to her repertoire, including watching television, which she'd previously avoided because she thought it wasn't productive. However, she realized that watching cooking shows energized her desire to cook. When she cooked more, she ate more food of better quality, and she felt less of an urge to drink alcohol. Isabel also started doing art as a distraction tactic, which fed her value of Creativity.

Isabel also expanded her repertoire of strategies. She learned a variety of different cognitive reappraisal tools from her therapist,

TABLE 9.1. Strategies and Tactics

Strategy	Example tactics (There are many possible options here!)
Problem-solving	• Create a boundary with a person causing problems in your life. • Go to your professor's office hours to get tips on successful studying. • Hire a house cleaner (throw money at the problem). *In general, identifying and defining the problem, setting clear and measurable goals, and generating a variety of solutions can help here!*
Distraction	• Take a nap. • Change the subject. • Crack a joke. • Watch an episode of *Zoey's Extraordinary Playlist* (see Chapter 8). • Call a friend and ask them to talk about themselves.
Reinterpretation	• Think about the silver lining (positive aspects of the situation). • Think about a mental image or visual image as unreal. • Generate multiple examples of what the future consequences might be. • Imagine yourself as able to change the situation. • Think about what you are capable of; remember your successes. • Ask a close other to help you see what you might be missing.

(continues)

TABLE 9.1. Strategies and Tactics (*Continued*)

Strategy	Example tactics (There are many possible options here!)
Distancing	• Narrate the situation in the third person, using your own name rather than "I." • Visually picture what you might look like if you were on reality TV. • Use language like "I'm having the thought that . . ."
Change physiology	• Put an ice cube in your hand or your mouth and let it melt. • Go for a run (or do whatever sporting activity you like).
Grounding	• Describe your environment verbally, with nonjudgmental detail. • Mindfully rub a soothing stone. • Mindfully eat a Lemonhead or a Hot Tamale.
Emotional expression	• Do some expressive writing via journaling. • Call a friend and directly tell them how you're feeling, using emotional labels. • Use a friend as a sounding board to talk through a situation. • Cry in front of a mirror. • Ask for a hug.

including reinterpretation and distancing. She also heard one of her friends say the phrase, "Not my circus, not my monkeys" and realized this could be a useful tactic for her. She had the tendency to try to take charge of situations and take on responsibilities that weren't really hers, so she started trying to identify situations where she could let go by telling herself, "Not my circus, not my monkeys." She found it funny, which helped her feel looser and less physically tense. She also felt more capable of letting go of her tendency to assign herself to fix other people's problems.

Remember that broadening your repertoire is about trying strategies and practicing them, not just learning about them. People often think that a given strategy won't be helpful, or need a reminder that "helpful" can have a long time frame. Just as building physical strength and endurance takes time and effort, so too does cultivating a broad repertoire of strategies. Owning a set of tools doesn't help if you don't know how to use them.

Monitoring and Feedback

When people are flexible in their emotion regulation, they monitor whether the strategy is working and take steps to add additional strategies or change strategies as needed. When that happens in the moment of the emotional experience, it's typically called *monitoring*, and when a person checks in with themselves after the fact, it's called *feedback*. Both monitoring and feedback are a type of checking in—where am I at right now? Where do I want to be? What strategies did I try, and did things play out the way I thought they would?

Remember that whether a strategy works or not depends entirely on the goal. Does "working" mean reducing the emotion and, if so, to what level? Does "working" mean helping you take steps toward your long-term goals, or finding emotion relief now? The clearer the goal, the better the monitoring can be.

Isabel learned this firsthand when she started thinking about monitoring and feedback. She realized that "I don't want to feel anxious" was an unrealistic goal because completely getting rid of an emotion is a tough task (and probably not a useful one, because emotions have functions!). She also recognized that "I want to feel less anxious" wasn't a clear goal. What exactly is "less"? How do you know when "less" has happened? Good goals should be specific, measurable, and feasible.

Isabel learned that assigning numbers to her emotional states helped her set realistic and achievable goals. In Chapter 1, we talked about rating scales (Tanner, 2012) on which feelings are rated from 0 (*none at all*) to 100 (*extreme levels, the worst it could possibly be*). Isabel focused on anxiety by asking herself, "Where am I right now? I'm at an 85." Doing that helped her articulate to herself that her emotion was strong and that she could set a goal to "reduce anxiety to below 50," which is a much clearer target.

If you know where you're starting from and approximately where you'd like to go, monitoring becomes much easier. Are you generally moving in the direction you want to go in, or are your efforts backfiring and the emotion is going in the opposite direction of what you want? Or is nothing changing at all?

Another important aspect of monitoring and feedback is the expected speed of change. Sometimes people give up on their current strategy because it isn't working as quickly as expected.

For example, I've worked with a number of clients whom I've asked to practice deep breathing, which is a relaxation-focused skill to try to decrease physiological reactivity (Jerath et al., 2015). When anger or anxiety or other hot emotions (Metcalfe & Mischel, 1999) are particularly high, deep breathing can help slow down the autonomic nervous system.

One client, Allison, came to the next session and said, "That didn't work." I asked, "What does 'work' mean to you?" She said that "worked" meant decreasing her anxiety. I asked her to share what happened. She said, "Well I tried deep breathing for a minute, but my mind was still racing and my heart was still pounding, so then I smoked some weed, and that helped." One minute is probably not enough to down-regulate the body's physiological activity! She could have tried for longer before turning to her go-to drug.

The opposite problem to giving up on strategies too quickly is continuing with strategies that are not working as intended. Accurate monitoring involves recognizing when a strategy isn't helping and then adjusting accordingly. That could involve adding a new strategy on top of the prior one or switching to a new strategy entirely. But continuing a strategy because it's worked before can be an inflexible monitoring problem if it's not helping now.

Longer term feedback also matters, because it is only over time that people can see the benefits of some strategies. For example, Isabel started trying to be more emotionally expressive at work, sharing some of her stress and frustration in commiseration with others rather than just saying "It's fine, I'll take care of it!" She found this very anxiety inducing at first. She thought about going back to her old, less expressive ways, but she decided to stick with it for a month. After a month, she checked back in and realized that she'd gotten more comfortable with sharing at work. She wasn't feeling as anxious, and she felt far more authentic. She felt like she was getting to know her coworkers much better and that they were getting to know the real her. The small changes she experienced over time weren't obvious on the day-to-day level, but the "wait a month and then see" type of feedback was illuminating.

In fact, Isabel also asked for feedback from the coworker she felt the most comfortable with. She asked her coworker if she'd noticed Isabel sharing more of her feelings. Her coworker thought for a second and said, "You know, I hadn't noticed. I did notice you seemed more interested in me, though, which was nice!"

Monitoring how the emotions are responding now in response to the selected strategy is one part of the puzzle. The other part is trying to see how strategies you use seem to work on a long time scale. Both are crucial parts of regulating flexibly.

APPLICATION TO EMOTIONAL MESSAGES

What on earth does emotion regulation flexibility have to do with emotional messages? Everything.

Throughout this book, I have subtly advocated for flexibility. If emotions are messages, sent from your values, then aren't those messages important to listen to? Emotions try to be helpful, though sometimes they get in the way. When emotions are desirable or helpful, feel them and use them. When they aren't desirable or helpful, regulate.

Yet figuring out which emotions are helpful to you in a given situation is hard. You are your own unique person, with your own experiences, values, preferences, attitudes, and personality. How situations affect you are different than how situations affect other people. Part of the function of this book is to give you more information about how your feelings work and how they might work differently in different situations. Ultimately, it is you who will have to make some decisions about what might help you navigate your feelings more flexibly.

Revisiting Mail Flexibility

In Chapter 6, we talked about two problematic ways people deal with their emotional messages: throwing away the envelope before reading the message (i.e., trying to avoid, escape from, ignore, or squash the emotion), and hanging on to an envelope longer than necessary (i.e., rumination and worry). We talked about these strategies as understandable but not beneficial to long-term emotional health.

But are there ever reasons to throw a message away, or hang on to it? If the idea of emotion regulation flexibility is that no strategies are inherently bad and that strategies should fit the situation, are there situations in which these strategies are useful? Yes! That said, it's hard to clearly identify those situations broadly, because they are specific to the situation and the person. So, let's talk about a specific person and situations she finds herself in!

When to Hang On to Emotional Envelopes

As Isabel started thinking about emotion regulation flexibility, she and her therapist talked a lot about her use of the so-called "maladaptive" strategies. Isabel had a tendency to ruminate and worry—particularly worry. Remember that this is a hanging-onto-the-emotional-envelope-longer-than-necessary kind of problem (see Chapter 6).

Isabel was future focused. She thought a lot about how her actions would affect others, and she worried how other people viewed her. She was particularly prone to worrying in the evening hours, when she was alone. In fact, her nighttime worrying was fairly constant and draining. One of the reasons she drank alcohol was to drown her mind chatter, because her worries seemed to slow down and fade away when she was drunk.

Isabel didn't want to get rid of worry entirely. She recognized the value of worrying as helping her attend to details. Worry made her invaluable at work, because she was quite good at thinking of how things might go wrong and so was able to plan for circumventing disasters.

Isabel decided to use journaling as a way to think through situations in which worry was objectively helpful and in which situations worry seemed to hurt. She first made a list of all of the times in the past week she'd found herself worrying and what kinds of things she worried about. It was a long list! She then tried to sort the list into times worrying seemed to pay off for her as opposed to times worrying sent her into a shame spiral.

She unknowingly stumbled into a useful "If . . . then . . ." strategy (Mischel & Shoda, 1995). The idea is that *if* some to-be-identified contextual elements are evident, *then* use one strategy, but *if* other elements are in place, *then* try something else. Isabel figured out that *if* she was trying to plan a project, a trip, or a definable set of actions, *then* worry seemed to be useful. But *if* she was thinking about how other people thought of her, or other kinds of broad, general, fuzzy future concepts, *then* it would better for her to say "Not my circus, not my monkeys." She basically decided that *if* the situation was her circus and her monkeys, she could worry, otherwise she'd be better off with a different strategy.

Throwing Away Envelopes Without Reading Them

Isabel also relied on other maladaptive strategies, namely, avoidance (e.g., the throwing-away-envelopes-without-reading-them problem). She found her feelings uncomfortable and aversive. In particular, she considered her feelings of sadness and anxiety pesky because they got in the way of her productivity—which was a core value for her.

She'd talked to her therapist about the rationale for opening the envelope and exploring her feelings in more detail, and Isabel intellectually understood the purpose of this. But she also pointed out that people were depending on her to think quickly and make decisions, particularly at work, and that she didn't have time to explore her emotions at those times. Isabel thought maybe this was a time to exert flexibility—that she could push her emotions into the hall closet of her mind on occasion to be able to focus on her tasks.

This is akin to seeing an envelope and saying, "Ugh, yes, I know I have to pay this bill but I don't have time right now." Can you set it aside without opening it? Absolutely. If you see the return address and have a pretty good idea of what's in the envelope, set it aside for awhile while you do other tasks. But then remember to go back and open the envelope later.

There are some kinds of emotional messages that are better to set aside than others. For example, some emotions are *muddy* (Orsillo & Roemer, 2016). *Clear* emotions are generated in direct response to a trigger, but muddy emotions tend to bring past experiences into the situation. For example, I once worked with a client I'll call Jamie. She was in her 50s, and she had a volatile relationship with her adult daughter Emily. They were at a barbecue together one summer afternoon, and Emily loudly chastised Jamie for flirting with one of their neighbors. Jamie lost it, screaming at Emily to mind her own business, and the two women didn't talk for a week.

Jamie's reaction seemed out of proportion to the situation. Yes, being criticized in a social situation doesn't sound nice, but Jamie was extremely angry. When we talked about it in session, we unpacked how this was a **muddy emotion**. Jamie was divorced, and her ex-husband was an alcoholic who had regularly cheated on her. He had also repeatedly accused Jamie of cheating, even though she never did. At the barbecue, Jamie was reacting to her past as much as the present.

Muddy emotions are still messages from values, but values that have been threatened, ignored, or challenged in the past, to the point that they are extra sensitive. I like to think of these as *inflamed values*. When inflamed (e.g., a sunburn is inflamed skin), only a little touch hurts it. In Jamie's situation, she valued Loyalty, which was violated when her husband cheated and accused her of cheating. Her Loyalty value was inflamed and easily ignited. Another person without her history wouldn't have felt as strongly.

The idea isn't to throw away muddy emotional messages but to try to clean them off. Muddy emotions are less helpful than clear emotions, because they aren't (just) about the situation at hand.

Muddy emotions are ones that tend to be hung on to more closely, because they feel strong and meaningful.

Isabel recognized that her emotions were often muddy. Her father was a police officer and her mother was a teacher, and both had high expectations of her. She realized that some of her anxiety around being good enough stemmed from the kinds of things her parents said to her when she was a child.

Isabel asked her therapist, "What can I *do* with muddy emotions?" Her therapist told her that muddy emotions can be another type of "If . . . then . . ." decision. Emotions are often muddy when they seem complex and layered, or when you get some feedback (i.e., facial expressions or body language from other people) that your reaction is out of proportion to the situation. *If* you are in the presence of a muddy emotion, *then* use distraction, distancing, or grounding to help you cool off and think more clearly. It can then be easier to tease apart the degree to which the feeling is about now versus the degree to which the feeling is about the past. If the feeling is more than 25% about the past, it's probably a "duplicate" message, and you can just go ahead and recycle it.

Being flexible with emotion regulation means acknowledging the value of emotional messages, but also acknowledging the realities of the situation. A quick peek at the emotional message may give you an indication that now isn't the best time to read the message in detail. Maybe the message should be recycled or pinned to a bulletin board. There is a time and a place for virtually every regulation strategy—you just have to figure out which strategies to use when.

BALANCE OF GOALS AND MOTIVES

There is one other piece of information about emotion regulation flexibility that I think is important. People need to cultivate balance in the types of emotion regulation goals they pursue, sometimes intentionally choosing to modulate or change emotions and sometimes intentionally choosing to allow the feelings to be present (Crum et al., 2020). Both of these goals are important. Why?

Because emotions serve functions, they have a purpose. Always regulating emotions conveys the belief that emotions are useless and unhelpful. But never regulating emotions conveys either the belief that emotions cannot be controlled or that they should not be reined in (Ford & Gross, 2019). To be flexible and balanced, we need both types of goals.

The other reason why people need a variety of emotional goals is that (as we discussed in Chapter 6) there are distinctions between *desired* feelings and *helpful* feelings (Southward et al., 2021). Desired feelings reflect what you want to feel, but helpful feelings are those that can serve you. Both matter. If a person never feels what they want to feel, their values will shrivel, and they will feel unfulfilled. But if a person pursues only desired feelings, they will forever remain on the treadmill, running faster and faster toward a future they will never actually reach (Diener et al., 2006).

Feeling happy all of the time isn't the secret to living a good life. A good life is one with plenty of happiness, yes. But people who report living a good life also report a life that has meaning, and psychological richness, which is about variety, curiosity, novelty, and the ability to shift perspectives (Oishi & Westgate, 2022).

I would argue that emotional health is consistent with the good life. Feeling pleasure is important, but some values are less about pleasure and more about meaning. Duty, Loyalty, Responsibility, and Caring often bring meaning, but aren't always happy and fun. For example, Responsibility is one of my values. I try to respond to student emails quickly and follow the traffic laws even when I'd be happier watching TV or speeding at 70 miles an hour down my residential street.

Feeling emotions that are not desirable can sometimes help you nourish your values or become the person you want to be. Getting a novel perspective on life means having a variety of experiences, showing curiosity toward people or situations that are unfamiliar, and recognizing that those undesirable feelings can be helpful, if you let them help you.

There are two attributes that are particularly important for flexibility of goals. The good news is that both of these attributes can be cultivated. They are self-efficacy and willingness.

Self-Efficacy

Self-efficacy is the "I think I can do it" idea exemplified by the *Little Engine That Could* (Piper, 1930/2011). In this classic children's story, a little blue train is hailed by some lost toys and dolls. Their prior train has broken down, and they asked several bigger and stronger trains to help them, but those trains ignored their pleas. The little blue train agrees to try. She's never been over the mountain, but she repeats "I think I can, I think I can" and chugs her way up and over the hill, much to the glee of the toys and dolls.

Self-efficacy is the perception that yes, you can accomplish tasks. Self-efficacy is specific to a given task, which means one person might have different levels of self-efficacy for different things. For example, I have low self-efficacy for making a four-course dinner, because I hardly ever cook and I feel quite incompetent in the kitchen. However, I have high self-efficacy for writing academic papers and running a 5K.

In the realm of emotion regulation, self-efficacy is incredibly important. People who have higher self-efficacy for emotion regulation are more flexible (Zimmer-Gembeck, 2021), and they actually experience less negative affect in response to stressful situations (Benfer et al., 2018). People with higher self-efficacy for emotion regulation also tend to be more mindful (Luberto et al., 2014).

Why is self-efficacy so important? Because when people believe they can do things, they are more likely to try. Think about it. Who likes failure? If you expect you won't be able to do something, you won't try. I don't think I can do any pull-ups, so I never try hanging from monkey bars. Because I never try, I never improve.

The same applies to emotion regulation, whether someone is actively trying to change emotions or actively allowing emotions to run their course. If someone believes that they can regulate their emotions, they will be more likely to try (De Castella et al., 2013). Similarly, if someone believes that they can allow their emotions to rise and fall without regulating them, they will be more likely to try letting their emotions fly free (Veilleux, 2023).

Many of the skills in this book were designed to try to get you to feel more capable of both changing and allowing your emotions. You *can* do it! Both regulation and just letting emotions follow their natural course can take practice to do well, but by taking the suggestions presented in this book you can cultivate greater skills and a greater sense that you have the capacity to use those skills.

Willingness

The belief that maybe—just maybe—emotions may be useful is theoretically associated with **willingness** to allow feeling and use feelings. Willingness is consenting to and being open to an experience. Unlike *wanting*, which is an actual wish or desire for an outcome, or *intending*, which is motivationally even stronger, willingness is just a slight openness. Willingness is merely not being unwilling.

In the realm of emotion and emotion regulation, unwillingness is a shut and locked door—the intention is to keep the feelings out, and if they happen to get in, to push them away. Willingness, however, is an openness to letting the feelings in. Perhaps it is just a small cracked window, or perhaps a wide open inviting door. Willingness involves all levels of openness and can change across time and in different contexts. A person who is willing to let the emotions in is open to the idea that emotions could maybe be helpful.

One major type of therapy, dialectical behavior therapy (Linehan, 1993) talks about unwillingness as *willfulness*. "Willfulness" is a word that is often applied to small children who refuse to do a task, such as refusing to put on their shoes to go to school, and it represents stubbornness. The same general concept could be applied here. Willfulness is a stubbornness, a "this won't be worth it" belief or a "this won't work" attitude. When people are willful or unwilling, they are not attending to the context, not seeing the situation for what it is, and often trying to apply ineffective problem-solving that worked elsewhere ("It worked once, so it MUST WORK now").

Isabel struggled mightily with willingness. She had less of a problem with self-efficacy because she generally adopted a "I can figure it out and do whatever is asked of me" mentality. She thought she could do just about anything, including allow and regulate emotions. But she was often unwilling to try, particularly in situations that would reveal her vulnerability. It was in the realm of willingness that Isabel had the most need for growth to enhance her flexibility. She often decided that a strategy wouldn't work or that expression would harm her, without actually trying it.

One of the biggest lessons in the world of emotion regulation is that behavior changes attitude. Thinking or attitudes rarely—if ever—change behaviors. Waiting to feel ready means you'll never do the thing. Trying to convince yourself rarely works. But *doing* changes thinking. *Doing* changes feeling. *Doing* changes beliefs. When people try new things, unexpected learning can happen (Baumeister et al., 2007).

Isabel realized that she was often unwilling to try. She was willful and stubborn and sure that her perspective was the right one. Yet when she finally started to open the window a bit, when she finally admitted to her therapist that she'd been unwilling, things started to change. Willingness is about seeing which way the wind is blowing, or how warm the breeze will be, rather than assuming on the front end.

Willingness is about curiosity. Try to be curious about what your values are trying to tell you and what growth your emotions can bring.

NO STRICT RECIPES

Perhaps you picked up this book because you wanted clear-cut answers about what you should do to experience emotional health. Throughout this book, I've shared scientific evidence with you about emotion and emotion regulation, evidence that includes some specific suggestions about best practices.

Yet at the end of the day, I can't give specific advice to you because I don't know you. And honestly, I don't give specific advice to my therapy clients all that often, either. That's because I don't live inside your head, in your body. You are the expert on you. The advice provided in this book isn't "Always do X" or "Never do Y" but "Think about your values, your goals, your emotions, and act accordingly."

Would you benefit from building up your toolbox, buying a few different letter openers, and figuring out a color-coded email folder system? Yes! But much of coping with emotions and managing emotional messages is learning to understand yourself and how to tune in to yourself in emotional moments.

Emotion regulation flexibility means attending to the situation and having a well-stocked toolbox ready to go for whatever is called for. For example, consider a new grandmother who visits her infant granddaughter in the hospital and is insulted when her son orders her to hold the baby in a specific way (Blanchard-Fields, 2007). A flexible response might be to gently excuse herself in the moment to avoid the lashing out that is at the tip of her tongue and then talk to her son at another time. Being able to use both passive (withdrawal, expressive suppression) and active (using anger to correct an injustice, seeking support) strategies can help manage emotions and maintain important relationships.

People often want clear-cut guidelines, or a recipe to follow. Yet emotion regulation flexibility is about doing what's needed, even when what's needed is a deviation from the recipe. Maybe the recipe says to include mushrooms, but you don't like mushrooms. Maybe the recipe said to add extra salt, but when you taste the dish it's already plenty salty. The idea here is to cultivate a sense of self-awareness and self-knowledge so that you can listen to yourself, know your own goals and values, and proceed accordingly. Trust that you don't always need more salt. But sometimes you do.

SUMMARY POINTS

- Emotion regulation flexibility is the idea that no strategy is universally good or bad. Instead, emotion regulation strategies need to be used flexibly to match the needs of the current context.
- There are three core aspects of flexibility:
  1. Context sensitivity, which involves paying attention to the physical and psychological aspects of the situation to get an idea about what strategies might best fit the moment.
  2. Breadth of repertoire, which is about building a well-stocked emotion regulation toolbox, with a variety of different emotion regulation strategies and multiple specific tactics within each strategy category.
  3. Monitoring and feedback, which are important to pay attention to what works in a given moment. Sometimes additional strategies need to be added, or switching strategies may be most helpful. Remember that whether or not a strategy works depends on the goals—and sometimes a longer time frame is needed to determine success.
- To be truly flexible, people also need to balance their goals and motives over time. Pursuing regulation is important sometimes,

but simply allowing the emotion to be present, or using the emotion to pursue a life goal, is important, too.

- Cultivating attitudes of willingness (i.e., an openness to and curiosity about emotions, an openness to trying new strategies) and self-efficacy (i.e., feeling capable of exerting change or of allowing emotions) are important for both regulation and allowing emotions.

- There is no clear recipe—learning about emotions can help you handle them, and your emotions are both like everyone else's and unique to you.

AFTERWORD

I'm going to let you in on a little secret, now that you've made it all the way through the book. The secret is this book has been aiming to improve your *distress tolerance.*

People who are intolerant of distress tend to be reactive to distress, suspicious of distress, and dislike their distress, and as a result they feel incapable of allowing or sitting with their unpleasant feelings (Veilleux, 2023). Low distress tolerance is linked with virtually every mental health problem under the sun (Leyro et al., 2010; Semcho et al., 2023; Zvolensky et al., 2010), but it tends to improve with psychotherapy (Heiland & Veilleux, 2024).

So, why not just call this a book on distress tolerance? Because distress tolerance sounds awful. Tolerance is about "putting up with." You have to tolerate your smelly uncle who screams his abhorrent political views at Thanksgiving dinner. That doesn't sound like a fun book to read, does it?

Yet the heart of distress tolerance is about recognizing that emotions might be useful. If we are open and willing to experience them, and develop skills to feel confident and self-efficacious in regulating them, emotions don't have to be so aversive. Tolerating distress is easier when emotions make more sense and when emotions are viewed as helpful messages sent from values rather than as junk mail.

Some people think that tolerating distress reflects resignation to distress, a sense of "I'm destined to feel this way forever." Not true—no feeling lasts forever. Feelings rise and fall. Other people think that tolerating distress is about approving of or liking distress. Although there may be times when that's the case, like wanting to feel scared out of your wits at a horror movie, most of the time distress is . . . distressing. It is stressful, unpleasant, and no fun at all.

Yet, living "the good life" isn't just about fun. Happiness matters, but remember, so does finding meaning in life and living a rich life full of growth and new experiences. Emotions are the key to meaning and richness. Emotions bring color, depth, and texture to our lives. Emotions help us cultivate long-lasting, deep relationships. Emotional expressions communicate our intentions and beliefs faster and more effectively than words. Emotions activate internal systems that help motivate us to approach what we want and help us avoid what can hurt us. Emotions teach us about ourselves and about the world.

Remember, *you can't have a feeling about things that don't matter*. If a feeling is there, importance is behind it. Seeing emotions as messages from values makes emotions meaningful and worth experiencing instead of seeing them as an infection to cure.

Maybe the goal shouldn't just be to tolerate distress but to embrace what emotions have to offer. Emotional health involves understanding, recognizing, allowing, and harnessing the power of emotions, and knowing how to regulate them.

Just remember that emotions are temporary, not permanent. Feeling them, allowing them—do that sometimes. Regulate other times. Balancing these goals, using a variety of strategies, expressing sometimes, and masking other times—all of these are skills that will let you see emotions as important, valuable, and necessary. Because whether you want them or not, you will have emotions. So you might as well embrace them.

GLOSSARY OF KEY TERMS

Affect: an umbrella term that covers feelings, moods, and. emotions; affect is typically described as positive (i.e., a pleasant feeling state) or negative (i.e., an unpleasant feeling state) (Chapter 1)

Alexithymia: a traitlike attribute (not a disorder) associated with difficulty being aware of, understanding, and labeling emotions (Chapter 2, Chapter 4, Chapter 8)

Appraisal: an interpretation, most often used to refer to the stage of emotion generation in which a person mentally interprets a situation (e.g., as good or bad, as certain or uncertain, as controllable or uncontrollable) (Chapter 2)

Avoidance-based coping: sometimes called *disengagement emotion regulation*, this includes strategies that involve escaping, circumventing, or avoiding upsetting thoughts, feelings, or situations (Chapter 6)

Cognitive reappraisal or **cognitive reframing:** highly effective "changing thoughts" emotion regulation strategies that involve thinking about situations from a different angle; includes reinterpretation (Chapter 7)

Contrahedonic goal: a goal to experience less pleasure and/or more unpleasant emotion (Chapter 6)

Coping ahead: strategies to use when not in a distressed state that decrease vulnerability to emotions and make upsetting feelings easier to handle (Chapter 5)

Corumination: often coinciding with *venting*, corumination involves ruminating with another person, revisiting details of emotional triggers, and rehashing them without reaching resolution or meaning (Chapter 8)

Defusion: another term for distancing that stems from acceptance and commitment therapy in which one tries to defuse or "unstick" from emotions (Chapter 7)

Distancing: a "changing thoughts" method of regulating emotion involving getting distance from thoughts and feelings by creating space with language, including talking to yourself in the third person (Chapter 7)

Distraction: an attentional emotion regulation strategy that involves shifting attention to a different stimulus or aspect of a situation (Chapter 7)

Emotion: a full-fledged emotion is a feeling state with a clear trigger, a middle, and an end, like a wave; tends to be more intense and shorter lived than a mood (Chapter 1)

Emotional awareness: the state of being attentive to and aware of an emotional response (Chapter 2)

Emotional expression: when the internal feelings of emotion are brought to the outside of the mind and body; often involves showing the emotion to others. Expression can be verbal or nonverbal, intentional or unintentional. (Chapter 8)

Emotional invalidation: after sharing emotions with someone else, getting feedback that the shared emotions are incorrect, inappropriate, or wrong (Chapter 1, Chapter 8)

Emotional labeling: the process of attaching a specific word (e.g., "angry," "anxious"), or several words, to an emotional experience (Chapter 4)

Emotional sensitivity: the biologically based personality characteristic associated with how internally responsive a person is to emotion. People who experience emotions more quickly, feel emotions more strongly, and have emotions that last longer are more emotionally sensitive. (Chapter 1)

Emotional sharing: a specific form of emotional expression that involves letting another person know (via words or nonverbal signaling) what emotions are experienced (Chapter 8)

Emotional vocabulary: the set of words that refer to emotional, mood, and affective states that a person has ready to use for emotional labeling (Chapter 4)

Emotion dysregulation: a term that summarizes the problems people have regulating their emotions effectively and adaptively; includes having limited strategies, underregulation, and misregulation (Chapter 7)

Emotion generation: the processes of how emotions come to be; a person experiences an emotional trigger, attends to an aspect of the situation, and interprets the situation before the emotion is felt (Chapter 2, Chapter 7)

Emotion regulation flexibility: the ability to flexibly choose an effective regulation strategy for the moment, taking into consideration contextual factors, availability of social support, and current resources (Chapter 9)

Emotion regulation strategies: sometimes called "coping" strategies, emotion regulation strategies include any method of trying to intentionally change the emotional experience (Chapter 4, Chapter 7)

Emotion regulation tactics: the specific ways an emotion regulation strategy is enacted in a moment of time (Chapter 9)

Energy resource: having enough energy and strength to be capable of handling distress by getting enough sleep, eating nourishing foods, limiting substance use, exercising, and taking medications as prescribed (Chapter 5)

Expressive flexibility: increasing emotional expressiveness in some situations and decreasing expressiveness in other situations, depending on the context (Chapter 8)

Expressive suppression: masking or hiding the expression of emotion from others (Chapter 8)

Feeling: the subjective component of emotion; often used as a synonym for "emotion" (Chapter 1)

Flow: the state of being one with an activity, when a person can become so engaged in an activity that they aren't even aware of time passing (Chapter 2)

Grounding: an emotion regulation strategy to dampen strong emotional responses that involves mindfully attending to sensory stimuli in the immediate environment (Chapter 7)

Hedonic goals: goals related to experiencing more pleasure and/or less unpleasant emotion (Chapter 6)

Interpersonal emotion regulation: efforts to change or manage emotions using other people (Chapter 8)

Metaemotion: an emotion about an emotion, sometimes called a "secondary emotion" because it's an emotional response to a primary emotion (e.g., anxious about feeling angry) (Chapter 6, Chapter 8)

Mindfulness: the act of present-moment awareness, intentionally attending to one thing (e.g., to one's breath, to sounds in the environment) and gently bringing the mind back to the task when it invariably wanders (Chapter 2)

Misregulation: a form of emotion dysregulation associated with using strategies that are generally less effective or strategies that are not well matched to the situation (Chapter 7, Chapter 9)

Mood: a diffuse, free-floating feeling state without a clear trigger; can last longer, but is typically less intense, than a full-fledged emotion (Chapter 1)

Muddy emotion: an emotional reaction that is not just about the present situation; it is "muddy" because it's also reacting to past situations and relationships (Chapter 9)

Negativity bias: the tendency to give greater weight to negative, stressful, unpleasant information compared to positive information (Chapter 5)

Opposite action: an emotion regulation strategy to dampen strong emotional responses that involves physically acting opposite to the current emotion (e.g., loosening the body for strong emotions, approaching rather than avoiding) (Chapter 7)

Pleasure: the experience of pleasant, positive emotions, including happiness, gratitude, awe, excitement, joy, love, and interest; a psychological resource that can buffer against stress (Chapter 5)

Polyregulation: the idea that people are often using multiple emotion regulation strategies at once (Chapter 7)

Psychological resources: psychological attributes that can help buffer against stress, including frequent experiences of pleasure, energy (e.g., eating nourishing food, getting enough sleep), and social connections (Chapter 5)

Privilege resource: an advantage or benefit granted to people who belong to a particular social group, such as advantages given to men, White people, able-bodied people, thin people, or wealthy people (Chapter 5)

Proactive selection: using an emotion regulation strategy before experiencing an emotion, planning ahead to not enter emotional situations (Chapter 7)

Problem-solving: an emotion regulation strategy focused on altering the trigger or changing the situation; recognizes that changing the underlying situation often changes the emotion (Chapter 7)

Procrastination: voluntarily delaying an important or necessary task even though the delay is irrational and has negative consequences (Chapter 7)

Reassurance seeking: the interpersonal emotion regulation strategy of sharing emotions with someone else to get reassurance that your reactions are reasonable and/or that everything will be OK. Reassurance seeking feels good in the short term but can be harmful when used excessively. (Chapter 8)

Reinterpretation: a form of cognitive reappraisal that involves reinterpreting what was attended to in the emotional trigger situation to change the emotional response (Chapter 7)

Reward sensitivity: a biologically based trait, the tendency to have strong emotional and physiological reactions to anticipated or experienced rewards (Chapter 1)

Rumination: an emotion regulation strategy that involves asking "why" and revisiting a thought or situation over and over, with the intention to understand but without actual meaning-making (Chapter 6)

Self-efficacy: the confidence in one's own ability to accomplish a task, the "I can do it" idea (Chapter 9)

Social connection: spending quality time with other people that results in feeling understood, loved, and tethered; a resource that helps reduce the pain of unpleasant emotions (Chapter 5)

States: temporary changes in the mind and body in response to a situation. Emotions are states—they fluctuate over time and across contexts. (Chapter 1)

Strategic delay: voluntarily delaying an important or necessary task strategically, for good reason, where the delay is helpful rather than having negative consequences (Chapter 7)

Stress: the subjective feeling of being overwhelmed by the pressures of life (i.e., without the resources to effectively handle stressors) (Chapter 5)

Stressors: events, situations, obligations, or other kinds of stimuli that occur in the environment that are demanding or challenging to deal with (Chapter 5)

Thought suppression: an avoidance-based cognitive emotion regulation strategy associated with trying to not think about stressful or emotional situations (Chapter 7)

Threat sensitivity: sometimes called "punishment sensitivity," a biologically based tendency to have strong emotional and physiological reactions to threatening, negative, or aversive situations (Chapter 1)

Traits: relatively stable personality characteristics that summarize tendencies of thinking, feeling, and behaving (Chapter 1)

Trigger: a situation (whether something in the environment that happens, or an internal situation, e.g., a thought) that kicks off the emotion generation process (Chapter 2)

Underregulation: a form of emotion dysregulation associated with failing to use emotion regulation strategies, or not putting enough effort into using them (e.g., not using them long enough to show an effect) (Chapter 7)

Validation: after sharing feelings, the feedback that the person (and their emotions) are normal, understandable, and loved (Chapter 8)

Values: chosen life directions, the attributes that are most important as guiding principles for your life; these are distinct from goals (which can be completed or checked off) (Chapter 3)

Venting: the airing out of emotions by talking about an emotional situation with another person. Venting often feels good in the short term but prolongs negative feelings and doesn't tend to produce emotional relief. (Chapter 8)

Willingness: consenting to and being open to an experience, even when not desired (Chapter 9)

Willpower: another word for "self-control," usually referred to as the energy to do something and the energy needed to resist impulses (Chapter 7)

Worry: an emotion regulation strategy involving concern about how the future will turn out and associated planning to prevent threatening outcomes from coming to be (Chapter 6)

REFERENCES

Aldao, A., Nolen-Hoeksema, S., & Schweizer, S. (2010). Emotion-regulation strategies across psychopathology: A meta-analytic review. *Clinical Psychology Review, 30*(2), 217–237. https://doi.org/10.1016/j.cpr. 2009.11.004

Aldao, A., Sheppes, G., & Gross, J. J. (2015). Emotion regulation flexibility. *Cognitive Therapy and Research, 39*(3), 263–278. https://doi.org/ 10.1007/s10608-014-9662-4

Allemand, M., & Flückiger, C. (2017). Changing personality traits: Some considerations from psychotherapy process–outcome research for intervention efforts on intentional personality change. *Journal of Psychotherapy Integration, 27*(4), 476–494. https://doi.org/10.1037/ int0000094

Andersen, H. C. (1985). *The princess and the pea.* North–South Books. (Original work published 1835)

Andrei, M. (2021). Why does electricity hum—And why is it a B flat in the US, and a G in Europe? *ZME Science.* https://www.zmescience.com/ feature-post/why-electricity-hum-07112017/

Assaz, D. A., Roche, B., Kanter, J. W., & Oshiro, C. K. B. (2018). Cognitive defusion in acceptance and commitment therapy: What are the basic processes of change? *The Psychological Record, 68*(4), 405–418. https://doi.org/10.1007/s40732-017-0254-z

Bagby, R. M., Parker, J. D. A., & Taylor, G. J. (1994). The twenty-item Toronto Alexithymia Scale—I. Item selection and cross-validation of the factor structure. *Journal of Psychosomatic Research, 38*(1), 23–32. https://doi.org/10.1016/0022-3999(94)90005-1

Baikie, K. A., & Wilhelm, K. (2005). Emotional and physical health benefits of expressive writing. *Advances in Psychiatric Treatment, 11*(5), 338–346. https://doi.org/10.1192/apt.11.5.338

Bailen, N. H., Wu, H., & Thompson, R. J. (2019). Meta-emotions in daily life: Associations with emotional awareness and depression. *Emotion, 19*(5), 776–787. https://doi.org/10.1037/emo0000488

Baker, J. P., & Berenbaum, H. (2007). Emotional approach and problem-focused coping: A comparison of potentially adaptive strategies. *Cognition and Emotion, 21*(1), 95–118. https://doi.org/10.1080/02699930600562276

Barata, P. C., Oliveira, C. F. P., Lima de Castro, S., & Rocha da Mota, A. M. P. (2019). A systematic review on substance addiction: Medical diagnosis or morality flaw? *European Journal of Psychiatry, 33*(4), 143–151. https://doi.org/10.1016/j.ejpsy.2019.07.001

Barney, J. L., Lillis, J., Haynos, A. F., Forman, E., & Juarascio, A. S. (2019). Assessing the valuing process in acceptance and commitment therapy: Experts' review of the current status and recommendations for future measure development. *Journal of Contextual Behavioral Science, 12*, 225–233. https://doi.org/10.1016/j.jcbs.2018.08.002

Bartoshuk, L. M., Duffy, V. B., & Miller, I. J. (1994). PTC/PROP tasting: Anatomy, psychophysics, and sex effects. *Physiology & Behavior, 56*(6), 1165–1171. https://doi.org/10.1016/0031-9384(94)90361-1

Battaglini, A. M., Rnic, K., Jameson, T., Jopling, E., & LeMoult, J. (2023). Interpersonal emotion regulation flexibility: Effects on affect in daily life. *Emotion, 23*(4), 1048–1060. https://doi.org/10.1037/emo0001132

Baumeister, R. F., Bratslavsky, E., Finkenauer, C., & Vohs, K. D. (2001). Bad is stronger than good. *Review of General Psychology, 5*(4), 323–370. https://doi.org/10.1037/1089-2680.5.4.323

Baumeister, R. F., Vohs, K. D., DeWall, C. N., & Zhang, L. (2007). How emotion shapes behavior: Feedback, anticipation, and reflection, rather than direct causation. *Personality and Social Psychology Review, 11*(2), 167–203. https://doi.org/10.1177/1088868307301033

Bazarova, N. N., Choi, Y. H., Whitlock, J., Cosley, D., & Sosik, V. (2017). Psychological distress and emotional expression on Facebook. *Cyberpsychology, Behavior, and Social Networking, 20*(3), 157–163. https://doi.org/10.1089/cyber.2016.0335

Behfar, K. J., Cronin, M. A., & McCarthy, K. (2020). Realizing the upside of venting: The role of the "challenger listener." *Academy of Management Discoveries*, 6(4), 609–630. https://doi.org/10.5465/amd.2018.0066

Benfer, N., Bardeen, J. R., & Clauss, K. (2018). Experimental manipulation of emotion regulation self-efficacy, perceived effort in the service of regulation, and affective reactivity. *Journal of Contextual Behavioral Science, 10*, 108–114. https://doi.org/10.1016/j.jcbs.2018.09.006

Bernstein, E. E., & McNally, R. J. (2017). Acute aerobic exercise helps overcome emotion regulation deficits. *Cognition and Emotion, 31*(4), 834–843. https://doi.org/10.1080/02699931.2016.1168284

Berridge, K. C., Robinson, T. E., & Aldridge, J. W. (2009). Dissecting components of reward: "Liking," "wanting," and learning. *Current Opinion in Pharmacology, 9*(1), 65–73. https://doi.org/10.1016/j.coph.2008.12.014

Bishop, S. R., Lau, M., Shapiro, S., Carlson, L., Anderson, N. D., Carmody, J., Segal, Z. V., Abbey, S., Speca, M., Velting, D., & Devins, G. (2004). Mindfulness: A proposed operational definition. *Clinical Psychology, 11*(3), 230–241. https://doi.org/10.1093/clipsy.bph077

Blackman, D., Feig, P., & Inkeles, D. (Executive Producers). (2020–2021). *Zoey's extraordinary playlist* [TV series]. Lionsgate Television; NBC Productions.

Blanchard-Fields, F. (2007). Everyday problem solving and emotion. *Current Directions in Psychological Science, 16*(1), 26–31. https://doi.org/10.1111/j.1467-8721.2007.00469.x

Blascovich, J., Mendes, W. B., Hunter, S. B., & Salomon, K. (1999). Social "facilitation" as challenge and threat. *Journal of Personality and Social Psychology, 77*(1), 68–77. https://doi.org/10.1037/0022-3514.77.1.68

Boden, M. T., & Thompson, R. J. (2017). Meta-analysis of the association between emotional clarity and attention to emotions. *Emotion Review, 9*(1), 79–85. https://doi.org/10.1177/1754073915610640

Boden, M. T., Thompson, R. J., Dizén, M., Berenbaum, H., & Baker, J. P. (2012). Are emotional clarity and emotion differentiation related? *Cognition and Emotion, 27*(6), 961–978. https://doi.org/10.1080/02699931.2012.751899

Bonanno, G. A., & Burton, C. L. (2013). Regulatory flexibility: An individual differences perspective on coping and emotion regulation.

Perspectives on Psychological Science, 8(6), 591–612. https://doi.org/10.1177/1745691613504116

Brans, K., Koval, P., Verduyn, P., Lim, Y. L., & Kuppens, P. (2013). The regulation of negative and positive affect in daily life. *Emotion, 13*(5), 926–939. https://doi.org/10.1037/a0032400

Brescoll, V. L., & Uhlmann, E. L. (2008). Can an angry woman get ahead? Status conferral, gender, and expression of emotion in the workplace. *Psychological Science, 19*(3), 268–275. https://doi.org/10.1111/j.1467-9280.2008.02079.x

Bresin, K. (2020). Toward a unifying theory of dysregulated behaviors. *Clinical Psychology Review, 80*, 101885. https://doi.org/10.1016/j.cpr.2020.101885

Bresin, K., & Mekawi, Y. (2022). Unpacking the construct of dysregulated behaviors using variable-centered and person-centered analytic approaches. *Substance Use and Misuse, 57*(4), 603–612. https://doi.org/10.1080/10826084.2022.2026966

Buck, C. (Director), & Lee, J. (Director). (2013). *Frozen* [Film]. Walt Disney Animation Studios; Walt Disney Pictures.

Burklund, L. J., Creswell, J. D., Irwin, M. R., & Lieberman, M. D. (2014). The common and distinct neural bases of affect labeling and reappraisal in healthy adults. *Frontiers in Psychology, 5*, 221. https://doi.org/10.3389/fpsyg.2014.00221

Bylsma, L. M., Morris, B. H., & Rottenberg, J. (2008). A meta-analysis of emotional reactivity in major depressive disorder. *Clinical Psychology Review, 28*(4), 676–691. https://doi.org/10.1016/j.cpr.2007.10.001

Bylsma, L. M., Vingerhoets, A. J. J. M., & Rottenberg, J. (2008). When is crying cathartic? An international study. *Journal of Social and Clinical Psychology, 27*(10), 1165–1187. https://doi.org/10.1521/jscp.2008.27.10.1165

Cameron, K., Ogrodniczuk, J., & Hadjipavlou, G. (2014). Changes in alexithymia following psychological intervention: A review. *Harvard Review of Psychiatry, 22*(3), 162–178. https://doi.org/10.1097/HRP.0000000000000036

Campbell, G. (Writer), Dombrowski, L. (Writer), & Leddy, B. (Director). (2001, May 12). Season 6, Episode 24. In D. Blasucci, Q. Jones, & D. Salzman (Executive Producers), *Mad TV*. Quincy Jones–David Salzman Entertainment.

Campos, B., Shiota, M. N., Keltner, D., Gonzaga, G. C., & Goetz, J. L. (2013). What is shared, and what is different? Core relational themes and expressive displays of eight positive emotions. *Cognition and Emotion*, 27(1), 37–52. https://doi.org/10.1080/02699931.2012.683852

Campos, J. J., Frankel, C. B., & Camras, L. (2004). On the nature of emotion regulation. *Child Development*, 75(2), 377–394. https://doi.org/10.1111/j.1467-8624.2004.00681.x

Carver, C. S., & Johnson, S. L. (2018). Impulsive reactivity to emotion and vulnerability to psychopathology. *American Psychologist*, 73(9), 1067–1078. https://doi.org/10.1037/amp0000387

Carver, C. S., Johnson, S. L., & Joormann, J. (2008). Serotonergic function, two-mode models of self-regulation, and vulnerability to depression: What depression has in common with impulsive aggression. *Psychological Bulletin*, 134(6), 912–943. https://doi.org/10.1037/a0013740

Chapman, A. L., Walters, K. N., & Dixon Gordon, K. L. (2012). Emotional reactivity to social rejection and negative evaluation among persons with borderline personality features. *Journal of Personality Disorders*, 28(5), 720–733. https://doi.org/10.1521/pedi_2012_26_068

Chawla, N., & Ostafin, B. (2007). Experiential avoidance as a functional dimensional approach to psychopathology: An empirical review. *Journal of Clinical Psychology*, 63(9), 871–890. https://doi.org/10.1002/jclp.20400

Cheli, S., & Cavalletti, V. (2021). The paradox of overcontrol, perfectionism and self-criticism: A cases series on gifted students. *Quaderni Di Psicoterapia Cognitiva*, 48(48), 59–73. https://doi.org/10.3280/qpc48-2021oa12141

Chen, S., Chen, T., & Bonanno, G. A. (2018). Expressive flexibility: Enhancement and suppression abilities differentially predict life satisfaction and psychopathology symptoms. *Personality and Individual Differences*, 126, 78–84. https://doi.org/10.1016/j.paid.2018.01.010

Cheng, C. (2001). Assessing coping flexibility in real-life and laboratory settings: A multimethod approach. *Journal of Personality and Social Psychology*, 80(5), 814–833. https://doi.org/10.1037/0022-3514.80.5.814

Cheng, C. (2003). Cognitive and motivational processes underlying coping flexibility: A dual-process model. *Journal of Personality and Social Psychology*, 84(2), 425–438. https://doi.org/10.1037/0022-3514.84.2.425

Chervonsky, E., & Hunt, C. (2017). Suppression and expression of emotion in social and interpersonal outcomes: A meta-analysis. *Emotion, 17*(4), 669–683. https://doi.org/10.1037/emo0000270

Clark, D. A. (2022). Cognitive reappraisal. *Cognitive and Behavioral Practice, 29*(3), 564–566. https://doi.org/10.1016/j.cbpra.2022.02.018

Cohen, S., Doyle, W. J., & Baum, A. (2006). Socioeconomic status is associated with stress hormones. *Psychosomatic Medicine, 68*(3), 414–420. https://doi.org/10.1097/01.psy.0000221236.37158.b9

Coles, N. A., Larsen, J. T., & Lench, H. C. (2019). A meta-analysis of the facial feedback literature: Effects of facial feedback on emotional experience are small and variable. *Psychological Bulletin, 145*(6), 610–651. https://doi.org/10.1037/bul0000194

Crum, A. J., Jamieson, J. P., & Akinola, M. (2020). Optimizing stress: An integrated intervention for regulating stress responses. *Emotion, 20*(1), 120–125. https://doi.org/10.1037/emo0000670

Dahl, J. (2015). Valuing in ACT. *Current Opinion in Psychology, 2*, 43–46. https://doi.org/10.1016/j.copsyc.2015.03.001

De Castella, K., Goldin, P., Jazaieri, H., Ziv, M., Dweck, C. S., & Gross, J. J. (2013). Beliefs about emotion: Links to emotion regulation, well-being, and psychological distress. *Basic and Applied Social Psychology, 35*(6), 497–505. https://doi.org/10.1080/01973533.2013.840632

De Castella, K., Platow, M. J., Tamir, M., & Gross, J. J. (2018). Beliefs about emotion: Implications for avoidance-based emotion regulation and psychological health. *Cognition and Emotion, 32*(4), 773–795. https://doi.org/10.1080/02699931.2017.1353485

DeYoung, C. G., & Tiberius, V. (2023). Value fulfillment from a cybernetic perspective: A new psychological theory of well-being. *Personality and Social Psychology Review, 27*(1), 3–27. https://doi.org/10.1177/10888683221083777

Dicker-Oren, S. D., Gelkopf, M., & Greene, T. (2022). The dynamic network associations of food craving, restrained eating, hunger and negative emotions. *Appetite, 175*, 106019. https://doi.org/10.1016/j.appet.2022.106019

Diener, E. (1984). Subjective well-being. *Psychological Bulletin, 95*(3), 542–575. https://doi.org/10.1037/0033-2909.95.3.542

Diener, E., Lucas, R. E., & Scollon, C. N. (2006). Beyond the hedonic treadmill: Revising the adaptation theory of well-being. *American Psychologist, 61*(4), 305–314. https://doi.org/10.1037/0003-066X.61.4.305

Dixon-Gordon, K. L., Haliczer, L. A., Conkey, L. C., & Whalen, D. J. (2018). Difficulties in interpersonal emotion regulation: Initial development and validation of a self-report measure. *Journal of Psychopathology and Behavioral Assessment*, 40(3), 528–549. https://doi.org/10.1007/s10862-018-9647-9

Docter, P. (Director), & Del Carmen, R. (Director). (2015). *Inside out* [Film]. Pixar Animation Studios, Walt Disney Studios Motion Pictures.

Edwards, E. R., Micek, A., Mottarella, K., & Wupperman, P. (2017). Emotion ideology mediates effects of risk factors on alexithymia development. *Journal of Rational-Emotive & Cognitive-Behavior Therapy*, 35(3), 254–277. https://doi.org/10.1007/s10942-016-0254-y

Edwards, E., Shivaji, S., & Wupperman, P. (2018). The Emotion Mapping Activity: Preliminary evaluation of a mindfulness-informed exercise to improve emotion labeling in alexithymic persons. *Scandinavian Journal of Psychology*, 59(3), 319–327. https://doi.org/10.1111/sjop.12438

Ehring, T., & Watkins, E. R. (2008). Repetitive negative thinking as a transdiagnostic process. *International Journal of Cognitive Therapy*, 1(3), 192–205. https://doi.org/10.1521/ijct.2008.1.3.192

Eid, M., & Diener, E. (2001). Norms for experiencing emotions in different cultures: Inter- and intranational differences. *Journal of Personality and Social Psychology*, 81(5), 869–885. https://doi.org/10.1037/0022-3514.81.5.869

Eman, S., Khalid, A., & Nicolson, R. I. (2019). A review of heterogeneous interpretations of emotional reactivity. *The International Journal of Emotional Education*, 11(2), 71–90.

Ent, M. R., Baumeister, R. F., & Tice, D. M. (2015). Trait self-control and the avoidance of temptation. *Personality and Individual Differences*, 74, 12–15. https://doi.org/10.1016/j.paid.2014.09.031

Erbas, Y., Ceulemans, E., Blanke, E. S., Sels, L., Fischer, A., & Kuppens, P. (2019). Emotion differentiation dissected: Between-category, within-category, and integral emotion differentiation, and their relation to well-being. *Cognition and Emotion*, 33(2), 258–271. https://doi.org/10.1080/02699931.2018.1465894

Evraire, L. E., & Dozois, D. J. A. (2011). An integrative model of excessive reassurance seeking and negative feedback seeking in the development and maintenance of depression. *Clinical Psychology Review*, 31(8), 1291–1303. https://doi.org/10.1016/j.cpr.2011.07.014

Fernandes, M. A., & Tone, E. B. (2021). A systematic review and meta-analysis of the association between expressive suppression and positive affect. *Clinical Psychology Review*, *88*, 102068. https://doi.org/10.1016/j.cpr.2021.102068

Fiori, M., Vesely-Maillefer, A. K., Nicolet-Dit-Félix, M., & Gillioz, C. (2023). With great sensitivity comes great management: How emotional hypersensitivity can be the superpower of emotional intelligence. *Journal of Intelligence*, *11*(10), 198. https://doi.org/10.3390/jintelligence11100198

Fischer, A., & LaFrance, M. (2015). What drives the smile and the tear: Why women are more emotionally expressive than men. *Emotion Review*, *7*(1), 22–29. https://doi.org/10.1177/1754073914544406

Föhr, T., Tolvanen, A., Myllymäki, T., Järvelä-Reijonen, E., Peuhkuri, K., Rantala, S., Kolehmainen, M., Korpela, R., Lappalainen, R., Ermes, M., Puttonen, S., Rusko, H., & Kujala, U. M. (2017). Physical activity, heart rate variability–based stress and recovery, and subjective stress during a 9-month study period. *Scandinavian Journal of Medicine & Science in Sports*, *27*(6), 612–621. https://doi.org/10.1111/sms.12683

Folkman, S., Lazarus, R. S., Dunkel-Schetter, C., DeLongis, A., & Gruen, R. J. (1986). Dynamics of a stressful encounter: Cognitive appraisal, coping, and encounter outcomes. *Journal of Personality and Social Psychology*, *50*(5), 992–1003. https://doi.org/10.1037/0022-3514.50.5.992

Ford, B. Q., & Gross, J. J. (2019). Why beliefs about emotion matter: An emotion-regulation perspective. *Current Directions in Psychological Science*, *28*(1), 74–81. https://doi.org/10.1177/0963721418806697

Ford, B. Q., Gross, J. J., & Gruber, J. (2019). Broadening our field of view: The role of emotion polyregulation. *Emotion Review*, *11*(3), 197–208. https://doi.org/10.1177/1754073919850314

Ford, B. Q., & Tamir, M. (2012). When getting angry is smart: Emotional preferences and emotional intelligence. *Emotion*, *12*(4), 685–689. https://doi.org/10.1037/a0027149

Ford, B. Q., & Troy, A. S. (2019). Reappraisal reconsidered: A closer look at the costs of an acclaimed emotion-regulation strategy. *Current Directions in Psychological Science*, *28*(2), 195–203. https://doi.org/10.1177/0963721419827526

Forgas, J. P. (2013). Don't worry, be sad! On the cognitive, motivational, and interpersonal benefits of negative mood. *Current Directions in Psychological Science, 22*(3), 225–232. https://doi.org/10.1177/0963721412474458

Fredrickson, B. L., & Losada, M. F. (2005). Positive affect and the complex dynamics of human flourishing. *American Psychologist, 60*(7), 678–686. https://doi.org/10.1037/0003-066X.60.7.678

Friedman, H. L., & Brown, N. J. L. (2018). Implications of debunking the "critical positivity ratio" for humanistic psychology: Introduction to special issue. *Journal of Humanistic Psychology, 58*(3), 239–261. https://doi.org/10.1177/0022167818762227

Friedman, R. S., & Förster, J. (2010). Implicit affective cues and attentional tuning: An integrative review. *Psychological Bulletin, 136*(5), 875–893. https://doi.org/10.1037/a0020495

Frijda, N. H. (1988). The laws of emotion. *American Psychologist, 43*(5), 349–358. https://doi.org/10.1037/0003-066X.43.5.349

Frijda, N. H., Kuipers, P., & ter Schure, E. (1989). Relations among emotion, appraisal, and emotional action readiness. *Journal of Personality and Social Psychology, 57*(2), 212–228. https://doi.org/10.1037/0022-3514.57.2.212

Fu, Y., & Depue, R. A. (2019). A novel neurobehavioral framework of the effects of positive early postnatal experience on incentive and consummatory reward sensitivity. *Neuroscience and Biobehavioral Reviews, 107*, 615–640. https://doi.org/10.1016/j.neubiorev.2019.09.026

Funder, D. C. (2016). Taking situations seriously: The situation construal model and the Riverside Situational Q-Sort. *Current Directions in Psychological Science, 25*(3), 203–208. https://doi.org/10.1177/0963721416635552

Gable, P., & Harmon-Jones, E. (2010). The motivational dimensional model of affect: Implications for breadth of attention, memory, and cognitive categorisation. *Cognition and Emotion, 24*(2), 322–337. https://doi.org/10.1080/02699930903378305

Galla, B. M., & Duckworth, A. L. (2015). More than resisting temptation: Beneficial habits mediate the relationship between self-control and positive life outcomes. *Journal of Personality and Social Psychology, 109*(3), 508–525. https://doi.org/10.1037/pspp0000026

Geisler, F. C. M., & Schröder-Abé, M. (2015). Is emotion suppression beneficial or harmful? It depends on self-regulatory strength. *Motivation and Emotion, 39*(4), 553–562. https://doi.org/10.1007/s11031-014-9467-5

Goodman, W. (2022). *Toxic positivity: Keeping it real in a world obsessed with being happy.* Penguin House.

Gottman, J. M. (1993). A theory of marital dissolution and stability. *Journal of Family Psychology, 7*(1), 57–75. https://doi.org/10.1037/0893-3200.7.1.57

Gottman, J. M., & Silver, N. (2015). *The seven principles for making marriage work: A practical guide from the country's foremost relationship expert* (rev. ed). Harmony.

Gratz, K. L., & Roemer, L. (2004). Multidimensional assessment of emotion regulation and dysregulation: Development, factor structure, and initial validation of the Difficulties in Emotion Regulation Scale. *Journal of Psychopathology and Behavioral Assessment, 26*(1), 41–54. https://doi.org/10.1023/B:JOBA.0000007455.08539.94

Gross, J. J. (1998a). Antecedent- and response-focused emotion regulation: Divergent consequences for experience, expression, and physiology. *Journal of Personality and Social Psychology, 74*(1), 224–237. https://doi.org/10.1037/0022-3514.74.1.224

Gross, J. J. (1998b). The emerging field of emotion regulation: An integrative review. *Review of General Psychology, 2*(3), 271–299. https://doi.org/10.1037/1089-2680.2.3.271

Gross, J. J. (2015). Emotion regulation: Current status and future prospects. *Psychological Inquiry, 26*(1), 1–26. https://doi.org/10.1080/1047840X.2014.940781

Gross, J. J., & Barrett, L. F. (2011). Emotion generation and emotion regulation: One or two depends on your point of view. *Emotion Review, 3*(1), 8–16. https://doi.org/10.1177/1754073910380974

Gross, J. J., & John, O. P. (1995). Facets of emotional expressivity: Three self-report factors and their correlates. *Personality and Individual Differences, 19*(4), 555–568. https://doi.org/10.1016/0191-8869(95)00055-B

Gross, J. J., & John, O. P. (2003). Individual differences in two emotion regulation processes: Implications for affect, relationships, and well-being. *Journal of Personality and Social Psychology, 85*(2), 348–362. https://doi.org/10.1037/0022-3514.85.2.348

Gross, J. J., Sheppes, G., & Urry, H. L. (2011). Emotion generation and emotion regulation: A distinction we should make (carefully). *Cognition and Emotion, 25*(5), 765–781. https://doi.org/10.1080/02699931.2011.555753

Gross, J. J., Uusberg, H., & Uusberg, A. (2019). Mental illness and well-being: An affect regulation perspective. *World Psychiatry*, *18*(2), 130–139. https://doi.org/10.1002/wps.20618

Grossmann, I., Dorfman, A., Oakes, H., Santos, H. C., Vohs, K. D., & Scholer, A. A. (2021). Training for wisdom: The distanced-self-reflection diary method. *Psychological Science*, *32*(3), 381–394. https://doi.org/10.1177/0956797620969170

Haga, S. M., Kraft, P., & Corby, E.-K. (2009). Emotion regulation: Antecedents and well-being outcomes of cognitive reappraisal and expressive suppression in cross-cultural samples. *Journal of Happiness Studies*, *10*, 271–291. https://doi.org/10.1007/s10902-007-9080-3

Hamm, J. M., Wrosch, C., Barlow, M. A., & Kunzmann, U. (2021). A tale of two emotions: The diverging salience and health consequences of calmness and excitement in old age. *Psychology and Aging*, *36*(5), 626–641. https://doi.org/10.1037/pag0000512

Hari, J. (2018). *Lost connections: Uncovering the real causes of depression, and the unexpected solutions*. Bloomsbury.

Harris, R. (2006). Embracing your demons: An overview of acceptance and commitment therapy. *Psychotherapy in Australia*, *12*(4), 2–8.

Hartmann, S., Pruessner, L., & Barnow, S. (2024). Contextual variations in emotion polyregulation: How do regulatory goals shape the use and success of emotion regulation strategies in everyday life? *Emotion*, *24*(3), 574–588. https://doi.org/10.1037/emo0001285

Hatfield, E., Cacioppo, J. T., & Rapson, R. L. (1993). Emotional contagion. *Current Directions in Psychological Science*, *2*(3), 96–100. https://doi.org/10.1111/1467-8721.ep10770953

Hayes, J. E., & Keast, R. S. J. (2011). Two decades of supertasting: Where do we stand? *Physiology & Behavior*, *104*(5), 1072–1074. https://doi.org/10.1016/j.physbeh.2011.08.003

Hayes, S. C. (2005). *Get out of your mind and into your life: The new acceptance and commitment therapy*. New Harbinger.

Hayes, S. C. (2019). *A liberated mind: How to pivot toward what matters*. Avery.

Headley, J. (2013, May 22). *It's not about the nail* [Video]. YouTube. https://www.youtube.com/watch?v=-4EDhdAHrOg&ab_channel=JasonHeadley

Heatherton, T. F., & Baumeister, R. F. (1991). Binge eating as escape from self-awareness. *Psychological Bulletin*, *110*(1), 86–108. https://doi.org/10.1037/0033-2909.110.1.86

Heiland, A. M., & Veilleux, J. C. (2024). Reductions in distress intolerance via intervention: A review. *Cognitive Therapy and Research, 48,* 833–853. https://doi.org/10.1007/s10608-023-10425-1

Hemming, L., Haddock, G., Shaw, J., & Pratt, D. (2019). Alexithymia and its associations with depression, suicidality, and aggression: An overview of the literature. *Frontiers in Psychiatry, 10,* 203. https://doi.org/10.3389/fpsyt.2019.00203

Henderson, H. M., Kane, S. J., Zabelina, D. L., & Veilleux, J. C. (2023). Creativity to prompt willpower: Feeling more creative predicts subsequent activated positive affect and increased willpower in daily life. *Psychology of Aesthetics, Creativity, and the Arts.* Advance online publication. https://doi.org/10.1037/aca0000566

Hervé, J., Mani, S., Behrman, J., Laxminarayan, R., & Nandi, A. (2024, April). *Food coma is real: The effect of digestive fatigue on adolescents' cognitive performance.* Institute of Labor Economics Discussion Paper No. 16909. https://docs.iza.org/dp16909.pdf

Hoemann, K., Nielson, C., Yuen, A., Gurera, J. W., Quigley, K. S., & Barrett, L. F. (2021). Expertise in emotion: A scoping review and unifying framework for individual differences in the mental representation of emotional experience. *Psychological Bulletin, 147*(11), 1159–1183. https://doi.org/10.1037/bul0000327

Hofmann, S. G., Carpenter, J. K., & Curtiss, J. (2016). Interpersonal Emotion Regulation Questionnaire (IERQ): Scale development and psychometric characteristics. *Cognitive Therapy and Research, 40*(3), 341–356. https://doi.org/10.1007/s10608-016-9756-2

Honkalampi, K., Jokela, M., Lehto, S. M., Kivimäki, M., & Virtanen, M. (2022). Association between alexithymia and substance use: A systematic review and meta-analysis. *Scandinavian Journal of Psychology, 63*(5), 427–438. https://doi.org/10.1111/sjop.12821

Hsieh, P. J., Colas, J. T., & Kanwisher, N. (2011). Pop-out without awareness: Unseen feature singletons capture attention only when top-down attention is available. *Psychological Science, 22*(9), 1220–1226. https://doi.org/10.1177/0956797611419302

Huang, S., Berenbaum, H., & Chow, P. I. (2013). Distinguishing voluntary from involuntary attention to emotion. *Personality and Individual Differences, 54*(8), 894–898. https://doi.org/10.1016/j.paid.2012.12.025

Ingram, R. E. (1990). Self-focused attention in clinical disorders: Review and a conceptual model. *Psychological Bulletin, 107*(2), 156–176. https://doi.org/10.1037/0033-2909.107.2.156

Ito, T., & Cacioppo, J. (2005). Variations on a human universal: Individual differences in positivity offset and negativity bias. *Cognition and Emotion, 19*(1), 1–26. https://doi.org/10.1080/02699930441000120

Izard, C. E. (2007). Basic emotions, natural kinds, emotion schemas, and a new paradigm. *Perspectives on Psychological Science, 2*(3), 260–280. https://doi.org/10.1111/j.1745-6916.2007.00044.x

Izard, C. E. (2010). The many meanings/aspects of emotion: Definitions, functions, activation, and regulation. *Emotion Review, 2*(4), 363–370. https://doi.org/10.1177/1754073910374661

Jamieson, J. P., Nock, M. K., & Mendes, W. B. (2012). Mind over matter: Reappraising arousal improves cardiovascular and cognitive responses to stress. *Journal of Experimental Psychology: General, 141*(3), 417–422. https://doi.org/10.1037/a0025719

Jerath, R., Crawford, M. W., Barnes, V. A., & Harden, K. (2015). Self-regulation of breathing as a primary treatment for anxiety. *Applied Psychophysiology and Biofeedback, 40*(2), 107–115. https://doi.org/10.1007/s10484-015-9279-8

Joiner, T. E., Jr., & Metalsky, G. I. (2001). Excessive reassurance seeking: Delineating a risk factor involved in the development of depressive symptoms. *Psychological Science, 12*(5), 371–378. https://doi.org/10.1111/1467-9280.00369

Kanter, J. W., Manos, R. C., Bowe, W. M., Baruch, D. E., Busch, A. M., & Rusch, L. C. (2010). What is behavioral activation? A review of the empirical literature. *Clinical Psychology Review, 30*(6), 608–620. https://doi.org/10.1016/j.cpr.2010.04.001

Kassam, K. S., & Mendes, W. B. (2013). The effects of measuring emotion: Physiological reactions to emotional situations depend on whether someone is asking. *PLoS One, 8*(6), e64959. https://doi.org/10.1371/journal.pone.0064959

Keltner, D., Sauter, D., Tracy, J., & Cowen, A. (2019). Emotional expression: Advances in basic emotion theory. *Journal of Nonverbal Behavior, 43*(2), 133–160. https://doi.org/10.1007/s10919-019-00293-3

Kennedy, M., & Franklin, J. (2002). Skills-based treatment for alexithymia: An exploratory case series. *Behaviour Change, 19*(3), 158–171. https://doi.org/10.1375/bech.19.3.158

Kennedy-Moore, E., & Watson, J. C. (2001). How and when does emotional expression help? *Review of General Psychology, 5*(3), 187–212. https://doi.org/10.1037/1089-2680.5.3.187

Kent, J. (2009). *There's no such thing as a dragon.* Dragonfly Books. (Original work published 1975)

Keough, M. E., Riccardi, C. J., Timpano, K. R., Mitchell, M. A., & Schmidt, N. B. (2010). Anxiety symptomatology: The association with distress tolerance and anxiety sensitivity. *Behavior Therapy, 41*(4), 567–574. https://doi.org/10.1016/j.beth.2010.04.002

Kessler, R. C., Chiu, W. T., Jin, R., Ruscio, A. M., Shear, K., & Walters, E. E. (2006). The epidemiology of panic attacks, panic disorder, and agoraphobia in the National Comorbidity Survey Replication. *Archives of General Psychiatry, 63*(4), 415–424. https://doi.org/10.1001/archpsyc.63.4.415

Khosravani, V., Ardestani, S. M. S., Mohammadzadeh, A., Bastan, F. S., & Amirinezhad, A. (2020). The emotional schemas and obsessive-compulsive symptom dimensions in people with obsessive-compulsive disorder. *International Journal of Cognitive Therapy, 13*(4), 341–357. https://doi.org/10.1007/s41811-020-00075-6

Kim, M. Y., Ford, B. Q., Mauss, I., & Tamir, M. (2015). Knowing when to seek anger: Psychological health and context-sensitive emotional preferences. *Cognition and Emotion, 29*(6), 1126–1136. https://doi.org/10.1080/02699931.2014.970519

Kinnaird, E., Stewart, C., & Tchanturia, K. (2019). Investigating alexithymia in autism: A systematic review and meta-analysis. *European Psychiatry, 55*, 80–89. https://doi.org/10.1016/j.eurpsy.2018.09.004

Klingsieck, K. B. (2013). Procrastination: When good things don't come to those who wait. *European Psychologist, 18*(1), 24–34. https://doi.org/10.1027/1016-9040/a000138

Klohnen, E. C. (1996). Conceptual analysis and measurement of the construct of ego-resiliency. *Journal of Personality and Social Psychology, 70*(5), 1067–1079. https://doi.org/10.1037/0022-3514.70.5.1067

Kneeland, E. T., Dovidio, J. F., Joormann, J., & Clark, M. S. (2016). Emotion malleability beliefs, emotion regulation, and psychopathology: Integrating affective and clinical science. *Clinical Psychology Review, 45*, 81–88. https://doi.org/10.1016/j.cpr.2016.03.008

Kneeland, E. T., Nolen-Hoeksema, S., Dovidio, J. F., & Gruber, J. (2016). Beliefs about emotion's malleability influence state emotion regulation.

Motivation and Emotion, *40*(5), 740–749. https://doi.org/10.1007/s11031-016-9566-6

Koven, N. S., & Thomas, W. (2010). Mapping facets of alexithymia to executive dysfunction in daily life. *Personality and Individual Differences*, *49*(1), 24–28. https://doi.org/10.1016/j.paid.2010.02.034

Kring, A. M., & Gordon, A. H. (1998). Sex differences in emotion: Expression, experience, and physiology. *Journal of Personality and Social Psychology*, *74*(3), 686–703. https://doi.org/10.1037/0022-3514.74.3.686

Kross, E., Bruehlman-Senecal, E., Park, J., Burson, A., Dougherty, A., Shablack, H., Bremner, R., Moser, J., & Ayduk, O. (2014). Self-talk as a regulatory mechanism: How you do it matters. *Journal of Personality and Social Psychology*, *106*(2), 304–324. https://doi.org/10.1037/a0035173

Ladis, I., Toner, E. R., Daros, A. R., Daniel, K. E., Boukhechba, M., Chow, P. I., Barnes, L. E., Teachman, B. A., & Ford, B. Q. (2023). Assessing emotion polyregulation in daily life: Who uses it, When is it used, and how effective is it? *Affective Science*, *4*(2), 248–259. https://doi.org/10.1007/s42761-022-00166-x

Laghai, A., & Joseph, S. (2000). Attitudes towards emotional expression: Factor structure, convergent validity and associations with personality. *British Journal of Medical Psychology*, *73*(3), 381–384. https://doi.org/10.1348/000711200160598

Lambert, N. M., Clark, M. S., Durtschi, J., Fincham, F. D., & Graham, S. M. (2010). Benefits of expressing gratitude: Expressing gratitude to a partner changes one's view of the relationship. *Psychological Science*, *21*(4), 574–580. https://doi.org/10.1177/0956797610364003

Lambie, J. A. (2009). Emotion experience, rational action, and self-knowledge. *Emotion Review*, *1*(3), 272–280. https://doi.org/10.1177/1754073909103596

Lane, R. D. (2020). The construction of emotional experience: State-related emotional awareness and its application to psychotherapy research and practice. *Counselling & Psychotherapy Research*, *20*(3), 479–487. https://doi.org/10.1002/capr.12331

Lane, R. D., Quinlan, D. M., Schwartz, G. E., Walker, P. A., & Zeitlin, S. B. (1990). The Levels of Emotional Awareness Scale: A cognitive-developmental measure of emotion. *Journal of Personality Assessment*, *55*(1–2), 124–134. https://doi.org/10.1080/00223891.1990.9674052

Lane, R. D., & Smith, R. (2021). Levels of emotional awareness: Theory and measurement of a socio-emotional skill. *Journal of Intelligence, 9*(3), 42. https://doi.org/10.3390/jintelligence9030042

Larsen, J. T., & McGraw, A. P. (2011). Further evidence for mixed emotions. *Journal of Personality and Social Psychology, 100*(6), 1095–1110. https://doi.org/10.1037/a0021846

Larsen, J. T., & Stastny, B. J. (2011). It's a bittersweet symphony: Simultaneously mixed emotional responses to music with conflicting cues. *Emotion, 11*(6), 1469–1473. https://doi.org/10.1037/a0024081

Lazarus, R. S. (1984). On the primacy of cognition. *American Psychologist, 39*(2), 124–129. https://doi.org/10.1037/0003-066X.39.2.124

Lazarus, R. S. (2006). Emotions and interpersonal relationships: Toward a person-centered conceptualization of emotions and coping. *Journal of Personality, 74*(1), 9–46. https://doi.org/10.1111/j.1467-6494.2005.00368.x

Lench, H. C., Tibbett, T. P., & Bench, S. W. (2016). Exploring the toolkit of emotion: What do sadness and anger do for us? *Social and Personality Psychology Compass, 10*(1), 11–25. https://doi.org/10.1111/spc3.12229

Lennarz, H. K., Hollenstein, T., Lichtwarck-Aschoff, A., Kuntsche, E., & Granic, I. (2019). Emotion regulation in action: Use, selection, and success of emotion regulation in adolescents' daily lives. *International Journal of Behavioral Development, 43*(1), 1–11. https://doi.org/10.1177/0165025418755540

Levant, R. F. (1995). Toward the reconstruction of masculinity. In W. S. Pollack & R. F. Levant (Eds.), *A new psychology of men* (pp. 229–251). Basic Books. (Reprinted in modified form from the *Journal of Family Psychology, 5*(3/4), 1992, pp. 379–402)

Levant, R. F., Hall, R. J., Williams, C. M., & Hasan, N. T. (2009). Gender differences in alexithymia. *Psychology of Men & Masculinities, 10*(3), 190–203. https://doi.org/10.1037/a0015652

Levy-Gigi, E., & Shamay-Tsoory, S. (2022). Affect labeling: The role of timing and intensity. *PLoS ONE, 17*(12), e0279303. https://doi.org/10.1371/journal.pone.0279303

Leyro, T. M., Zvolensky, M. J., & Bernstein, A. (2010). Distress tolerance and psychopathological symptoms and disorders: A review of the empirical literature among adults. *Psychological Bulletin, 136*(4), 576–600. https://doi.org/10.1037/a0019712

Lieberman, M. D., Inagaki, T. K., Tabibnia, G., & Crockett, M. J. (2011). Subjective responses to emotional stimuli during labeling, reappraisal, and distraction. *Emotion, 11*(3), 468–480. https://doi.org/10.1037/a0023503

Linehan, M. M. (1993). *Cognitive behavioral therapy of borderline personality disorders.* Guilford Press.

Linehan, M. M. (2015). *DBT skills training manual* (2nd ed.). Guilford Press.

Liu, D. Y., Strube, M. J., & Thompson, R. J. (2021). Interpersonal emotion regulation: An experience sampling study. *Affective Science, 2*(3), 273–288. https://doi.org/10.1007/s42761-021-00044-y

Luberto, C. M., Cotton, S., McLeish, A. C., Mingione, C. J., & O'Bryan, E. M. (2014). Mindfulness skills and emotion regulation: The mediating role of coping self-efficacy. *Mindfulness, 5*(4), 373–380. https://doi.org/10.1007/s12671-012-0190-6

Luminet, O., Nielson, K. A., & Ridout, N. (2021). Cognitive–emotional processing in alexithymia: An integrative review. *Cognition and Emotion, 35*(3), 449–487. https://doi.org/10.1080/02699931.2021.1908231

Macatee, R. J., & Cougle, J. R. (2013). The roles of emotional reactivity and tolerance in generalized, social, and health anxiety: A multimethod exploration. *Behavior Therapy, 44*(1), 39–50. https://doi.org/10.1016/j.beth.2012.05.006

Mankus, A. M., Boden, M. T., & Thompson, R. J. (2016). Sources of variation in emotional awareness: Age, gender, and socioeconomic status. *Personality and Individual Differences, 89*, 28–33. https://doi.org/10.1016/j.paid.2015.09.043

Matthews, G. D., & Wells, A. (1999). The cognitive science of attention and emotion. In T. Dalgleish & M. J. Power (Eds.), *Handbook of cognition and emotion* (pp. 171–191). Wiley. https://doi.org/10.1002/0470013494.ch9

McNally, R. J. (2002). Anxiety sensitivity and panic disorder. *Biological Psychiatry, 52*(10), 938–946. https://doi.org/10.1016/S0006-3223(02)01475-0

McRae, K., Ciesielski, B., & Gross, J. J. (2012). Unpacking cognitive reappraisal: Goals, tactics, and outcomes. *Emotion, 12*(2), 250–255. https://doi.org/10.1037/a0026351

Metcalfe, J., & Mischel, W. (1999). A hot/cool-system analysis of delay of gratification: Dynamics of willpower. *Psychological Review*, 106(1), 3–19. https://doi.org/10.1037/0033-295X.106.1.3

Michel, N. M., Rowa, K., Young, L., & McCabe, R. E. (2016). Emotional distress tolerance across anxiety disorders. *Journal of Anxiety Disorders*, 40, 94–103. https://doi.org/10.1016/j.janxdis.2016.04.009

Miller, M. (Director). (1989a). *The parent trap III* [Film]. Walt Disney Television.

Miller, M. (Director). (1989b). *The parent trap IV: Hawaiian honeymoon* [Film]. Walt Disney Television.

Mischel, W., & Shoda, Y. (1995). A cognitive–affective system theory of personality: Reconceptualizing situations, dispositions, dynamics, and invariance in personality structure. *Psychological Review*, 102(2), 246–268. https://doi.org/10.1037/0033-295X.102.2.246

Mitchell, M. D., Gehrman, P., Perlis, M., & Umscheid, C. A. (2012). Comparative effectiveness of cognitive behavioral therapy for insomnia: A systematic review. *BMC Family Practice*, 13(1), Article 40. https://doi.org/10.1186/1471-2296-13-40

Moors, A. (2014). Flavors of appraisal theories of emotion. *Emotion Review*, 6(4), 303–307. https://doi.org/10.1177/1754073914534477

Moser, J. S., Dougherty, A., Mattson, W. I., Katz, B., Moran, T. P., Guevarra, D., Shablack, H., Ayduk, O., Jonides, J., Berman, M. G., & Kross, E. (2017). Third-person self-talk facilitates emotion regulation without engaging cognitive control: Converging evidence from ERP and fMRI. *Scientific Reports*, 7(1), Article 4519. https://doi.org/10.1038/s41598-017-04047-3

Myin-Germeys, I., Krabbendam, P. A., Delespaul, P. E. A. G., & Van Os, J. (2003). Do life events have their effect on psychosis by influencing the emotional reactivity to daily life stress? *Psychological Medicine*, 33(2), 327–333. https://doi.org/10.1017/s0033291702006785

Nakamura, J., & Csikszentmihalyi, M. (2002). The concept of flow. In C. R. Snyder & S. J. Lopez (Eds.), *Handbook of positive psychology* (pp. 89–105). Oxford University Press.

Naragon-Gainey, K., McMahon, T. P., & Chacko, T. P. (2017). The structure of common emotion regulation strategies: A meta-analytic examination. *Psychological Bulletin*, 143(4), 384–427. https://doi.org/10.1037/bul0000093

Neff, K. D. (2003). Self-compassion: An alternative conceptualization of a healthy attitude toward oneself. *Self and Identity*, 2(2), 85–101. https://doi.org/10.1080/15298860309032

Niven, K. (2017). The four key characteristics of interpersonal emotion regulation. *Current Opinion in Psychology*, 17, 89–93. https://doi.org/10.1016/j.copsyc.2017.06.015

Nock, M. K., Wedig, M. M., Holmberg, E. B., & Hooley, J. M. (2008). The Emotion Reactivity Scale: Development, evaluation, and relation to self-injurious thoughts and behaviors. *Behavior Therapy*, 39(2), 107–116. https://doi.org/10.1016/j.beth.2007.05.005

Norman, H., Marzano, L., Coulson, M., & Oskis, A. (2019). Effects of mindfulness-based interventions on alexithymia: A systematic review. *Evidence-Based Mental Health*, 22(1), 36–43. https://doi.org/10.1136/ebmental-2018-300029

Nowakowski, M. E., McFarlane, T., & Cassin, S. (2013). Alexithymia and eating disorders: A critical review of the literature. *Journal of Eating Disorders*, 1(1), Article 21. https://doi.org/10.1186/2050-2974-1-21

O'Bryan, E. M., McLeish, A. C., & Johnson, A. L. (2017). The role of emotion reactivity in health anxiety. *Behavior Modification*, 41(6), 829–845. https://doi.org/10.1177/0145445517719398

O'Connor, L. E., Berry, J. W., Lewis, T., Mulherin, K., & Crisostomo, P. S. (2007). Empathy and depression: The moral system on overdrive. In T. F. D. Farrow & P. W. R. Woodruff (Eds.), *Empathy in mental illness* (pp. 49–75). Cambridge University Press. https://doi.org/10.1017/CBO9780511543753.005

O'Driscoll, C., Laing, J., & Mason, O. (2014). Cognitive emotion regulation strategies, alexithymia and dissociation in schizophrenia, a review and meta-analysis. *Clinical Psychology Review*, 34(6), 482–495. https://doi.org/10.1016/j.cpr.2014.07.002

Oishi, S., & Westgate, E. C. (2022). A psychologically rich life: Beyond happiness and meaning. *Psychological Review*, 129(4), 790–811. https://doi.org/10.1037/rev0000317

Oppenheim-Weller, S., Roccas, S., & Kurman, J. (2018). Subjective value fulfillment: A new way to study personal values and their consequences. *Journal of Research in Personality*, 76, 38–49. https://doi.org/10.1016/j.jrp.2018.07.006

Orsillo, S. M., & Roemer, L. (2016). *Worry less, live more: The mindful way through anxiety workbook.* Guilford Press.

Orvell, A., Vickers, B. D., Drake, B., Verduyn, P., Ayduk, O., Moser, J., Jonides, J., & Kross, E. (2021). Does distanced self-talk facilitate emotion regulation across a range of emotionally intense experiences? *Clinical Psychological Science, 9*(1), 68–78. https://doi.org/10.1177/2167702620951539

Osborne, D. W. S., & Williams, C. J. (2013). Excessive reassurance-seeking. *Advances in Psychiatric Treatment, 19*(6), 420–421. https://doi.org/10.1192/apt.bp.111.009761

Palmieri, P. A., Boden, M. T., & Berenbaum, H. (2009). Measuring clarity of and attention to emotions. *Journal of Personality Assessment, 91*(6), 560–567. https://doi.org/10.1080/00223890903228539

Pauw, L. S., Sauter, D. A., van Kleef, G. A., & Fischer, A. H. (2019). Stop crying! The impact of situational demands on interpersonal emotion regulation. *Cognition and Emotion, 33*(8), 1587–1598. https://doi.org/10.1080/02699931.2019.1585330

Pennebaker, J. W. (1997). Writing about emotional experiences as a therapeutic process. *Psychological Science, 8*(3), 162–166. https://doi.org/10.1111/j.1467-9280.1997.tb00403.x

Perciavalle, V., Blandini, M., Fecarotta, P., Buscemi, A., Di Corrado, D., Bertolo, L., Fichera, F., & Coco, M. (2017). The role of deep breathing on stress. *Neurological Sciences, 38*(3), 451–458. https://doi.org/10.1007/s10072-016-2790-8

Perel, E. (2001). A tourist's view of marriage: Cross-cultural couples—Challenges, choices, and implications for therapy. In P. Papp (Ed.), *Couples on the fault line* (pp. 178–204). Guilford Press.

Perry, M. (2022). *Friends, lovers, and the big terrible thing.* Flatiron Books.

Pickering, A. D., & Corr, P. J. (2008). J. A. Gray's reinforcement sensitivity theory (RST) of personality. In G. J. Boyle, G. Matthews, & D. H. Saklofske (Eds.), *The Sage handbook of personality theory and assessment: Vol. 1. Personality theories and models* (pp. 33–55). Sage.

Piper, W. (2011). *The little engine that could.* Grosset & Dunlap. (Original work published 1930)

Preece, D. A., Becerra, R., Robinson, K., Allan, A., Boyes, M., Chen, W., Hasking, P., & Gross, J. J. (2020). What is alexithymia? Using factor analysis to establish its latent structure and relationship with fantasizing and emotional reactivity. *Journal of Personality, 88*(6), 1162–1176. https://doi.org/10.1111/jopy.12563

Rauthmann, J. F., Gallardo-Pujol, D., Guillaume, E. M., Todd, E., Nave, C. S., Sherman, R. A., Ziegler, M., Jones, A. B., & Funder, D. C. (2014). The

Situational Eight DIAMONDS: A taxonomy of major dimensions of situation characteristics. *Journal of Personality and Social Psychology*, *107*(4), 677–718. https://doi.org/10.1037/a0037250

Rochat, M. J. (2023). Sex and gender differences in the development of empathy. *Journal of Neuroscience Research*, *101*(5), 718–729. https://doi.org/10.1002/jnr.25009

Rose, A. J. (2021). The costs and benefits of co-rumination. *Child Development Perspectives*, *15*(3), 176–181. https://doi.org/10.1111/cdep.12419

Roseman, I. J., Antoniou, A. A., & Jose, P. E. (1996). Appraisal determinants of emotions: Constructing a more accurate and comprehensive theory. *Cognition and Emotion*, *10*(3), 241–278. https://doi.org/10.1080/026999396380240

Roth, T. (2007). Insomnia: Definition, prevalence, etiology, and consequences. *Journal of Clinical Sleep Medicine*, *3*(5, Suppl.), S7–S10.

Rothbart, M. K., Ahadi, S. A., & Evans, D. E. (2000). Temperament and personality: Origins and outcomes. *Journal of Personality and Social Psychology*, *78*(1), 122–135. https://doi.org/10.1037/0022-3514.78.1.122

Rozin, P., & Royzman, E. B. (2001). Negativity bias, negativity dominance, and contagion. *Personality and Social Psychology Review*, *5*(4), 296–320. https://doi.org/10.1207/S15327957PSPR0504_2

Rush, J., Ong, A. D., Piazza, J. R., Charles, S. T., & Almeida, D. M. (2024). Too little, too much, and "just right": Exploring the "Goldilocks zone" of daily stress reactivity. *Emotion*, *24*(5), 1249–1258. https://doi.org/10.1037/emo0001333

Russell, J. A. (2012). Introduction to special section: On defining emotion. *Emotion Review*, *4*(4), 337. https://doi.org/10.1177/1754073912445857

Rutherford, M. R. (2019). *Perfectly hidden depression: How to break free from the perfectionism that masks your depression.* New Harbinger.

Sabey, C. V., Charlton, C., & Charlton, S. R. (2019). The "magic" positive-to-negative interaction ratio: Benefits, applications, cautions, and recommendations. *Journal of Emotional and Behavioral Disorders*, *27*(3), 154–164. https://doi.org/10.1177/1063426618763106

Salovey, P., & Grewal, D. (2005). The science of emotional intelligence. *Current Directions in Psychological Science*, *14*(6), 281–285. https://doi.org/10.1111/j.0963-7214.2005.00381.x

Samur, D., Tops, M., Schlinkert, C., Quirin, M., Cuijpers, P., & Koole, S. L. (2013). Four decades of research on alexithymia: Moving toward clinical applications. *Frontiers in Psychology, 4,* 861. https://doi.org/10.3389/fpsyg.2013.00861

Sauer-Zavala, S., Wilner, J. G., & Barlow, D. H. (2017). Addressing neuroticism in psychological treatment. *Personality Disorders, 8*(3), 191–198. https://doi.org/10.1037/per0000224

Sauer-Zavala, S., Wilner, J. G., Cassiello-Robbins, C., Saraff, P., & Pagan, D. (2019). Isolating the effect of opposite action in borderline personality disorder: A laboratory-based alternating treatment design. *Behaviour Research and Therapy, 117,* 79–86. https://doi.org/10.1016/j.brat.2018.10.006

Schei, V. (2013). Creative people create values: Creativity and positive arousal in negotiations. *Creativity Research Journal, 25*(4), 408–417. https://doi.org/10.1080/10400419.2013.843336

Scherer, K. R. (2005). What are emotions? And how can they be measured? *Social Sciences Information, 44*(4), 695–729. https://doi.org/10.1177/0539018405058216

Schneider, T. R. (2004). The role of neuroticism on psychological and physiological stress responses. *Journal of Experimental Social Psychology, 40*(6), 795–804. https://doi.org/10.1016/j.jesp.2004.04.005

Schrauf, R. W., & Sanchez, J. (2004). The preponderance of negative emotion words in the emotion lexicon: A cross-generational and cross-linguistic study. *Journal of Multilingual and Multicultural Development, 25*(2–3), 266–284. https://doi.org/10.1080/01434630408666532

Schreiber, R. E., & Veilleux, J. C. (2022). The Self-Invalidation Due to Emotion Scale: Development and psychometric properties. *Psychological Assessment, 34*(10), 937–951. https://doi.org/10.1037/pas0001155

Schwartz, S. H. (2012). An overview of the Schwartz theory of basic values. *Online Readings in Psychology and Culture, 2*(1), 1–20. https://doi.org/10.9707/2307-0919.1116

Schwartz, S. H. (2017). The refined theory of basic values. In S. Roccas & L. Sagiv (Eds.), *Values and behavior: Taking a cross-cultural perspective* (pp. 51–72). Springer. https://doi.org/10.1007/978-3-319-56352-7_3

Schwartz, S. H., Cieciuch, J., Vecchione, M., Davidov, E., Fischer, R., Beierlein, C., Ramos, A., Verkasalo, M., Lönnqvist, J.-E., Demirutku, K., Dirilen-Gumus, O., & Konty, M. (2012). Refining the theory of basic individual values. *Journal of Personality and Social Psychology, 103*(4), 663–688. https://doi.org/10.1037/a0029393

Schwarz, N., & Clore, G. L. (1983). Mood, misattribution, and judgments of well-being: Informative and directive functions of affective states. *Journal of Personality and Social Psychology, 45*(3), 513–523. https://doi.org/10.1037/0022-3514.45.3.513

Segerstrom, S. C., Tsao, J. C. I., Alden, L. E., & Craske, M. G. (2000). Worry and rumination: Repetitive thought as a concomitant and predictor of negative mood. *Cognitive Therapy and Research, 24*(6), 671–688. https://doi.org/10.1023/A:1005587311498

Sels, L., Tran, A., Greenaway, K. H., Verhofstadt, L., & Kalokerinos, E. K. (2021). The social functions of positive emotions. *Current Opinion in Behavioral Sciences, 39*, 41–45. https://doi.org/10.1016/j.cobeha.2020.12.009

Semcho, S. A., Southward, M. W., Stumpp, N. E., MacLean, D. L., Hood, C. O., Wolitzky-Taylor, K., & Sauer-Zavala, S. (2023). Aversive reactivity: A transdiagnostic functional bridge between neuroticism and avoidant behavioral coping. *Journal of Emotion and Psychopathology, 1*(1), 23–40. https://doi.org/10.55913/joep.v1i1.9

Shapero, B. G., Abramson, L. Y., & Alloy, L. B. (2016). Emotional reactivity and internalizing symptoms: Moderating role of emotion regulation. *Cognitive Therapy and Research, 40*, 328–340. https://doi.org/10.1007/s10608-015-9722-4

Shariff, A. F., & Tracy, J. L. (2011). What are emotion expressions for? *Current Directions in Psychological Science, 20*(6), 395–399. https://doi.org/10.1177/0963721411424739

Shaver, J. A., Veilleux, J. C., & Ham, L. S. (2013). Meta-emotions as predictors of drinking to cope: A comparison of competing models. *Psychology of Addictive Behaviors, 27*(4), 1019–1026. https://doi.org/10.1037/a0033999

Sheppes, G., Scheibe, S., Suri, G., & Gross, J. J. (2011). Emotion-regulation choice. *Psychological Science, 22*(11), 1391–1396. https://doi.org/10.1177/0956797611418350

Simon-Thomas, E. R., Keltner, D. J., Sauter, D., Sinicropi-Yao, L., & Abramson, A. (2009). The voice conveys specific emotions: Evidence from vocal burst displays. *Emotion, 9*(6), 838–846. https://doi.org/10.1037/a0017810

Sirois, F. M., & Pychyl, T. (2013). Procrastination and the priority of short-term mood regulation: Consequences for future self. *Social and Personality Psychology Compass, 7*(2), 115–127. https://doi.org/10.1111/spc3.12011

Slatcher, R. B., & Pennebaker, J. W. (2006). How do I love thee? Let me count the words: The social effects of expressive writing. *Psychological Science, 17*(8), 660–664. https://doi.org/10.1111/j.1467-9280.2006.01762.x

Smillie, L. D., Pickering, A. D., & Jackson, C. J. (2006). The new reinforcement sensitivity theory: Implications for personality measurement. *Personality and Social Psychology Review, 10*(4), 320–335. https://doi.org/10.1207/s15327957pspr1004_3

Smith, C. A., & Ellsworth, P. C. (1985). Patterns of cognitive appraisal in emotion. *Journal of Personality and Social Psychology, 48*(4), 813–838. https://doi.org/10.1037/0022-3514.48.4.813

Smith, C. A., & Kirby, L. D. (2001). Affect and cognitive appraisal processes. In J. P. Forgas (Ed.), *Handbook of affect and social cognition* (pp. 75–92). Erlbaum.

Smith, R., Killgore, W. D. S., & Lane, R. D. (2018). The structure of emotional experience and its relation to trait emotional awareness: A theoretical review. *Emotion, 18*(5), 670–692. https://doi.org/10.1037/emo0000376

Smith, R., & Lane, R. D. (2016). Unconscious emotion: A cognitive neuroscientific perspective. *Neuroscience & Biobehavioral Reviews, 69*, 216–238. https://doi.org/10.1016/j.neubiorev.2016.08.013

Smolinski, J. (Writer), & Asher, R. (Director). (2019). The retreat (Season 5, Episode 6) [TV series episode]. In M. Kaufmann & H. J. Morris (Executive Producers), *Grace and Frankie*. Okay Goodnight; Skydance Television.

Soto, J. A., Perez, C. R., Kim, Y. H., Lee, E. A., & Minnick, M. R. (2011). Is expressive suppression always associated with poorer psychological functioning? A cross-cultural comparison between European Americans and Hong Kong Chinese. *Emotion, 11*(6), 1450–1455. https://doi.org/10.1037/a0023340

Southward, M. W., Sauer-Zavala, S., & Cheavens, J. S. (2021). Specifying the mechanisms and targets of emotion regulation: A translational framework from affective science to psychological treatment. *Clinical Psychology, 28*(2), 168–182. https://doi.org/10.1037/cps0000003

Steele, C. M., & Josephs, R. A. (1990). Alcohol myopia: Its prized and dangerous effects. *American Psychologist, 45*(8), 921–933. https://doi.org/10.1037/0003-066X.45.8.921

Storm, C., & Storm, T. (1987). A taxonomic study of the vocabulary of emotions. *Journal of Personality and Social Psychology, 53*(4), 805–816. https://doi.org/10.1037/0022-3514.53.4.805

Strack, F., Martin, L. L., & Stepper, S. (1988). Inhibiting and facilitating conditions of the human smile: A nonobtrusive test of the facial feedback hypothesis. *Journal of Personality and Social Psychology, 54*(5), 768–777. https://doi.org/10.1037/0022-3514.54.5.768

Strauss, G. P., Ossenfort, K. L., & Whearty, K. M. (2016). Reappraisal and distraction emotion regulation strategies are associated with distinct patterns of visual attention and differing levels of cognitive demand. *PLoS One, 11*(11), e0162290. https://doi.org/10.1371/journal.pone.0162290

Sweeny, K., & Dooley, M. D. (2017). The surprising upsides of worry. *Social and Personality Psychology Compass, 11*(4), e12311. https://doi.org/10.1111/spc3.12311

Tackman, A. M., & Srivastava, S. (2016). Social responses to expressive suppression: The role of personality judgments. *Journal of Personality and Social Psychology, 110*(4), 574–591. https://doi.org/10.1037/pspp0000053

Tamir, M. (2016). Why do people regulate their emotions? A taxonomy of motives in emotion regulation. *Personality and Social Psychology Review, 20*(3), 199–222. https://doi.org/10.1177/1088868315586325

Tamir, M., Schwartz, S. H., Cieciuch, J., Riediger, M., Torres, C., Scollon, C., Dzokoto, V., Zhou, X., & Vishkin, A. (2016). Desired emotions across cultures: A value-based account. *Journal of Personality and Social Psychology, 111*(1), 67–82. https://doi.org/10.1037/pspp0000072

Tangney, J. P., Miller, R. S., Flicker, L., & Barlow, D. H. (1996). Are shame, guilt, and embarrassment distinct emotions? *Journal of Personality and Social Psychology, 70*(6), 1256–1269. https://doi.org/10.1037/0022-3514.70.6.1256

Tanner, B. A. (2012). Validity of global physical and emotional SUDS. *Applied Psychophysiology and Biofeedback, 37*(1), 31–34. https://doi.org/10.1007/s10484-011-9174-x

Taylor, S. (2003). Anxiety sensitivity and its implications for understanding and treating PTSD. *Journal of Cognitive Psychotherapy, 17*(2), 179–186. https://doi.org/10.1891/jcop.17.2.179.57431

Taylor, S. E., & Stanton, A. L. (2007). Coping resources, coping processes, and mental health. *Annual Review of Clinical Psychology, 3*(1), 377–401. https://doi.org/10.1146/annurev.clinpsy.3.022806.091520

Thompson, B. L., Luoma, J. B., & Lejeune, J. T. (2013). Using acceptance and commitment therapy to guide exposure-based interventions for posttraumatic stress disorder. *Journal of Contemporary Psychotherapy*, *43*(3), 133–140. https://doi.org/10.1007/s10879-013-9233-0

Thompson, R. J., Dizén, M., & Berenbaum, H. (2009). The unique relations between emotional awareness and facets of affective instability. *Journal of Research in Personality*, *43*(5), 875–879. https://doi.org/10.1016/j.jrp.2009.07.006

Tice, D. M., & Bratslavsky, E. (2000). Giving in to feel good: The place of emotion regulation in the context of general self-control. *Psychological Inquiry*, *11*(3), 149–159. https://doi.org/10.1207/S15327965PLI1103_03

Torre, J. B., & Lieberman, M. D. (2018). Putting feelings into words: Affect labeling as implicit emotion regulation. *Emotion Review*, *10*(2), 116–124. https://doi.org/10.1177/1754073917742706

Torrubia, R., Ávila, C., Moltó, J., & Caseras, X. (2001). The Sensitivity to Punishment and Sensitivity to Reward Questionnaire (SPSRQ) as a measure of Gray's anxiety and impulsivity dimensions. *Personality and Individual Differences*, *31*(6), 837–862. https://doi.org/10.1016/S0191-8869(00)00183-5

Troy, A. S., Shallcross, A. J., & Mauss, I. B. (2013). A person-by-situation approach to emotion regulation: Cognitive reappraisal can either help or hurt, depending on the context. *Psychological Science*, *24*(12), 2505–2514. https://doi.org/10.1177/0956797613496434

Tsai, J. L. (2007). Ideal affect: Cultural causes and behavioral consequences. *Perspectives on Psychological Science*, *2*(3), 242–259. https://doi.org/10.1111/j.1745-6916.2007.00043.x

Tversky, A., & Kahneman, D. (1981, January 30). The framing of decisions and the psychology of choice. *Science*, *211*(4481), 453–458. https://doi.org/10.1126/science.7455683

Tyra, A. T., Fergus, T. A., & Ginty, A. T. (2024). Emotion suppression and acute physiological responses to stress in healthy populations: A quantitative review of experimental and correlational investigations. *Health Psychology Review*, *18*(2), 396–420. https://doi.org/10.1080/17437199.2023.2251559

Vaish, A., Grossmann, T., & Woodward, A. (2008). Not all emotions are created equal: The negativity bias in social–emotional development. *Psychological Bulletin*, *134*(3), 383–403. https://doi.org/10.1037/0033-2909.134.3.383

van Doorn, J. (2018). Anger, feelings of revenge, and hate. *Emotion Review*, *10*(4), 321–322. https://doi.org/10.1177/1754073918783260

van Overveld, W. J. M., de Jong, P. J., Peters, M. L., Cavanagh, K., & Davey, G. C. L. (2006). Disgust propensity and disgust sensitivity: Separate constructs that are differentially related to specific fears. *Personality and Individual Differences, 41*(7), 1241–1252. https://doi.org/10.1016/j.paid.2006.04.021

van Zutphen, L., Siep, N., Jacob, G. A., Goebel, R., & Arntz, A. (2015). Emotional sensitivity, emotion regulation and impulsivity in borderline personality disorder: A critical review of fMRI studies. *Neuroscience and Biobehavioral Reviews, 51*, 64–76. https://doi.org/10.1016/j.neubiorev.2015.01.001

Västfjäll, D., Slovic, P., Burns, W. J., Erlandsson, A., Koppel, L., Asutay, E., & Tinghög, G. (2016). The arithmetic of emotion: Integration of incidental and integral affect in judgments and decisions. *Frontiers in Psychology, 7*, 325. https://doi.org/10.3389/fpsyg.2016.00325

Veilleux, J. C. (2023). A theory of momentary distress tolerance: Toward understanding contextually-situated choices to engage with or avoid distress. *Clinical Psychological Science, 11*(2), 357–380. https://doi.org/10.1177/21677026221118327

Veilleux, J. C., Caldwell, A. R., Johnson, E. C., Kavouras, S., McDermott, B. P., & Ganio, M. S. (2020). Examining the links between hydration knowledge, attitudes and behavior. *European Journal of Nutrition, 59*(3), 991–1000. https://doi.org/10.1007/s00394-019-01958-x

Veilleux, J. C., Chamberlain, K. D., Baker, D. E., & Warner, E. A. (2021). Disentangling beliefs about emotions from emotion schemas. *Journal of Clinical Psychology, 77*(4), 1068–1089. https://doi.org/10.1002/jclp.23098

Veilleux, J. C., Clift, J. B., Schreiber, R. E., Shelton, D. K., Henderson, H. M., & Gregory, C. (2024). What goals do people have for who they want to be emotionally? Exploring long-term emotional goals. *Emotion.* https://doi.org/10.1037/emo0001453

Veilleux, J. C., Hyde, K. C., Chamberlain, K. D., Higuera, D. E., Schreiber, R. E., Warner, E. A., & Clift, J. B. (2022). The "thinking threshold": A therapeutic concept guided by emotion regulation flexibility. *Practice Innovations, 7*(1), 28–39. https://doi.org/10.1037/pri0000166

Veilleux, J. C., Pollert, G. A., Skinner, K. D., Chamberlain, K. D., Baker, D. E., & Hill, M. A. (2021). Individual beliefs about emotion and perceptions of belief stability are associated with symptoms of psychopathology and emotional processes. *Personality and Individual Differences, 171,* 110541. https://doi.org/10.1016/j.paid.2020.110541

Veilleux, J. C., Schreiber, R. E., Warner, E. A., & Brott, K. H. (2024). Development and validation of a brief version of the Emotion Reactivity Scale: The B-ERS. *Current Psychology, 43,* 12586–12600. https://doi.org/10.1007/s12144-023-05323-4

Veilleux, J. C., Warner, E. A., Baker, D. E., & Chamberlain, K. D. (2021). Beliefs about emotion shift dynamically alongside momentary affect. *Journal of Personality Disorders, 35*(Suppl. A), 83–113. https://doi.org/10.1521/pedi_2020_34_491

Veilleux, J. C., Warner, E. A., Chamberlain, K. D., Brott, K. H., Schreiber, R. E., & Clift, J. B. (2023). Contextual variation in beliefs about emotion and associated emotion regulation efforts. *Motivation and Emotion, 47*(3), 308–322. https://doi.org/10.1007/s11031-022-09992-9

Verduyn, P., Delvaux, E., Van Coillie, H., Tuerlinckx, F., & Van Mechelen, I. (2009). Predicting the duration of emotional experience: Two experience sampling studies. *Emotion, 9*(1), 83–91. https://doi.org/10.1037/a0014610

Vine, V., Bernstein, E. E., & Nolen-Hoeksema, S. (2019). Less is more? Effects of exhaustive vs. minimal emotion labelling on emotion regulation strategy planning. *Cognition and Emotion, 33*(4), 855–862. https://doi.org/10.1080/02699931.2018.1486286

Volkaert, B., Wante, L., Van Beveren, M. L., Vervoort, L., & Braet, C. (2020). Training adaptive emotion regulation skills in early adolescents: The effects of distraction, acceptance, cognitive reappraisal, and problem solving. *Cognitive Therapy and Research, 44*(3), 678–696. https://doi.org/10.1007/s10608-019-10073-4

Wahl, K., Schönfeld, S., Hissbach, J., Küsel, S., Zurowski, B., Moritz, S., Hohagen, F., & Kordon, A. (2011). Differences and similarities between obsessive and ruminative thoughts in obsessive-compulsive and depressed patients: A comparative study. *Journal of Behavior Therapy and Experimental Psychiatry, 42*(4), 454–461. https://doi.org/10.1016/j.jbtep.2011.03.002

Wall, K., Kalpakci, A., Hall, K., Crist, N., & Sharp, C. (2018). An evaluation of the construct of emotional sensitivity from the perspective of emotionally sensitive people. *Borderline Personality Disorder and Emotion Dysregulation, 5*(1), Article 14. https://doi.org/10.1186/s40479-018-0091-y

Waller, R., & Wagner, N. (2019). The Sensitivity to Threat and Affiliative Reward (STAR) model and the development of callous–unemotional traits. *Neuroscience and Biobehavioral Reviews, 107,* 656–671. https://doi.org/10.1016/j.neubiorev.2019.10.005

Walley-Jean, J. C. (2009). Debunking the myth of the "angry Black woman": An exploration of anger in young African American women. *Black Women, Gender + Families, 3*(2), 68–86.

Watkins, E. R. (2016). *Rumination-focused cognitive-behavioral therapy for depression.* Guilford Press.

Webb, T. L., Lindquist, K. A., Jones, K., Avishai, A., & Sheeran, P. (2018). Situation selection is a particularly effective emotion regulation strategy for people who need help regulating their emotions. *Cognition and Emotion, 32*(2), 231–248. https://doi.org/10.1080/02699931.2017.1295922

Webb, T. L., Miles, E., & Sheeran, P. (2012). Dealing with feeling: A meta-analysis of the effectiveness of strategies derived from the process model of emotion regulation. *Psychological Bulletin, 138*(4), 775–808. https://doi.org/10.1037/a0027600

Wegner, D. M., Schneider, D. J., Carter, S. R., III, & White, T. L. (1987). Paradoxical effects of thought suppression. *Journal of Personality and Social Psychology, 53*(1), 5–13. https://doi.org/10.1037/0022-3514.53.1.5

Weissman, D. G., Nook, E. C., Dews, A. A., Miller, A. B., Lambert, H. K., Sasse, S. F., Somerville, L. H., & McLaughlin, K. A. (2020). Low emotional awareness as a transdiagnostic mechanism underlying psychopathology in adolescence. *Clinical Psychological Science, 8*(6), 971–988. https://doi.org/10.1177/2167702620923649

Wenzel, M., Rowland, Z., Weber, H., & Kubiak, T. (2019). A round peg in a square hole: Strategy–situation fit of intra- and interpersonal emotion regulation strategies and controllability. *Cognition and Emotion, 34*(5), 1003–1009. https://doi.org/10.1080/02699931.2019.1697209

Westphal, M., Seivert, N. H., & Bonanno, G. A. (2010). Expressive flexibility. *Emotion, 10*(1), 92–100. https://doi.org/10.1037/a0018420

Wheaton, B., & Montazer, S. (2010). Stressors, stress, and distress. In T. L. Scheid & T. N. Brown (Eds.), *A handbook for the study of mental health: Social contexts, theories, and systems* (2nd ed., pp. 171–199). Cambridge University Press.

Wilson, K. G., Sandoz, E. K., Kitchens, J., & Roberts, M. (2010). The Valued Living Questionnaire: Defining and measuring valued action within a behavioral framework. *Psychological Record, 60,* 249–272. https://doi.org/10.1007/BF03395706

Winkielman, P., & Berridge, K. C. (2004). Unconscious emotion. *Current Directions in Psychological Science, 13*(3), 120–123. https://doi.org/10.1111/j.0963-7214.2004.00288.x

Wolgast, M., & Lundh, L. G. (2017). Is distraction an adaptive or maladaptive strategy for emotion regulation? A person-oriented approach. *Journal of Psychopathology and Behavioral Assessment, 39*(1), 117–127. https://doi.org/10.1007/s10862-016-9570-x

Yik, M., Russell, J. A., & Barrett, L. F. (1999). Structure of self-reported current affect: Integration and beyond. *Journal of Personality and Social Psychology, 77*(3), 600–619. https://doi.org/10.1037/0022-3514.77.3.600

Zaki, J., & Williams, W. C. (2013). Interpersonal emotion regulation. *Emotion, 13*(5), 803–810. https://doi.org/10.1037/a0033839

Zhang, Y., Fu, R., Sun, L., Gong, Y., & Tang, D. (2019). How does exercise improve implicit emotion regulation ability: Preliminary evidence of mind–body exercise intervention combined with aerobic jogging and mindfulness-based yoga. *Frontiers in Psychology, 10,* 1888. https://doi.org/10.3389/fpsyg.2019.01888

Zielinski, M. J., Hill, M. A., & Veilleux, J. C. (2018). Is the first cut really the deepest? Frequency and recency of nonsuicidal self-injury in relation to psychopathology and dysregulation. *Psychiatry Research, 259,* 392–397. https://doi.org/10.1016/j.psychres.2017.10.030

Zielinski, M. J., & Veilleux, J. C. (2018). The Perceived Invalidation of Emotion Scale (PIES): Development and psychometric properties of a novel measure of current emotion invalidation. *Psychological Assessment, 30*(11), 1454–1467. https://doi.org/10.1037/pas0000584

Zimmer-Gembeck, M. J. (2021). Coping flexibility: Variability, fit and associations with efficacy, emotion regulation, decentering and responses to stress. *Stress & Health, 37*(5), 848–861. https://doi.org/10.1002/smi.3043

Zvolensky, M. J., Vujanovic, A. A., Bernstein, A., & Leyro, T. (2010). Distress tolerance: Theory, measurement, and relations to psychopathology. *Current Directions in Psychological Science, 19*(6), 406–410. https://doi.org/10.1177/0963721410388642

INDEX

Acceptance, 60, 68, 74
Accuracy, of emotional labels, 97, 102
Achievement, 60, 68, 74, 78, 101, 140, 234
Action tendencies of emotions (action urges)
  acting opposite of, 183–184
  awareness of, 29, 41
  compulsion to follow, 184
  deciding to enact, 151–152
  defined, 10
  emotional labeling to use, 85–86
  function of, 55
  reading, 138–141
Active emotion regulation strategies, 163–190, 249
Adventure, 60, 64, 69–70, 118
Affect, 10, 153, 255
Agency, 171, 205
Aggression, 39
Alexithymia
  defined, 38, 255
  emotional expression and, 194
  emotional labeling with, 39, 82, 91
  emotional sharing with, 214–215
  mindfulness practices and, 48
  opening the envelope approach with, 136
Ambition, 60, 74

Amusement family of emotions, 88, 94
Amygdala, 84
Anger
  action tendency of, 10
  appraisal associated with, 34, 57, 176
  challenged values and, 67, 76
  complex emotions involving, 100
  cultural norms of expression of, 39, 219
  as family of emotions, 88, 92, 139
  goal pursuit and, 85–86
  metaemotions associated with, 140–141
  opposite action response for, 183–184
  physiological changes with, 182, 183
  usefulness of, 55, 144
Antecedent emotion regulation strategies, 182–186
  mental grounding, 184–186
  opposite action, 183–184
  targeting physiological changes, 182–183
Anxiety disorder, 4, 6, 194
  controllability beliefs and symptoms of, 188
  emotional awareness and, 28
  emotional sensitivity and, 20, 40

Anxiety disorder (*continued*)
  expressive suppression and
    symptoms of, 202
  involuntary attention to emotion
    and, 37
Anxiety or anxiousness, 10
  about uncertainty, 168–169
  action urge associated with, 140
  in appraisal theory of emotion, 57
  challenged values and, 67, 76
  as family of emotions, 139
  message of, 88
  in mixed emotions, 101
  norms of expression for, 39, 194
  panic attacks and, 27
  physiological changes with, 182
  threat sensitivity and, 18
  usefulness of, 145–146
Appraisal
  defined, 255
  in emotion generation, 33, 34, 165,
    176
  with involuntary attention to
    emotion, 37–38
  regulation strategies that change,
    166, 176–179
  theories of emotion, 56–57, 176–177
  variability in response and, 56
Asking for what you want, 219–221
Attention
  awareness vs., 31, 35, 37
  high emotional sensitivity and, 31–32
  in emotion generation, 32–34
  emotions to direct, 55, 58
  in Mail With Sticky Glue problem,
    36–38
  in mindfulness activities, 42
  in negativity bias, 110–111
  in Watching the Mailbox problem,
    35–38
  regulation strategies that shift, 166,
    171–175
  self-focused, 37
  sharing to redirect, 213–215

for thought suppression, 173
  variability in response and, 56
Attitude, behavior and, 248
Authenticity, 79
Authority, 60, 78
Autism, 39
Automatic thoughts, 177
Avoidance-based coping (disengage-
    ment emotion regulation),
    154–156
  controllability beliefs and, 188
  coping ahead vs., 107
  defined, 255
  distraction in, 172–174
  flexible use of, 242–244
  proactive selection vs., 169
  research on, 227
Awareness
  attention vs., 35, 37
  of emotion generation stage, 32
  mindful, 36, 41, 135
  in mindfulness vs. flow, 45
  of triggers, 50–51
Awe family of emotions, 88, 94

Beauty, 61, 78, 118
Behavior, attitude and, 248
Belonging, 61, 65, 78, 79, 87, 101, 118
Black women, expression of anger by,
    219
Blame, 24, 177, 179, 205–207, 222
Blended emotions, 99–100
Bodily sensations
  awareness of, 29, 40
  labeling current, 99
  labeling past, 97–99
Body language
  emotional labeling based on, 97
  in emotional sharing, 198
  feedback in terms of, 244
  imbuing, with emotions, 9
  information communicated by, 55
  media that dampen or lack, 221
  in opposite action, 184

Bonding, 55, 144, 200, 208, 209, 215
Borderline personality disorder, 20,
   28, 40
Brief Emotional Reactivity Scale, 16–19
Broadcaster, 195
   asking for what you want as,
      219–221
   benefits of sharing for, 210–215
   blaming by, 206–207
   knowing what you want as, 217–218
   suppression for protection of, 205
Bucket lists, 59

Caring, 61, 87, 245
Cathartic emotional expression,
   195–197, 208
Challenged values (triggered values),
   67, 74–76, 101
Clear emotions, 243
Cognitive behavioral therapy, 120,
   176, 179
Cognitive biases, 37
Cognitive reappraisal (cognitive
   reframing)
   barriers to using, 181
   beliefs supporting, 189
   context for using, 230
   defined, 176, 255
   distancing vs., 179, 180
   emotional sharing and, 214
   reinterpretation, 176–179, 187, 227,
      235, 260
   tips for, 178
Cognitive reinterpretation. *See* Cognitive
   reappraisal
Collectivist (interdependent) cultures,
   142, 202–203
Communication
   around emotional expression,
      193–194
   emotions to facilitate, 55, 192, 199
   medium for, 221
Compassion, 8, 108
Complex emotions, 99–101, 141

Conflicting values, 67, 77–78, 89
Conservation cluster of values, 70–72,
   76, 77, 142–143
Contempt, 207
Contentment, 55, 88, 94
Context sensitivity, 228–233
Contrahedonic goals, 143, 255
Controllability
   of emotions, 187–189, 209
   of situation, 230
Coping ahead, 105–129
   and beliefs about emotions, 189
   and breadth of repertoire, 233
   coping with generated emotions vs.,
      108–109
   defined, 256
   emotional conditioning for, 107–108
   energy resource for, 119–125
   grounding techniques and, 186
   and need for emotion regulation, 164
   overcoming barriers to, 125–127
   physical health for, 119–122
   with pleasure, 113–119
   preparing for emotional distress,
      127–128
   as psychological protective gear,
      105–106
   psychological resources for, 111–119
   social connection for, 123–124
   and stress vs. resilience, 109–111
Coping strategies. *See also* Emotion
   regulation strategies
   coping ahead vs. using, 108–109
   emotional sensitivity and reliance
      on, 20
   seeking therapy to cultivate, 5–6,
      164
   substance use as proxy for, 121
Corumination, 208–209, 256
Couples therapy, 114, 193–194, 207,
   210–212, 214
Creativity, 61, 68, 72, 78, 234
Criticism, 158, 207, 212
Crossed signals, 199, 200, 221–222

Crying, solo, 195
Cultural norms
    desired emotions and, 142–143
    of emotional expression, 39, 194,
        202–203, 205, 219
    Receiver standards based on, 219
    recognizing, 216–217
Curiosity, 61, 72, 78, 118

Decision making, about emotion
    regulation, 151–154
Deep breathing, 153, 182, 238–239
Defense (value), 61, 72
Defensiveness, 207
Defusion, 179, 256. See also Distancing
Delivery Unsuccessful problem, 36,
    38–41, 48, 49
Denial, 97
Dependability, 61
Depression, 4, 6, 108, 193, 194
    alexithymia and, 39, 40
    controllability beliefs and symptoms
        of, 188
    disconnection and, 69
    emotional awareness and, 28
    emotional sensitivity and, 18,
        20, 40
    expressive suppression and
        symptoms of, 202
    involuntary attention to emotion
        and, 37
    nonverbal cues of, 198
    pursuing pleasant feelings and, 117,
        144
Describe Your Environment technique,
    185–186
Desired emotions, 240
    in emotional goal setting, 142–143
    long-term goals based on, 148–149
    synergy of long-term goals,
        short-term goals and, 150–151
    useful emotions vs., 146, 245
Dialectical behavior therapy, 183, 248
Disconnection, 69, 124, 125, 202, 203

Disengagement emotion regulation.
    See Avoidance-based coping
Disgust, 18, 88, 93, 100, 139, 144
Distancing, 176, 178–181, 236, 256
Distraction, 83, 171–176
    as avoidance, 172–174
    beliefs supporting, 189
    defined, 171, 256
    emotional sharing for, 214, 220
    grounding techniques and, 186
    for healthy emotion regulation,
        174–175
    during mindfulness activities, 44
    in polyregulation, 187
    social context for using, 231
    tactics for, 234, 235
Distress tolerance, 253–254
Divorce, 207
Down-regulation, 134, 164
Down-to-Earth (value), 61, 64
Duty, 61, 118, 245

Eating disorders, 28, 39
Embarrassment, 98
Emotion(s). See also specific emotions
    by name
    aversion to use of term, 17
    complex, 99–101, 141
    components of, 9–10
    controllability of, 187–189, 209
    defined, 9, 256
    distinctions between terms for, 10–14
    facilitation of communication by,
        55, 192, 199
    feeling vs., 10, 258
    functions/purpose of, 3–4, 54–58,
        85, 132, 192, 199, 245
    meta-, 140–141, 211, 258
    mixed, 100–101
    mood vs., 10–14, 256, 259
    muddy, 243–244, 259
    multifaceted, 99–101
    physical and mental components
        of, 119

pleasant/positive. *See* Pleasant
  emotions (positive emotions)
reactivation of, 157–158
recognition of others', 96
relationship of values and, 67,
  86–89
as signals of what matters, 4, 55–58,
  254
social nature of, 191–192
unpleasant/negative. *See* Unpleasant
  emotions (negative emotions)
Emotional awareness, 27–52
assessing your, 29–31
attentiveness to emotions and,
  31–32, 35–41
and awareness of triggers, 50–51
and breadth of repertoire, 233
broad and balanced, 36, 41
defined, 28–29, 256
in Delivery Unsuccessful problem,
  36, 38–41
for emotional labeling, 82
involuntary attention with narrowed, 35–38
in Mindful Awareness profile, 36, 41
mindfulness activities to improve,
  41–50
in opening the envelope approach,
  135
in panic attacks, 27–28
sweet spot of, 50
with Watching the Mailbox problem,
  35–38
Emotional channels
nonverbal, 198, 199, 221–222
synergy of, 221–222
verbal, 198, 199, 221–222
Emotional conditioning, 47, 107–108,
  127, 128
Emotional distress
about distress, 211
coping ahead and, 106–107
emotional labeling to reduce,
  84–85

emotional sensitivity and, 19
during expressive writing, 197
preparing for, 106–107, 127–128
problem-solving to reduce, 170
rating scale for, 12, 238
tolerating, 253–254
Emotional expression, 9
with alexithymia, 39
and breadth of repertoire, 233
cathartic, 195–197, 208
cultural norms of, 39, 194, 202–203,
  219
defined, 194, 256
emotional sensitivity and, 15
flexibility in, 204, 216–217, 223,
  230–231, 258
labeling others emotions based on,
  96–97
long-term goals related to, 147, 149
opposite action and, 184
as regulation strategy, 222
sharing type of. *See* Emotional
  sharing
social context for, 231
and social nature of emotions,
  191–192
suppressing. *See* Expressive
  suppression
tactics for, 236
types of, 193–199
variability in, 5
without sharing, 195–197
Emotional goals, 141–151
balance in, 244–249
desired emotions component of,
  142–143
identifying, 141–150
labeling to set, 136
long-term, 146–150, 153–154,
  239–240
matching up components of,
  150–151
monitoring regulation strategies
  against, 186–187, 237–240

Emotional goals (*continued*)
  short-term, 143–146, 150–151,
    237–240
  useful emotions component of,
    143–150
Emotional harm, 138, 205
Emotional health, 5–6, 226
  advice on, 249–250
  cathartic emotional expression for,
    197
  cultivating meaning for, 245
  emotional awareness for, 31, 51
  labeling for, 101–102
  physical health and, 120, 122–123
Emotional intelligence, 19, 28, 149
Emotional intensity. *See* Intensity of
  emotion
Emotional invalidation
  defined, 20, 256
  expressive suppression after, 218
  of high emotional sensitivity, 20–21,
    23, 25
  of low emotional sensitivity,
    21–22, 25
  with reinterpretation, 181
  responses to, 25
  in response to sharing, 205, 206
  unintentional, 206, 219
Emotional labeling, 81–104
  accuracy in, 97, 102
  with alexithymia, 39, 82, 91
  and beliefs about emotions, 189
  and breadth of repertoire, 233
  for complex, multifaceted, or mixed
    emotions, 99–101
  for current emotion, 99
  defined, 81, 82, 257
  emotional awareness required for, 82
  emotional sharing and, 211,
    214–215
  emotional vocabulary for, 90–96
  as emotion regulation strategy,
    83–85, 164
  in expressive writing, 197

  to facilitate goal pursuit, 85–86
  importance of, 83
  improving at, 90–99
  in opening the envelope approach,
    136
  of others' emotional expressions,
    96–97
  of past emotional states, 97–99
  pitfalls to watch out for with,
    101–103
  problem-solving after, 170–171
  to recognize values, 86–89
  self-assessment of skill, 89–90
  specificity in, 102
  thoroughness in, 102–103
Emotional messages. *See also* Mail
    metaphor for emotional messages;
    Opening the envelope approach
  discarding, too early, 154–156, 172
  distraction and, 171
  emotion regulation flexibility and,
    240
  in families of emotions, 87–88
  reading information and implied
    action of, 136–141, 233
  retaining, too long, 156–158
  unhelpful, 158–160
  values as senders of, 78–79, 137–141,
    192, 254
Emotional response
  in appraisal theory of emotions,
    57–58
  complexity of, 100
  dampening, 181–187, 189, 204, 212
  deciding to experience, 152–153,
    245, 254
  in emotion generation, 32–34, 56
  in emotion regulation cycle, 165
  experiencing, as long-term goal,
    147, 149
  experiencing crest and fall of,
    132–133
  mood and, 11–13
Emotional self, 5

Emotional sensitivity, 7–26. *See also*
    High emotional sensitivity
  "correct" amount of, 18–22
  defined, 14–15, 257
  intentionally changing, 8–9
  long-term goals related to, 147, 149
  low, 21–22, 24, 38, 40
  moderate levels of, 19
  parallels between supertasting and,
    22–24
  of Princess vs. Detective, 7, 18
  reflection on, 24–25
  self-assessment of, 217
  spectrum of, 7, 16–18
Emotional sharing
  asking for what you want in,
    219–221
  benefits of, 201, 210–216
  considering the Receiver in, 218–219
  defined, 194–195, 257
  drawbacks of, 201, 205–209
  effects of, for Broadcaster, 205,
    210–215
  emotional expression without,
    195–197
  feedback on, 239–240
  invalidation and blaming in
    response to, 206–207
  knowing what you want from,
    217–218
  relational effects of, 215–216
  selecting medium for, 221
  for social connection, 55
  synergy of emotional channels in,
    221–222
  tips for successful, 216–222
  as type of emotional expression,
    198–199
  venting or excessive reassurance
    seeking, 207–209
Emotional tunnel vision, 213–215
Emotional vocabulary, 90–96, 257
Emotional vulnerability, reducing,
    113–125

Emotion dysregulation, 166–167, 257
Emotion generation
  alexithymia and, 39
  defined, 257
  with involuntary attention to
    emotion, 37–38
  and regulation, 164–167, 182
  stages of, 32–34, 51, 176
  triggers in, 50–51
  and variability in emotional
    response, 56
Emotion regulation, 163–190
  balancing experiencing emotions
    with, 254
  belief in your skills of, 188
  breadth of repertoire, 233–237
  and controllability beliefs, 187–189
  decision making about, 151–154
  dysregulation, 166–167, 257
  emotional sharing for, 223
  emotion generation and, 164–167
  flexibility in. *See* Emotion regulation
    flexibility
  identification stage of, 133–134
  long-term goals related to, 147
  mind–body connection for, 122
  misregulation, 167, 259
  monitoring and feedback on,
    237–240
  need for, 142
  overlabeling of emotion and, 103
  planning for, 153
  polyregulation, 186–187, 259
  science of, 4–5
  self-efficacy for, 246–247
  slowing down, 132–133
  strategies for. *See* Emotion regulation
    strategies
  underregulation, 167, 261
  willingness to attempt, 247–248
  willpower and, 163
Emotion regulation flexibility
  balance in goals for, 244–249
  breadth of repertoire for, 233–237

Emotion regulation flexibility
  (*continued*)
  context sensitivity in, 228–233
  defined, 227–228, 257
  for emotional health, 226
  monitoring and feedback for,
    237–240
  in opening the envelope approach,
    240–244
  recipes for, 249–250
Emotion regulation strategies, 168–186
  active, 163–190, 249
  antecedent, 182–186
  changing triggers, 168–171, 187, 213
  cultivating, 163–164
  dampening emotional responses,
    181–187, 189, 204, 212
  defined, 257
  disengagement. *See* Avoidance-based
    coping
  distancing, 176, 178–181, 236, 256
  distraction. *See* Distraction
  emotional expression as, 222
  emotional labeling as, 83–85, 164
  emotion controllability and
    effectiveness of, 187–189
  in emotion regulation cycle,
    133–134
  expressive suppression as, 202, 204
  failure of implementation for, 167
  incorporating other people in, 167
  mental grounding, 184–186
  opposite action, 183–184, 256
  passive, 249
  proactive selection, 168–170, 260
  problem-solving. *See*
    Problem-solving
  reinterpretation, 176–179, 187, 227,
    235, 260
  selection of, 165
  shifting thoughts, 176–181, 187,
    214
  tactics for enacting, 183, 233–237,
    258

  targeting physiological changes,
    182–183
  toolbox of, 166–167
Emotion regulation tactics, 183,
    233–237, 258
Emotions
  useful/helpful. *See* Useful emotions
    (helpful emotions)
Emotion science, 4–5
Empathy, 19, 194
Energy resource, 119–127
  defined, 119–125, 258
  for emotional health, 122–123
  exercise to build, 121–122
  interactions between components,
    127
  medications to improve, 121
  nourishing food for, 119–120
  overcoming barriers to building,
    126–127
  sleep to replenish, 120
  substance use and, 121–122
Environmental context, 228–229
Environmental triggers, 11
Equality, 61
Esteem, 61, 79, 87, 89
Excitement, mixed emotions involving,
    101
Exercise, 121–122, 126, 183
Expressive flexibility, 204, 216–217,
    223, 230–231, 258
Expressive suppression, 200
  after emotional invalidation, 218
  benefits of, 192–193, 201, 203–205
  cultural norms and effects of,
    202–203
  defined, 258
  drawbacks of, 193, 201–203
  as emotion regulation strategy, 202,
    204
  self-assessment of, 217
Expressive writing, 196–197, 210
External experience, mindfulness of,
    48, 49

Facial expression
emotional labeling based on, 97
in emotional sharing, 198
feedback in terms of, 244
imbuing, with emotions, 9
information communicated by, 55
media that lack, 221
in opposite action, 184
Faith, 61
Families, expressive suppression
norms in, 203, 216–217
Fear
action tendency of, 10
challenged values and, 76
in complex emotions, 100
of emotional labeling, 84–85
as family of emotions, 88, 92, 139
usefulness of, 144
Feedback, on emotion regulation
strategies, 237–240
Feelings
awareness of, 29
defined, 10, 258
differentiating between, 82, 90
irrational, 86, 87
regulation strategies that dampen,
166
Feeling-to-word method of labeling,
99–100
Financial resources, 112
5-4-3-2-1 technique, 185, 186
Flow, 44–45, 258
Food choices, nourishing, 119–120,
126
Frozen (film), 195
Fulfillment, 54, 245

Generated emotions
coping strategies for, 108–109
labeling, 99
overattentiveness to, 36–38
regulation strategies for, 165
Goal pursuit, 85–86, 132

Goals. *See also* Emotional goals
contrahedonic, 143, 255
of emotional sharing, 217–221
hedonic, 142–143, 147, 258
values vs., 59, 262
Gottman, John, 114, 207
Grace and Frankie (TV series), 143
Gratitude, 88, 94, 144
Grief, 170, 193, 206
Grounding, 184–186, 230, 236, 258
Growth, mindfulness for, 47–48, 50
Guilt, 179
action tendency of, 10
as family of emotions, 88, 93, 139
in interdependent cultures, 143
malnourished values and, 67, 69

Happiness, 10, 202, 245
Hayes, Stephen, 67
Health (value), 62
Hedonic goals, 142–143, 147, 258
Helpful emotions. *See* Useful
emotions
Helpfulness, 62
High emotional awareness, 28, 31, 35.
See also Watching the Mailbox
problem
High emotional sensitivity
alexithymia with, 40
and aversion to term "emotion," 17
benefits and drawbacks of, 19–21
emotional charts for, 15
emotional labeling by people
with, 96
emotional tunnel vision with,
213–215
nonverbal emotional channel use
with, 198–199
and overattentiveness to emotion,
31–32
supertasting as parallel for, 22–24
Honesty, 62, 68
Humility, 62
Humor, 62, 72

Identification stage of emotion
  regulation
  importance of, 133–134
  opening the envelope in, 134–154
  revisiting, 154
"If. . .then . . ." strategies, 242, 244
Ignored values, 70–75
Impulsive behavior, 18, 29, 163
Independence, 59, 62, 72, 78
Individualistic cultures, 142, 202–203
Inflamed values, 243–244
Information, in emotional messages, 137
Inside Out (film), 144
Insomnia, 120
Intending, willingness vs., 247
Intensity of emotion
  for coping ahead, 109
  distraction to reduce, 174
  emotional sharing and, 211
  labeling, 91–96
  and lack of food, 119
  physical health and, 122–123
  regulation strategy selection based
    on, 181, 230
  thinking threshold and, 187
Interdependent (collectivist) cultures,
  142, 202–203
Interest family of emotions, 95
Internal experience, mindfulness of,
  48, 49
Internal triggers, 11
Interpersonal emotion regulation.
  See also Reassurance seeking;
    Venting
  benefits for Broadcaster of, 210–215
  defined, 258
  drawbacks of, 207–209
Intimacy, 62, 65, 74, 87, 140, 141
Involuntary attention to emotions,
  35–38, 48
Irrational feelings, 86, 87
Irrational thinking, 29
Isolation, 193
"It's Not the Nail" (video), 219

Jealousy, 88, 93, 139
Journaling, 195–197, 209, 241–242
Joy, 10, 88, 95

Knowing what you want, 217–218

Leadership, 62
Leisure, 62
Life goals, emotional goals based on,
  144, 145
Life satisfaction, 19, 50, 54, 153, 204
Life-threatening situations, 57–58, 91,
  110
Little Engine That Could (Piper), 246
Loneliness, 123, 182, 202
Long-term emotional goals, 146–151,
  153–154, 239–240
Love family of emotions, 95
Low emotional awareness, 28, 36,
  38–41, 48
Low emotional sensitivity, 21–22, 24,
  38, 40
Loyalty, 62, 72, 243, 245
Lust, 39

MadTV (TV series), 163
Mail metaphor for emotional
    messages, 3–4. *See also* Opening
    the envelope approach
  with alexithymia, 40
  coping ahead in, 106
  emotional awareness in, 28, 36
  emotional expression in, 192
  emotional labeling in, 81–82
  emotional sensitivity in, 23
  emotion regulation strategies in,
    166, 168
  values in, 67
Mail With Sticky Glue problem,
  36–38, 135
Malnourished values, 67, 69–75, 79
Masking emotions, 97, 191–193, 227.
  See also Expressive suppression

Meaning, cultivating, 54, 197, 245, 254
Meaningful activities, 117–119, 124–125
Medications, taking, 121, 126
Men, norms of emotional expression
    for, 39, 194
Metaemotions (secondary emotions),
    140–141, 211, 258
Mind–body connection, 122
Mindful awareness, 36, 41, 135
Mindful body scan, 49
Mindful eating, 49
Mindfulness, 41–48, 186
    being "good" at, 43–45
    and beliefs about emotions, 189
    defined, 41, 258
    emotion regulation with, 164
    to external experiences, 49
    hating, 43, 45–48
    to internal experiences, 49
    nonjudgment in, 43
    specific focus in, 42, 43
    to breath, 41–42, 45–48, 50
    to feelings, 49
    to sound, 41–44, 46–48, 50
    to thoughts, 49
    walking, 49
Misregulation, 167, 259
Mixed emotions, 100–101
Monitoring emotion regulation
    strategies, 237–240
Mood, 10–14, 47, 256, 259
Muddy emotions, 243–244, 259
Multifaceted emotions, 99–101

Near Tier values, 66, 72, 73, 75
Negative affect, 10, 153, 255
Negativity bias, 110–111, 114–115,
    177, 259
Neurotransmitters, 121–122
Nonjudgment, 43, 46–47, 50
Nonverbal emotional channel, 198,
    199, 221–222
Normalization, asking for, 220

Obedience, 62, 79
Obsessive thinking, 157
Opening the envelope approach,
    131–161
    and beliefs about emotions, 189
    discarding envelopes too early,
        154–156, 172
    emotional goal setting in, 141–151
    emotional labeling in, 136
    emotion regulation flexibility in,
        240–244
    hanging on to envelopes too long,
        156–158
    and identification stage of regulation,
        133–134
    mindful awareness in, 135
    problem-solving after, 170–171
    reading information and implied
        action in, 136–141
    regulation decision making in,
        151–154
    slowing down regulation process
        with, 132–133
    throwing away envelopes without
        reading them, 242–244
    unhelpful messages from values in,
        158–160
    when to hand on to envelopes,
        241–242
Openness to Change cluster of values,
    70–72, 77
Opposite action, 183–184, 259
Outsourcing problem-solving, 213,
    219–221
Overgeneralization, 177

Paced breathing. *See* deep breathing
Panic attacks, 20, 27–28, 34, 36, 39,
    50–51
Passive emotion regulation strategies,
    249
Past emotional states, labeling, 97–99
Pennebaker, J. W., 196
Perry, Matthew, 166–167

Personality traits, 112–113
Perspective-taking, 214–215, 218, 220
Physical context, 228–229
Physical health and resources, 119–123, 231
Physiological changes
  with emotions, 9
  with expressive suppression, 202
  in panic attacks, 27–28
  regulation targeting, 182–183
  tactics for managing, 236
Physiological context, 229
Pleasant emotions (positive emotions)
  contrahedonic goals to feel less, 143
  distraction to increase, 171
  emotional vocabulary for, 91
  expression of, 199–200
  functions of, 54
  in individualistic cultures, 142
  mixed emotions and, 100
  nourished values and, 67
  useful, 143–144
Pleasure
  balancing negativity bias with, 114–115
  in coping ahead, 113–119
  cultivating meaning and, 245
  defined, 113, 259
  from meaningful activities, 115–119
  overcoming barriers to, 126–127
  recognizing sources of, 118–119
  as value, 62
Polyregulation, 186–187, 259
Positive affect, 10, 153, 255
Positive judgments, 46–47
Positivity, 115, 177
Posttraumatic stress disorder, 20, 28, 169
Pride family of emotions, 88, 95
Primary emotions, expressing, 211
The Princess and the Pea (Andersen), 7, 18
Privilege resources, 112, 259

Proactive selection, 168–170, 260
Problem-solving, 168, 170–171, 180
  beliefs supporting use of, 188
  defined, 260
  outsourcing, 213, 219–220
  polyregulation involving, 187
  tactics for, 235
  venting/corumination and, 209
Problem-solving therapy, 170
Procrastination, 174–175, 260
Progressive muscle relaxation, 182–183
Prosperity, 62
Protection, 63, 72
Proximity, social connection and, 123
Psychological context, 229
Psychological resources, 106, 111–119, 259
Punishment sensitivity. *See* Threat sensitivity
Purpose
  finding, 53–54
  as a value, 63, 78, 79

Quality time, with others, 123–124

Reassurance seeking, 205, 208, 209, 260
Receiver, 195
  Broadcaster's selection of, 218–219
  expressive suppression by, 204–205
  unintentional invalidation by, 206, 219
  validation and support from, 212
Recognition, 63, 74
Reframing. *See* Cognitive reappraisal
Reinterpretation. *See* Cognitive reappraisal
Relationships
  balancing negative and positive experiences in, 114
  communication around emotional expression in, 193–194

effect of emotional invalidation on, 206

effect of emotional sharing on, 215–216

effect of expressive suppression on, 202–203

social nature of emotions about, 191–192

unsolvable problems in, 170

values conflicts in, 77–78

Relaxation, mindfulness for, 47

Resilience, 110–113, 115

Respect, 63, 65, 72, 78

Responsibility, 63, 245

Reward sensitivity, 18, 260

Rumination, 157, 158, 184, 241, 260

Sadness, 55, 67, 69

action tendency of, 10

appraisal leading to, 176

in complex emotions, 100

as family of emotions, 88, 93, 139

norms of expression of, 39, 194

opposite action response for, 184

physiological changes with, 182

reinterpretation of, 179

usefulness of, 144

Safety, 63, 76, 78, 79, 87, 89, 138, 141, 192

Schizophrenia, 39

Self-confidence, 189

Self-control. *See* Willpower

Self-criticism, 158, 212

Self-efficacy, 246–248, 260

Self-Enhancement cluster of values, 70, 71, 77, 142

Self-focused attention, 37

Self-invalidation, 21–22, 230

Self-regulation, 84

Self-Transcendence cluster of values, 70, 71, 77

Shame, 67, 69, 179–180

Sherlock Holmes (character), 7

Shifting thoughts, 176–181, 187, 214

Short-term emotional goals, 143–146, 150–151, 237–240

Sleep, 120, 126, 127

Social anxiety disorder, 132, 169

Social connection
for coping ahead, 123–125
defined, 260
disconnection, 69, 124, 125, 202, 203
emotional sharing for, 55
long-term goals related to, 147
low emotional sensitivity and, 21
overcoming barriers to, 126

Social context, 230–231

Social justice, 63, 65–66, 78

Social media, 198, 213

Social rejection, 18

Social support
asking for, 220
emotional sharing to seek, 212–213, 218, 219, 221
research on, 227
from "supportive" people, 123–125, 206

Solo crying, 195

Sounding-board sharing, 210–211, 220

States, defined, 9, 261

Stonewalling, 207

Strategic delay, 174–175, 244–245, 261

Stress
deep breathing to reduce, 182
defined, 109, 261
expressive flexibility and, 204
negativity bias and, 110–111
resilience vs., 110
stressors vs., 109–110
use of term, for emotion, 17

Stressors, 109–111, 122, 261

Subliminal messaging, 35–36

Substance use, 39, 121–122, 126, 127, 173

Supertasting, 22–24

Surprise family of emotions, 88, 92, 138–140

Synergy
  of emotional channels, 221–222
  of emotional goals, 150–151

Task lists, 59
Temperature changes, regulation with, 183
There's No Such Thing as a Dragon (Kent), 155–156
Thinking threshold, 187
Third-perspective, distancing with, 180
Thoughts
  association of emotions and, 10
  avoidance-based coping for, 155
  labeling, in distancing, 180
  during mindfulness activities, 44
  shifting, 176–181, 187, 214
Thought suppression, 172–174, 261
Threatened, feeling, 55, 76
Threat sensitivity, 18, 110–111, 261
Thrill seeking, 58
Tolerance, 63
Tone of voice, 9, 55, 195, 198, 221
Top Tier values, 66, 72, 73, 75, 215
Tradition (value), 63, 78, 118
Traits, defined, 9, 17, 261
Trigger(s)
  awareness of, 34, 50–51
  changing, 166, 168–171, 187, 213
  defined, 11, 261
  in emotion generation, 165
  repeated emotions related to same, 14
  shifting attention away from.
    See Distraction
  as stage of emotion generation, 32–34
  substance use and effect of, 122
Triggered values. *See* Challenged values
Trust, building, 215–216
Try mail, 159–160

Uncertainty, 168–169
Uncontrollable situations, 230
Underregulation, 167, 261

Unhelpful emotional messages, 158–160
Unity with Nature (value), 63
Unpleasant emotions (negative emotions), 3, 6
  avoiding, 155–156
  and challenged values, 76
  contrahedonic goals related to, 143
  coping ahead vs. circumventing, 106–107
  distraction to reduce, 171
  emotional labeling of, 84
  emotional vocabulary for, 91, 92
  expressive suppression of, 200, 204
  functions of, 54–55
  malnourished values and, 67
  mixed emotions and, 100
  regulation of, 132, 134
  reinterpretation of, 177
  sensitivity to, 18
  useful, 144
  values as senders of, 138
Up-regulation, 134, 164
Useful emotions (helpful emotions), 143–150, 240
  desired emotions vs., 245
  functions of, 55–56
  for long-term goals, 146–150
  for short-term goals, 143–146
  synergy of desired emotions and, 150–151

Validation. *See also* emotional invalidation
  asking for, 220
  defined, 261
  emotional sharing for, 212–213, 219, 221
  labeling emotional intensity for, 91, 96
  venting and corumination for, 209
Values, 53–80. *See also specific values and clusters by name*
  articulating, as regulation strategy, 164
  avoiding messages from, 155–156

challenged/triggered, 67, 74–76, 101
changes in, over time, 65
conflicting, 67, 77–78, 89
defined, 58–59, 262
emotional messages sent by, 78–79,
    137–141, 192, 254
and emotions as signals of what
    matters, 55–58
and finding purpose, 53–54
goals vs., 59, 262
identifying your, 60–67
ignored, 70–75
inflamed, 243–244
labeling to recognize, 86–89
malnourished, 67, 69–75, 79
Near Tier, 66, 72, 73, 75
pleasurable activities that align with,
    117–119
relationship of emotions and, 67,
    86–89
Top Tier, 66, 72, 73, 75, 215
unhelpful messages from, 158–160
well-nourished, 67, 68, 118–119
Values Clarification activity, 60–67
Variety (value), 63, 72, 78
Venting, 83, 205
    and corumination, 208–209, 256
    defined, 208, 262
    sounding-board sharing vs., 210–211

Verbal emotional channel, 198, 199,
    221–222
Vocal bursts, 198

Wanting
    asking for what you want, 219–221
    knowing what you want, 217–218
    willingness vs., 247
Wariness, 99
Watching the Mailbox problem,
    35–38, 41, 48, 49
Water, drinking enough, 120
Wealth, 63
Well-nourished values, 67, 68,
    118–119
White bear study, 173
Willfulness, 248
Willingness, 247–249, 262
Willpower (self-control), 163, 169,
    262
Women, norms of emotional expression
    for, 194, 219
Word-to-feeling method of labeling,
    99
Worry, 157–158, 184, 227, 241–242,
    262

Zoey's Extraordinary Playlist
    (TV series), 191, 222

ABOUT THE AUTHOR

Jennifer C. Veilleux, PhD, is a professor in the Department of Psychological Science at the University of Arkansas and a licensed clinical psychologist who focuses on helping people navigate their emotional lives with greater skill and flexibility. Dr. Veilleux's research has been funded by the National Institute of Mental Health, the National Institute on Drug Abuse, the American Psychological Foundation, and the John Templeton Foundation. She focuses her work on applying the basic science of emotion and self-regulation to people suffering from mental health concerns, with an emphasis on understanding contextual and dynamic features underlying the emotion, coping, and self-control decisions people make in their daily lives. Her particular emphasis is on understanding the beliefs people have about emotions, and the ways in which people are unwilling and/or feel incapable of tolerating their uncomfortable emotions. Dr. Veilleux is married with two children. She loves musical theater, young adult fiction, and taking weekend hikes with her kids through the Ozark mountains.